Communities and Caring

Communities and Caring

The Mixed Economy of Welfare

Marjorie Mayo

First published in Great Britain 1994 by
MACMILLAN PRESS LTD
Houndmills, Basingstoke, Hampshire RG21 6XS
and London
Companies and representatives
throughout the world

A catalogue record for this book is available
from the British Library.

ISBN 0–333–56750–1 hardcover
ISBN 0–333–56751–X paperback

 First published in the United States of America 1994 by
ST. MARTIN'S PRESS, INC.,
Scholarly and Reference Division,
175 Fifth Avenue,
New York, N.Y. 10010

ISBN 0–312–12027–3

Library of Congress Cataloging-in-Publication Data
Mayo, Marjorie.
Communities and caring : the mixed economy of welfare / Marjorie Mayo.
p. cm.
Includes bibliographical references and index.
ISBN 0–312–12027–3
1. Community development—Great Britain. 2. Public welfare—Great
Britain. 3. Great Britain—Social policy. I. Title.
HN400.C6M39 1994
307 . 1'4'0941—dc20   94–37356
                                                         CIP

---

11 10 9 8 7 6 5 4 3 2
04 03 02 01 00 99 98 97

Printed in Hong Kong

To Clyde and Scarlet

Contents

Acknowledgements

I owe very particular thanks to the community organisations who shared their experiences, and especially so to the Afro-Caribbean Organisation, Alexandra and Ainsworth, Kilburn Vale and Highgate Newtown Tenants Organisations, Camden Federation of Tenants and Residents, Ferguslie League of Action Groups, and the Pinehurst People's Centre.

Many thanks, too, to colleagues at Ruskin College, Oxford, and the William Temple Foundation, Manchester, who worked together on the Communities in Crisis programmes of community education, experiences which raised a number of the questions that appear in this book.

I should also like to thank a number of individuals who commented upon drafts of specific chapters and made extremely constructive criticisms and suggestions, including Bill Bryant, Richard Bryant, Pauline Conroy, David Marsden and Ines Newman. Any remaining errors are, of course, mine.

My thanks, too, to Jo Campling, who as editor has been consistently supportive and constructive, as well as personally encouraging, and to Frances Arnold and Keith Povey.

And last but by no means least, my thanks to Laurence, Clyde and Scarlet Harris, whose support has included the most patient assistance and encouragement in combating my technophobia with the word processor, and to Sue Coles, who then took on the task of turning the draft into a more professionally presented typescript.

MARJORIE MAYO

Introduction: The Changing Parameters of Debate

Looking at the future of welfare – and to the future of communities in relation to welfare – in the latter half of the 1990s and beyond to the twenty-first century, the starting point has to reflect change and uncertainty. The 1980s have been characterised as a decade of change (Johnson, 1990), and so may the 1990s. Since the mid-1970s there have been key changes in the economic context within which welfare policies have been developed and implemented. These underlying economic changes have been experienced in interrelated ways, and across national boundaries with the increasing globalisation of the economy.

In parallel there have been key changes in approaches to welfare. It is not just that welfare policies and practices have changed. The very nature of the debate has changed. 'Welfare state debate has shifted emphasis during the last decade', argued Abrahamson, for example, as 'the immediate certainty of both Social Democratic welfare state protagonists and Marxist critics of the welfare state project of the 1970s have been followed by uncertainty in the 1980s'. The shift in emphasis over this period was in response to rethinking on both the right and the left.

This book is concerned to explore some of the implications of these changes in terms of community participation, community care and community development. As the emphasis of debates on the state's role in welfare shifted, so the role of the non-state sector, including the role of the 'community sector', took on new potential significance. Voluntarism, self-help, community participation and community development acquired a novel interest, albeit for fundamentally different reasons and with contradictory implica-

1

tions, differences which in turn were related to alternative and competing theoretical perspectives.

Community-participation, self-help and community-development strategies have traditionally been promoted for alternative and conflicting aims and objectives. Chapter 2 explores some of the tensions and contradictions that, historically, have been inherent in the very concept of community. More generally this book sets out to explore some of the competing and contrasting ways in which community-participation, self-help, community-care and community-development strategies have been developing and reemerging in widely differing contexts across the First, Second and Third Worlds since the 1970s.

The changes in the nature of the welfare-state debate have been, at least in part, the result of the strategies of the new right. In Britain the conservative government, under the leadership of Margaret Thatcher, who was prime minister, from 1979 to 1990, set out to change attitudes as well as policies and to emphasise the role of the free market and individualism in place of public ownership, planning and collectivism in social welfare. 'I really think that [my government] was the turning of the tide. We were slipping so fast into a socialist state, that the individual mattered less and the collective more', commented Margaret Thatcher on the significance of the Conservative Party victory in 1979 (quoted in Rentoul, 1989). Margaret Thatcher was specifically concerned to ensure that the basis for such socialist ideas in Britain should be undermined: 'Economics are the method', she commented earlier, but more fundamentally, 'the object is to change the soul' (*The Sunday Times*, 3 May 1981). By the time of her final election victory in 1987, Margaret Thatcher considered that she had made significant progress towards this objective of changing the soul, or at least of shifting the parameters of political, economic and social debate: 'We are well on the way to making Britain safe from Socialism', she told the *Sunday Express* (17 May 1987).

The extent to which that latter objective had been achieved by the end of Thatcher's prime ministership has itself been, the subject of debate. There has also been continuing debate about how far John Major, her successor has been committed to the more extreme versions of the Thatcherite new-right project. Margaret Thatcher expressed strong views on these issues in the aftermath of the conservative election victory in 1992, arguing for the continuation of her project: 'Don't undo what I have done' (the *Guardian*, 22 April 1992).

And there has been continuing debate about the extent to which new-right ideologies have been espoused by the wider public in Britain. The empirical evidence from opinion surveys certainly did not suggest a massive swing of support away from state welfare spending towards a greatly enhanced role for private-sector provision, or for a greatly enhanced role for charitable, voluntary and community-based welfare provision. In fact at the beginning of the 1990s there was some evidence that attitudes had actually shifted towards increased support for direct government social expenditure and greater public spending on the National Health Service (Jowell *et al.*, 1989), although such support did not necessarily translate into votes in the 1992 General Election, of course. Most significantly, in terms of the focus of this book on voluntary and community effort, there was evidence of over-whelming support for the view that governments ought to provide more and that charities should not have to be relied on to provide money to those in need (89 per cent believed this in 1990, according to the Charities Household Survey).

So the point to emphasize here is that the new right certainly did not sweep the board with their ideas from the late 1970s to the 1990s, or even that new right-policies were uniformly applied to economic and social policies in Britain. As Glennerster and Midgely, for instance, have argued, whilst new-right policies challenged the centrist consensus and implemented measures that had 'negative consequences for the welfare state ideal . . . the extent to which they have significantly altered institutionalized approaches to govern-ment welfare provision is debatable' (Glennerster and Midgely, 1991, p. xi). Given that new-right policies included, they suggested, different and not entirely compatible strands, economic individual-ism, cultural traditionalism and authoritarian populism, this apparent lack of consistent and coherent impact may not be altogether surprising.

One view has been that despite the rhetoric of rolling back state provision, the new right in Britain did not actually succeed in significantly dismantling the structures of state welfare provision. As Le Grand has suggested, 'One of the more curious features of the first two Conservative administrations under Mrs Thatcher was how little impact they had on the welfare state. With the major exception of council house sales, the basic structure of the welfare state in 1987 was much the same as in 1979' (Le Grand, 1990).

But to argue that the new right did not entirely dismantle the welfare state in the 1980s, or fatally undermine its last vestiges of popular support, is absolutely not to argue that nothing was fundamentally changed. On the contrary, in fact, the processes of change could be seen to be both increasingly significant and increasingly sophisticated. Le Grand went on to argue that potentially more fundamental changes were subsequently initiated, not by dismantling public welfare provision but by restructuring it, particularly through the introduction of internal markets or quasi markets. Quasi markets were introduced with the intention of reducing the state's dual role of funder and provider of welfare services. 'Instead it is to become primarily a funder, with services being provided by a variety of private, voluntary and public suppliers, all operating in competition with one another' (Le Grand, 1990, p. 2).

Privatisation has taken a variety of forms, involving not only the privatisation of direct public-service provision, but also a reduction of public intervention in the provision of subsidies and in the regulation of service provision (Le Grand and Robinson, 1984; Papadakis and Taylor Gooby, 1987). In addition to the development of internal or quasi markets, public subsidies have been applied to promote the role of the private sector. For example, until the National Health Service and Community Care Act, private rather than local-authority residential care for the elderly was effectively subsidised through the social-security system. The growth of private-sector provision, which more than doubled between 1981 and 1990, and the 13 per cent reduction in local-authority provision over the same period can be related to this effective subsidy. Meanwhile increased charges for public services reinforced the relative advantages of private alternatives; for example council-house tenants faced increased rents but those tenants who opted to buy their council homes were offered discounts on the market value of the houses. More generally private-market mechanisms were stimulated, through reductions in such state regulations as minimum-wage legislation and health and safety regulations, regulations that had been designed to protect the health and welfare of those who are most vulnerable.

Finally, new-right strategies have involved systematic efforts to reduce the power and influence of organisations whose interests conflict with those of the government, organisations such as trade unions and local authorities with mandates to pursue alternative policies. The 'enabling state' has been seen as including the means of enabling the break-up of national pay bargaining, and 'enabling the break-up of trade union organisation through the fragmentation of the workforce into different contracts and employers' (Whitfield, 1992, p. 71). And the 'enabling state' has been seen as a means of promoting commercialisation in the public sector, whilst bypassing and marginalising local authorities' potential for promoting alternative agendas based upon social criteria, rather than market led criteria.

The end result of such a process, it has been argued, could be more fragmented and poorer-quality services, with public bodies being left with those services which are neither profitable for the private sector nor attractive to voluntary organisations (Whitfield, 1992). Commenting on the significance of the new right policies developed towards the end of the 1980s, Le Grand concluded that 'If these reforms are carried through to their conclusion, the welfare state in the 1990s will be a very different animal from the welfare state of the previous 45 years' (Le Grand, 1990, p. 2).

So there has been and continues to be fundamental change, even if the welfare state had not been dismantled per se by the early 1990s. The reality of welfare-state restructuring, as this book will attempt to demonstrate, has been both complex and contradictory. The particular point to reemphasise here is that the parameters of the debate have been shifted. Fundamental assumptions have been challenged, including fundamental challenges about the role of the state, the private sector and the voluntary and community sectors. Even without the continued presence of some of the most prominent politicians identified with the new right in the 1980s, the terrain of the debate in the 1990s, is no longer the same, from whichever side of the political spectrum it is approached.

This shift in the nature of the debate about welfare is by no means unique to Britain. In fact there are powerful parallels between debates in Britain and debates in USA, despite the the two countries' differing histories and policy traditions. As Glennerster and Midgely and others have demonstrated, the rise of radical-right ideas in the 1970s and 1980s was particularly linked with developments in both Britain and the USA (Glennerster and Midgely, 1991). And these ideas were exported, as Glennerster and Midgely also demonstrated, to Third-World countries through academic exchanges, such as in the case of the Chilean economists, the 'Chicago Boys', who applied the new-right approaches developed by Friedman in Chicago to Pinochet's Chile. New-right strategies were also exported through the influences exerted by international agencies such as the International Monetary Fund (IMF) (Glennerster and Midgely, 1991, p. x).

J. K. Galbraith has summarised some of the key features of this common line of thought in terms of an essentially theological view that 'government interventions in, or regulation of, the economy were not only economically perverse but also morally suspect. God, speaking through the works of Adam Smith, David Ricardo and Herbert Spencer (who gave the world the doctrine of the survival of the fittest), was essentially a benign and solicitous Republican. Leave matters to Him and to the market and all would be well' (although, as Galbraith also points out, this interpretation would have disturbed the more pragmatic Adam Smith; not that the relevant policy advisors in the White House, or indeed Reagan himself, had necessarily read Adam Smith's work in any case.) In parallel, the rich and the would-be rich were to be stirred to maximum effort by the incentive of even more money and less tax. 'Meanwhile, a reduction in various welfare payments to the poor would lead to their greater effort and also greater production and income; as the affluent needed the spur of more income the poor, it was said, needed the spur of their poverty.' (J. K. Galbraith, 'Back to the Future', *Observer*, 30 December 1990).

Each of these assumptions has been the subject of extensive debate. Galbraith himself has been amongst the more forceful critics of both the theories and the policies of the new right, which he saw as problematic. Meanwhile he argued that the practical results of the policies in USA could be seen in terms of recession and rising unemployment, despite earlier successes based upon speculation in the finance and property-development sectors. New-right policies failed to generate sustained economic growth, although they did succeed in generating increasing social polarisation and poverty. A similar conclusion on the economic impact of the Reagan years has been drawn, for instance, by Harrison and Bluestone (1988), who refer to the period in terms of the 'Illusion of Solid Growth'.

Once again the point being made here is not that the new right had it all their own way in terms of the arguments, let alone that new-right policies were successfully implemented or even consistently applied. Each of these views has been contested. Karger, for instance, has argued that 'Despite his public posturing, Reagan was not able to dismantle any of the major components of the welfare state' (Karger, 1991, p. 69). But once again, as in the case of Britain, this is in no way to underestimate the long term significance of the new right. Reagan's policies did promote changes that resulted in increasing poverty and income polarisation (ibid. 1991) And both new-right arguments and new-right policies reset the framework for debate, both in Britain under Major and in the USA in the Clinton era.

These changes in the terms of debates have in turn related to wider international changes in the framework of debate, as other industrialised countries have attempted to grapple with their own specific versions of broader economic pressures. There have been both similarities and important differences in the ways in which different countries have developed their responses to increasingly global trends. The differential impact of these changes have been explored in a range of contexts including Canada, Australia, New Zealand, European Community (EC) countries, Scandinavian countries and Israel (Mishra, 1990; Glennerster and Midgely, 1991). Whilst there has been increasing interest in learning from international comparisons and contrasts in general, there has also been increasing interest in focusing particularly upon EC countries and upon the EC itself, with the arrival of the single market in 1992 (an interest which has been shared by a growing number of voluntary and community organisations as well as by academics and policy-makers). Chapter Four focuses upon some examples of the various and contrasting ways in which different states have approached the changing framework of debate, in principle and in practice, before looking at some of the ways in which voluntary and community organisations have been attempting to grapple with the need to operate within an increasingly international framework, and especially so in relation to the EC.

The changing context, and the impact of new-right policies

Of course it is not just the parameters of the debate that have changed, or even the concepts. There have been key changes in the world economy, which has itself become increasingly globalised, changes which have had major consequences in terms of the growth of social needs and the new-right's development or curtailment of social welfare policies and provision which might meet, or fail to meet, these social needs.

As has been suggested, the new right have argued that the free market is the most effective generator of growth, which can then trickle down to benefit the wider population. Friedman has even argued that 'contrary to popular conception, capitalism leads to less inequality than alternative systems of organization and the development of capitalism has greatly lessened the extent of inequality' (Friedman 1962 p. 169).

The reality has been that, in this changing global context, there has been increasing polarisation between and within nations and between and within regions. In the early 1980s there was concern about the north–south divide, between the richer countries of the industrialised north, and the poorer countries of the less developed south. Brandt described north–south relations as 'the great social challenge of our time' in his introduction ('Plea for Change: Peace, Justice, Jobs') to the Report of the Independent Commission on International Development Issues, which he chaired (Brandt, 1980). Since then the combined effects of recession, global restructuring and international debt have led to greater inequality, and a report for the United Nations Development Programme published in 1992, for example, revealed rising world poverty. The gap between rich and poor was estimated to have doubled over the previous thirty years, with the richest fifth receiving one hundred and fifty times the income of the poorest fifth. Absolute levels of poverty and hunger have grown dramatically, with the sharpest effects being experienced by the poorest peoples in the least-developed countries, especially in Africa and Latin America. An estimated 1.2 billion people were suffering absolute poverty. The author of this UNDP report, Dr Mahbub ul Haq, commented that 'The evidence of human despair rooted in poverty is worldwide, in drugs, pollution, terrorism, Aids, instability (Brittain, 1992).

This is the context in which the imposition of structural adjustment programmes has led to higher food prices, and in which privatisation programmes, including the imposition of higher charges for services, have seriously affected major social and community programmes, including health and education. This is also the context in which community participation, community development and self-help programmes have been attempting to operate.

Meanwhile in Britain and the USA, as has already been suggested, recession and restructuring have also led to increasing polarisation. Harrison and Bluestone have argued that 'For more than a decade [the late 1970s and 1980s] the United States has been evolving as an increasingly unequal society' (Harrison and Bluestone, 1988, p. 3). With recession and increased international competition from the early to the mid-1970s, they argued, American businesses embarked upon corporate-restructuring programmes, including policies to shift investment to more profitable sectors and areas and policies to reduce costs, at the expense of labour. The results of this included speculative booms in finance and property, the loss of domestic jobs, and the growth of low-wage, insecure and unorganised employment, increasing poverty and the growth of social problems such as homelessness. New-right strategies to reduce expenditure on welfare compounded this increasing social misery. By the outset of the 1980s these trends had already been identified. Bowles, Gordon and Weisskopf (1984, p. 227) quoted Tobin's (1981) analysis of the effects of new-right policies. 'The only sure results', he argued, 'are redistribution of income, wealth, and power – from government to private enterprises, from workers to capitalists, and from poor to rich. A revolution is in process all right'. There was continuous polarisation and increasing poverty, the effects of which were compounded by cuts in welfare spending. Between 1979 and 1990 the national percentage share of adjusted family income (after tax) plus food and housing benefits in the USA rose from 39 per cent to 41.9 per cent for the highest quintile, but it fell from 6.4 per cent to 5.6 per cent for the lowest quintile (US House of Representatives, 1992). By 1990 Phillips had concluded that the USA led the major industrialised countries in the gap dividing rich and poor (Phillips, 1990). This was the legacy that Clinton had to tackle in 1993.

Increasing polarisation as a result of government strategies has also taken place in Britain, where once again increasing inequalities have not been accompanied or compensated by overall growth trickling down to raise the living standards of the relatively poor. On the contrary there has been an overall increase in the incidence of absolute poverty, along with an increase in the incidence of such social problems as homelessness. For example 170 000 households were classified homeless in 1992, some three times the number at the end of the 1970s (*Social Trends*, 1992). Overall, official estimates of those living in poverty rose from almost five million, or some 9 per cent of the population of Britain, in 1979 to some 11.75 million, or almost 22 per cent of the population, in 1988 (Millar, 1991, p. 25). Similar figures emerged from the Breadline Britain surveys, which found some 7.5 million poor in 1983 compared with about 11 million in 1990 (Millar, 1991, p. 26).

Growing unemployment was a major cause of this increasing incidence of poverty, together with the trend towards the increasing incidence of lower pay and casual, 'precarious' employment, which was particularly associated with women's jobs and those held by other disadvantaged groups, including black and ethnic-minority workers. The gap between the better paid and the low paid widened, and taxation failed to reduce this process of polarisation (in 1977 the top fifth of households received 37 per cent of total post-tax income, compared with the higher proportion of 44 per cent, enjoyed by the top fifth of households by 1988) (*Social Trends*, 1992). Taken together the impact of economic and social welfare restructuring has borne most harshly upon those in greatest social and economic need.

The importance of these changes for communities, however defined, and most especially for the most disadvantaged communities, can scarcely be overstated. One of the sub-themes of this book is the link between economic and employment policies on the one hand, and social welfare and community development policies on the other. In the context of developing countries in the Third World, community development has traditionally included related strategies for local economic development, employment and training. In First-World countries there have been differing traditions, with Britain providing an example of an approach based upon some degree of separation between economic policies and social and community policies. As Chapter 3 explores, however, from the 1960s and 1970s, and especially from the 1980s, there has been increasing interest in local economic strategies, including community-based employment and training strategies. More generally there has also been developing interest in the potential offered by voluntary work and community involvement in gaining confidence, skills and experience, which could in turn improve people's chances of gaining employment and training in the wider labour market. Chapter 7 provides some examples of the ways in which community-based experiences have opened the door to improved opportunities for individuals and social groups who have been struggling to overcome disadvantages and discrimination in the labour market.

Whilst communities and community participation and development have been massively affected by changes in the global economy, the deteriorating economic climate and the polarisation of opportunities, this does not mean that all these changes have been in one direction, however. As has already been suggested, the reality has been both more complex and more contradictory. Despite all the odds, and even in sharply deteriorating economic contexts, communities have struggled to preserve local services and jobs, both paid and unpaid, and open up wider opportunities for those who have suffered economic and social disadvantage and discrimination.

But however valuable their contributions have been, and continue to be, one of the themes of this book is that communities cannot be expected to take on increasing responsibilities with regard to welfare, effectively substituting for essential public provision. Even if they wanted to do this (and there is no systematic evidence to suggest that they do), it will be argued that this would be absolutely unrealistic unless communities are underpinned with continuing systems of public support. Neither voluntary effort in general, nor community-based self-help in particular, can be expected to fill the widening gap between social needs and public provision. On the contrary, both have been struggling with the impact of recession and welfare-state restructuring. New-right policies towards communities are fundamentally contradictory. If communities are realistically to play an enhanced role in a restructured welfare state they will have to be provided with the public resources to make that option viable.

Meanwhile alternative approaches have also been developed in policy debates and in practice over the past decades. Rejecting new-right strategies for restructuring based upon privatisation and the enhancement of market mechanisms (including internal or quasi market mechanisms), others have been attempting to shift the boundaries of the mixed economy of welfare in a different direction. Key elements of these alternative approaches have included the promotion of more democratic accountability and more pluralism within the public sector, with an enhanced role for community participation, collective forms of self-help and community development. The next section of this chapter sets out some of the key features of the changing parameters of debate, in the changing global context, by looking at alternative debates on the left of the political spectrum. This sets the scene for a more specific introduction to the chapters which follow.

The changing parameters of debate and left-wing alternatives: community participation, democratic accountability, quality services and pluralism *within* the public sector

So far the discussion has concentrated upon the role of the new right in redefining the terms of the debate. But, as has been suggested, whilst the new right has held the key, there have been other strands to the developing debates. The new right took forward criticisms of welfare that had been developed from alternative perspectives. On the left, and particularly on the libertarian socialist left, there had been criticism of state provision as bureaucratic and paternalistic, controlling and regulating the poor. The state was charged with being primarily concerned with social reproduction for the interests of capital, and with the reproduction of social divisions in terms of class, race and gender.

As Duncan has argued, '"Roll back the frontiers of the state" has a Left as well as a Right variant' (Duncan, 1989, p. 298). One left-wing interpretation of the 1979 electoral victory of the new-right in Britain was that this demonstrated widespread disillusion with the welfare state. After thirty years or so of statist bureaucracy the electorate opted instead for the private market, individualism and freedom of choice. Corrigan, for example, wrote that there was a 'distinct vote against the Welfare State' (Corrigan, 1979).

The empirical evidence for these assertions may have been lacking (in fact such evidence as there was, in the form of opinion polls, cast doubts on such views) but they do point to a more general aspect of the debates on the left; and to a wider fragmentation and loss of confidence within particular sections of the left, both during that period and subsequently. Structuralist, deterministic versions of Marxism were subjected to fundamental criticisms, and along with these forms of questioning there were basic criticisms of other aspects of left-wing approaches, including left-wing approaches to the role of the state in general, to planning and to the welfare state in particular.

One form in which such criticisms subsequently developed, related in turn to the development of post-modernist perspectives. In her discussion of urban planning, for example, Wilson (1991) demonstrated how the 'fashionable postmodern solution' to urban problems was based upon the rejection of plans in favour of piecemeal initiatives. Now that the municipal authority is 'billed as a Stalinist juggernaut', she went on to argue, 'the private developer may re-emerge in the guise of an Enlightenment benefactor. . . The post-modern solution may seem an elegant one to those who have followed Jane Jacobs in targeting public-development projects as the source of the urban crisis'. But Wilson concluded that the post-modern solution of the anarchic city, in which individuals and communities spontaneously create the exciting fabric of the cosmopolitan city, failed to take account of the power of property and capital. 'Such arguments appear surprisingly compatible', she argued, 'with the views of New Right economists such as Milton Friedman and Friedrich Hayek' (Wilson, 1991, p. 151).

Summarising the ensuing dilemma she concluded, 'Critical of the disasters of utopian planning, we are in danger of forgetting that the unplanned city still *is* planned, equally undemocratically, by big business and the multinational corporation. Women, ethnic minorities and the working class in general have been caught between a paternalistic form of planning in which surveillance and regulation played a key role, and a profit-driven capital development that has been unbelievably destructive of urban space, and thus of supportive communities, killing whole cultures as the loved and familiar buildings and streets were bulldozed away' (ibid, p. 152).

In the wake of the defeat of communist governments in East and Central Europe in 1989 and the fragmentation of the former USSR, there was increased interest in debates about the negative aspects of state planning. One left-wing approach to this process of rethinking, which has been characterised as 'new realism', concluded that the new right had triumphed globally. All that was possible in these circumstances, it was argued, was the more humane management of capitalism, rather than its ultimate replacement.

But in contrast with this view there has also been renewed debate about the potential for revitalising the socialist project, an approach which was presented, for example, by Blackburn and others in a collection of essays entitled 'After the Fall', which set out to tackle some of the issues involved in understanding past failures with a view to reinvigorating socialist theory and practice. One of the key themes in this discussion was that of socialist democracy. As Miliband argued, any positive approach to the lessons of the experiences of communism must include the importance of the subject of democracy. One of the main tasks of socialists, he continued, must be to defend democratic gains in capitalist regimes and to act as 'the best advocates of a social order in which democracy is at long last liberated from constrictions which capitalist domination imposes upon it.' in a more democratic future socialist society (Miliband, (1991) p. 16).

Meanwhile, on a far more immediate and practical level, there were also positive approaches from the left of the political spectrum, including the social-democratic left. Hambleton and Hoggett, for example, argued for a progressive alternative to new-right criticisms of the welfare state. This alternative was based upon collectivist rather than individualistic solutions to problems of bureaucratic and paternalistic welfare provision. And they argued for progressive pluralism within the framework of public-sector provision. They emphasised the potential contribution of strategies for decentralisation and democratisation in improving the quality and appropriateness of welfare services. Self-management initiatives, such as the development of tenant self-management schemes, provided examples of such approaches within the public sector (for example in Scandinavian countries) (Hoggett and Hambleton, 1987). The public sector in Britain also provided examples of public resources being made available to community organisations to enable them to participate more effectively and directly organise their own specific services. There was then, as Hoggett argued, a left-wing alternative strategy of decentralisation and democratisation with a radical potential for developing a post-bureaucratic welfare state (Hoggett, 1990). Whilst it was clear that decentralisation, for example, could be used in different ways, ways which were not necessarily linked to increasing democracy let alone automatically leading to an improvement in the quality of services, these ingredients were considered to have potential relevance in the construction of an alternative and progressive agenda.

More generally, too, the issue of consumer involvement in the development of consumer-responsive quality services has emerged as an important theme in social policy debates (Deakin and Wright,

1990; Stewart and Walsh, 1990; Gaster, 1991). Similar concerns have been the subject of debate in different local government contexts in Europe (Batley and Stoker, 1991). These themes emerge, in subsequent chapters, in a variety of attempts to make welfare-state provision more responsive and more appropriate to the needs of individuals and communities.

Collective versus individualistic approaches

In the meantime, some of the criticisms of the welfare state that had been voiced by the more disillusioned, or at least the more ambivalent, sections of the left in Britain had been taken up and developed in very different ways by the new right. The very terms of the debate became increasingly contradictory and problematic.

Privatisation was justified by the new right not just in terms of the promotion of economic growth, efficiency and value for money, it was also justified in terms of choice for the consumer. The public sector was to have its boundaries shifted so that the power of professionals and bureaucrats could be more effectively curtailed. But this could also be used to justify attacks on front-line public-service workers and public-sector trade unionism. Decentralisation could lead to greater scope for community control, But it could also be used to justify central government's abdication from particular areas of responsibility. Decentralisation, for instance can, as van Rees has argued, 'go hand in hand with changes of ideology which are shifting from collective responsibilities to individual ones and organising welfare and care as a commodity on the market' (van Rees, 1991, p. 137). Likewise debureaucratisation could enhance the scope for community initiatives based upon self-help and self-reliance, or it could effectively increase the burden upon individuals, families and communities already struggling to provide informally for those in need of care.

More recently there has been increasing emphasis on individual consumer rights, as exemplified for example by debates about the Citizens' Charter in Britain. But there have been criticisms of this new emphasis on consumerism, too. Berry, for example, suggested that there was 'greater emphasis upon the glossy brochure than on the process of achieving consumer involvement'. More fundamentally, she argued that there were specific problems with consumerism in relation to services aimed at the poor, since poor people are unable to pay directly for these services, and certain services are, in any case, aimed at 'unwilling or unpopular groups' who may not have chosen to be consumers at all. Whilst Berry concluded with some serious reservations about the limitations of an individualised approach to consumerism, she recognised that there are nevertheless common goals as well as important differences between consumerism and community development, goals which include accountability, participation and local involvement (Berry, 1988, pp. 266–72).

So whilst there was room for debate and fundamental disagreement about the basis and meaning of the election of new-right governments, in both Britain, and the USA in the 1980s, and early 1990s, there was perhaps more agreement about the importance of responding to the challenges raised by the new emphasis on consumer/user rights. Issues concerning consumer rights, participation and user accountability were placed more firmly on the agenda for the 1990s and beyond.

This was viewed by some on the left with caution and scepticism, but others were more welcoming of the changes. Duncan, for instance, illustrates the views of those who have embraced the scenario of community welfare. 'The goal', Duncan argues 'is emphatically that, as far as possible conditions should be established, that encourage people to do more things for themselves. This requires an increase both of opportunities and of the capacity to recognize and take advantage of them, both an increase of the field of choice and a strengthening of agency which are intimately linked' (Duncan, 1989, p. 298) 'One of the crucial tasks for Socialists', Duncan went on to argue, 'given legitimate doubts about traditional state-provided services, is to devise a welfare system in which consumer choice and client participation play a much larger role than is common now' (ibid. p. 313). 'The pleas from Left and Right for more decentralisation, more genuine choice, and fuller democratisation at lower levels have a lot of contemporary appeal, and can be used to prompt positively both social imagination and social experimentation' (ibid. 1989, p. 314). There have been both positive features and serious limitations to this type of approach, it will be argued, whether coming from the left or from the right.

In subsequent chapters it will be suggested that these issues had already been and were still on the agendas of a range of community organisations, both in Britain and beyond. Community organisations, women's organisations and black and ethnic-minority groups have campaigned (both separately and as part of wider coalitions) to gain an effective voice in key planning decisions affecting the future of their areas. Despite the very real difficulties of the underlying material situation, subsequent chapters will attempt to demonstrate that community organisations have refused to disappear. They have attempted to apply pressure, to participate, and to gain improvements in the quality and relevance of services, or at least to prevent their deterioration. There are examples of communities organising for these purposes in Britain, the USA, Third-World countries and countries in Eastern and Central Europe.

Whether or not they have been successful is another matter of course. In some cases failure to obtain their goals within the public sector has led community organisations to organise their own alternative forms of provision. In other cases direct-service provision, by community organisations themselves, was chosen as the only realistic option. Some organisations have specifically chosen direct provision because they wish to run the service themselves, in their own way, without external bureaucratic or professional controls. And women's organisations and black and ethnic-minority organisations have chosen to run services themselves because this is, they believe, necessary if they are to receive services that are organised and delivered in anti-discriminatory ways. Subsequent chapters will consider examples of each of these strategies.

But one of the underlying themes of this book is that neither equal opportunities specifically, nor community participation, community development and self-help more generally, can simply be left to the operations of the free market. Despite the difficulties of the background situation, community organisations, women's groups and black and ethnic-minority groups have been active both in trying to participate in service provision, as users of services, and to operate as direct providers of services to their constituencies. But, as will be argued, there is no reason to suppose that, left to themselves, such organisations will be able to continue to operate at their present level, let alone to play a more significant role in the direct provision of services. On the contrary, there is evidence from the experiences of organisations in the USA to suggest that contracting services out to the voluntary sector, in the current context of the mixed economy of welfare, may strengthen the largest and best established organisations but at the potential cost of pressurising them into adopting increasingly commercialised and/or bureau-cratised ways of operating. Meanwhile the smaller more directly community-based organisations may be far less able to participate in the mixed economy of welfare. As Lipsky and Smith have also pointed out, there have been inherent tensions between the goals of equity, fairness and accountability, as represented through public responsibility and public provision on the one hand, and the goals of flexibility and community initiative, motivation and identity on the other (Lipsky and Smith, 1989–90).

Nor is there any reason to suppose that, left to themselves, community organisations will necessarily or automatically resolve the tensions and impediments which block progress towards equal opportunities. On the contrary, it will be argued that if the boundaries of the public sector are to be shifted, with a new balance between public and voluntary/not for profit sectors, then community organisations, and especially organisations representing the poor or disadvantaged communities, will only benefit if their participation is systematically resourced and they are provided with adequate opportunities for education and training, including education and training for equal opportunities.

Of course this is not a novel argument, and there have been instances where the case for resourcing community participation has been given some quasi-official recognition. In Britain, for example, the speaker of the House of Commons Commission on Citizenship (1990. p. 35) accepted that 'Voluntary bodies need systematic funding' and that community partnerships 'are not cost free' but require a framework of support, including professional community-development work support.

Some of the tensions that are inherent in attempts to promote community participation and mobilise community self-help will be explored in subsequent chapters. In the mixed economy of welfare the case for greater community self-help within welfare provision has a contradictory history. There have, traditionally, been competing strands in this history, with both positive and negative features, depending upon the perspective. Abrahamson (1989) concludes his review of the case for community welfare with a clear caveat that there are no easy solutions.

The central issue here is not whether community welfare represents some panacea beyond the free market on the one hand, or over-centralised, bureaucratised statism on the other. The past history of community participation, community development and self-help does not provide evidence of panaceas (although there are relevant and positive case histories as well as negative ones). The issues considered in subsequent chapters are more concerned with the need to grapple with the changing parameters of the debate, and to explore ways in which criteria for the development of the community/voluntary sector can be developed and met as part of wider strategies to develop democratic accountability and pluralism within the public sector.

How can community participation and community development be developed and supported in such a way as to improve the quality of welfare services for the user and take account of equal opportunities considerations? To what extent can such improvements be achieved whilst maintaining principles of equity, ensuring that appropriate services are available to all on the basis of need rather than on the basis of what any particular community is able to press for, or even to provide for itself, with the best-resourced services being developed in the better-organised or economically more advantaged areas (even if these areas include the communities which need such services least)? To what extent can community-based services be developed without undermining those services which *are* still provided directly within the public sector, and without undermining the choice to remain within the public sector for those who do not choose, or do not have the time or energy to choose, to become involved in community-based provision or self-help schemes? To what extent can the community-based sector be developed and supported without undermining the jobs and conditions of public-service workers, who may themselves be members of that same community (typically the case, for instance, for home-care workers, who tend to be local women working part time for relatively low pay)? And to what extent can such improvements be achieved without placing an unbearable strain on the most vulnerable in the community, including those women who are already struggling with their triple role of worker, wife and mother, as well as community organiser and activist, the triple burden that has been described with powerful effect in relation to women in the Third World (Moser, 1989)?

These questions run through the following chapters and reemerge in the concluding chapter, together with some of the potential implications for the development of policies and the provision of resources (including resources for education and training) for community participation and community development.

Chapter 1 focuses on unravelling some of the myths surrounding the term 'mixed economy of welfare' and explores some of the ways in which the 'mix' has been subjected to change. It identifies some of the possible choices, together with their underlying assumptions and potentially alternative implications for different individuals and communities.

Chapter 2 focuses more specifically on the concept of 'community' and explores some of the contrasting ways in which the term has been used, both historically and in more recent debates, in relation to community participation, community development and community care, in the mixed economy of welfare.

Chapter 3 considers some of the ways in which community-participation and community-development strategies have linked into strategies for local economic development, employment and training, both in Third-World contexts and increasingly, in response to economic recession and restructuring in industrialised contexts, such as in Britain and the USA.

Chapter 4 makes some international comparisons between Britain, the USA and a selection of European countries (including some of the experiences of Eastern Europe). The chapter concludes by focusing more specifically on voluntary-sector and community-based initiatives to form networks at the European level in response to increasing recognition of the importance of effective responses to European integration.

Chapter 5 develops the discussion of international perspectives, by looking at community participation and community development in the Third World. This chapter starts from the view that comparative social policy learning between the First and Third Worlds is not just a one-way process, and that Western social-policy analysis stands to gain from becoming less Eurocentric.

Chapter 6 returns to the First World, and specifically to Britain, to explore some of the ways in which the changing climate of the mixed economy of welfare has actually been developing in practice. This chapter looks at some of the ways in which, despite all the pressures and difficulties, the voluntary sector and community-based organisations have been responding to change, together with some of the ways in which a number of local authorities have been attempting to develop positive responses to community participation and community development.

Chapter 7 provides some examples of the different ways in which community organisations have been grappling with issues and problems of community participation and community-based service provision.

Finally, the Conclusion summarises some of the implications of these experiences for community education and training, together with some of the wider implications for policy development. Community-based strategies for community participation and community development can in no way substitute for the wider economic and social strategies and policies that are urgently needed in the face of global recession and restructuring. But community-participation and community-development strategies could complement such wider strategies, potentially making a modest contribution to the development of more democratically accountable and more appropriate and responsive public policies and services.

1

The Mixed Economy of Welfare: Unravelling Some Myths and Identifying Some Choices

The term 'the mixed economy of welfare' has been around for some time. And so has the reality that this term encapsulates. Welfare systems as different from each other as Britain's and the USA's have in practice included a range of welfare provisions, some services being directly provided by the state whilst others have been provided through the private market or through voluntary organisations. Typically, for the personal social services, the most significant source of care has been the informal sector; meaning that, in practice, family, friends and neighbours together constitute the front-line of caring, whether this is for children, the elderly, or those with physical disabilities, learning difficulties or mental illness. The balance that has been struck between the different sectors – state, private, voluntary or non-profit, informal has varied in important ways from country to country and over time. But even the more reluctant welfare states such as the USA have developed significant areas of state provision; conversely, even socialist states have expected their citizens to supplement state welfare provision, for instance, through informal caring, and communal self help.

This chapter sets out to unravel some of the myths around the notion of the 'mixed economy of welfare.' What does the term actually mean, when applied to different contexts? And why has the 'mixed economy of welfare' been so widely advocated as the way forward towards the twenty-first century?

The final part of the chapter looks at some of the issues involved in making positive choices about different balances for the mixed economy of welfare. The choice of mixture will vary, it will be argued, depending on the differing interests of those who are exercising their options, and depending on their differing theoretical approaches to the state and to economic and social planning more generally.

Britain and the USA have been both compared and contrasted in terms of their different mixes of welfare. Wilensky and Lebeaux considered that 'All major political parties in the rich countries of the free world claim the maintenance of the "Welfare State" as an article of faith' but that there were alternative approaches to welfare (Wilensky and Lebeaux, 1965, p. v). The USA has in the past, been characterised, they argued, by its reluctance to accept state intervention, which was tended to be seen as a last resort when the 'normal structures of supply, the family and the market, break down' (ibid., p. 138). This 'residual' conception of welfare, with minimum (federal) state intervention, represented one end of the spectrum in the compromise between 'The values of economic individualism and free enterprise on the one hand, and security, equality and humanitarianism on the other' (ibid., p. 138–9). But Wilensky and Lebeaux considered that, following rapid social change with the development of advanced industrialisation, there was increasing acceptance of an alternative 'institutional' conception of social welfare as a legitimate function of modern industrial society. According to this view, both public and voluntary organisations had their place alongside private organisations and the family. So both conceptions fitted into the overall framework of the mixed economy of welfare, but they represented different ends of the spectrum. Over time, with continuing industrialisation and social change, Wilensky and Lebeaux considered that the residual conception would become weaker and the institutional conception increasingly dominant (ibid., p. 147). *Industrial Society and Social Welfare* was published at the end of the 1950s and republished in the mid-1960s, the period when the federal government's increased social welfare initiatives and 'War on Poverty' seemed to reflect moves towards a more 'institutional' approach. Fifteen years later the USA was pursuing policies to revert to the other end of the spectrum, the residual conception of welfare. To what extent the Democratic presidency from 1993 will reverse these trends remains to be seen.

But in the 1980s, the trend was towards a more residual approach, a welfare pattern which could also be based in Britain. In his study, *The Welfare State in Capitalist Society,* Mishra (1990) presents the examples of Britain and the USA to exemplify new-right responses to crisis, from the mid-1970s, through the retrenchment and restructuring of welfare. There is an element of irony here. The British and US strategies to shift the mix of the mixed economy of welfare were broadly comparable, despite their different starting points. Historically, Britain had typified the more 'institutional' end of the welfare spectrum, in contrast with the USA's more 'residual' approach.

Whilst there were similarities, however, there were also important differences. Mishra goes on to show how these differences affected the impact of new-right policies as these were applied in practice. In particular he argues that, in general, 'Ideological support for the welfare state has been a good deal weaker in the United States than in the United Kingdom' and universal services a good deal less developed (ibid., p. 25). Both these factors have been important. Universal services (that is, services such as the National Health Service in Britain that are available to the entire population on the basis of need for that service) have been shown to have survived attempts at retrenchment better than selective services (that is services that selectively target particular groups in the greatest need). This, it has been argued, is because universal services may be defended by those middle-class people who share an interest in using them, as well as by working-class people (Le Grand, 1985). In contrast, selective services, such as means-tested benefits targeted at the poor, have a far weaker constituency to defend them. So, despite the similarities between the overall strategies of governments in Britain and the USA from the mid-1970s, and especially in the 1980s, the outcomes of these strategies did vary. Part of the explanation for this variation lies in historical dissimilarities leading to different welfare models and ideologies in the two countries.

This fits into Mishra's wider approach. He identifies common trends and pressures on welfare states, including global economic pressures. But he also emphasises differences in response, differences which arise from political choices and which relate to differing balances of class forces, as well differences arising from history and ideology. So Mishra argues that, despite considerable pressures, the welfare state (at least during the 1980s) suffered less retrenchment in states with strong labour movements allied to social-democratic governments, such as Austria and Sweden, than in states such as the USA, where less effective broad coalitions have been organised to defend public welfare. The second part of this chapter will return to some of these different interests and competing political strategies, in deciding the balance between different mixes of the mixed economy of welfare.

Meanwhile the residual and institutional models may still be useful in depicting the two ends of the spectrum that covers the range of mixes that have actually been practised within the mixed economy of welfare, in modern, industrial, capitalist states.

Historically the British welfare state, as developed in the post-Second World War era, has been seen as representing the more institutional end of this spectrum. But this did not mean that the state intended to take over all welfare provision (or indeed that redistribution between social classes was a central goal for all services, including social insurance, which it was not). Beveridge, the key architect of the postwar social security system, had certainly not envisaged that universal state provision should take over to the extent that the voluntary sector would become redundant. It was those in the Labour Party who were associated with the Fabian Society's tradition of social reform through the state who were more highly sceptical about the voluntary sector. A common view amongst Fabian socialists of this time was that 'the voluntary sector would just wither away' (Brenton, 1985, p. 21). Brenton also quotes from the reflections of Richard Crossman, who was the labour government's secretary of state for social services in the late 1960s: 'Philanthropy was to us the odious expression of social oligarchy and churchy bourgeois attitudes. We detested voluntary hospitals maintained by flag days' (ibid., p. 265). 'From the 1920s on, the normal left-wing attitude has been opposed to middle class philanthropy, charity and everything else connected with do-gooding. Those of us who became socialists grew up with the conviction that we must in this point ally ourselves with the professionals and trades unions and discourage voluntary effort particularly since it was bound to reduce the number of jobs available' (Crossman, 1973, quoted in Brenton, 1985).

In fact, of course, voluntary effort by no means withered away. Crossman himself recognised the 'staggering extent of voluntary activity in our welfare state'. (Brenton, 1985, p. 274), which he subsequently came to value more positively. The voluntary sector was an essential ingredient of welfare provision and this continued to be the case, especially in the personal social services, which cater for the elderly, people with disabilities and children. There was effectively, as Brenton explains, a mixed economy of welfare built right into the postwar welfare state.

Webb and Wistow's study of the personal social services in Britain similarly traces the origins of the mixed economy of welfare, in this field, right back to the postwar period. Unlike the four pillars of the welfare state – income maintenance, health, education and housing – the personal social services, 'the fifth social service', were not brought together in any coherent way until the establishment of local-authority social-service departments following the Seebohm Report of 1968. Webb and Wistow describe the statutory core of the personal social services as having begun life as 'a distinctly mixed bag' (Webb and Wistow, 1987, p. 6).

Despite attempts at rationalisation and the provision of a more comprehensive local-authority service through the new social-service departments, in practice there has continued to be a mixed economy of welfare.

Whilst the personal social services in Britain have been particularly characterised by such a mix, the mixed economy of welfare has also been a feature of the welfare state more generally. Webb and Wistow (1987) give the example of housing, where owner occupation, cooperative ownership and private renting have coexisted with state-provided housing. In addition, private medicine has coexisted with the National Health Service, and private 'public' schools, voluntary schools and private insurance have coexisted with their state-run counterparts. Titmuss had much earlier identified the fact, too, that welfare covers a far wider area that simply those services provided directly by the state. He argued that both fiscal welfare (that is allowances through the tax system) and occupational welfare systems (such as company pension schemes and/or health-insurance cover) were also of key importance, and that through both of these systems the wealthier sections of society were being advantaged (Titmuss, 1963).

To summarise then, the mixed economy has been fundamental to the welfare state in Britain, although the mix has clearly varied between services and over time, just as the mix varies between Britain and the USA, for instance. As Mishra (1990) and others have argued, there is no necessary convergence between one type of mix and another. There may indeed have been mounting global economic pressures that have resulted in increasing social need amongst particular social groups, such as the unemployed on the one hand, and increasing efforts to contain public welfare spending on the other. But government responses have varied. Austria and Sweden (at least until the electoral defeat of the Swedish Social Democrats in 1991) provided examples of strategies to maintain a corporatist approach to the welfare state, with strong state intervention to maintain employment, and public welfare policies. In contrast both Britain and the USA, from their different starting points, in the 1970s and 1980s played a leading role in developing strategies for retrenchment, strategies which, particularly in Britain, were associated with attempts to shift the balance of welfare – to move towards a more residual model in general, and to promote the role of the private and voluntary sectors in particular.

Why was this? What was the basis for these attempts to roll back state involvement, to shift the balance, to alter the mix in the mixed economy of welfare? A number of different (and not necessarily consistent) arguments have been used in various combinations. The following list represents a summary of the most frequently encountered assertions.

1. The private sector and/or the voluntary sector can be more cost effective than public-sector provision.
2. Increasing the mix of provision within the mixed economy of welfare increases consumer/client choice.
3. State provision is inherently bureaucratic, whereas private and/ or voluntary provision can be less bureaucratic and paternalistic, which allows for greater innovation and flexibility.
4. The welfare state has reproduced patterns of inequality in terms of race and gender. Alternative forms of provision have therefore been essential as part of strategies to combat these structured inequalities.
5. More generally, voluntary welfare structures outside state provision, and self-help schemes, in particular, have a role in wider political strategies to promote active participation and democracy.

Before examining the factual and/or mythical nature of these assertions, it is important to emphasise just how diverse the mixed

economy of welfare really is. As has already been suggested, there
have been four major sectors. (The Wolfenden Committee, which
was set up in 1974 to review the 'role and function of voluntary
organisations in the UK over the next twenty-five years' identified
these four sectors as the informal sector, the commercial or private-
market sector, the statutory sector and the voluntary sector.) The
commercial or private-market sector ranges from small residential
day-care establishments – for example, day nurseries or child-
minders – at one end of the spectrum, through to major financial
institutions providing insurance, at the other. The voluntary sector
also covers an enormous range of organisations with widely
differing goals and functions. These range from well-established
national charities employing large numbers of professional staff (the
National Society for the Prevention of Cruelty to Children for
instance) through to informal local groupings and networks.

Broadly the functions of voluntary groups have been defined as
falling into three major categories; service-provision organisations
(examples include Dr Barnado's homes) self-help and mutual-aid
groups (such as support groups formed by or for people with
particular disabilities), and advocacy and self-advocacy groups and
pressure groups (including campaigning organisations such as
Shelter and Child Poverty Action Group) (Johnson, 1981). In
addition there are voluntary organisations that resource and
coordinate other forms of voluntary action (volunteer centres and
councils of voluntary service for instance) (Brenton, 1985).

In terms of goals and orientation these different types of
organisation cover the full spectrum too – from organisations that
still preserve elements of the patronising style of charitable 'do
gooding' that Crossman found so objectionable, through to some of
the more overtly radical, campaigning organisations that developed
when the welfare state's inadequacies and inbuilt biases (including
inbuilt sexism and racism) became the subject of more explicit
criticism, especially, from the 1960s onwards. Given this range, then,
it would be surprising if any of the supposed advantages of the
voluntary sector were to be found to be universally applicable. There
would seem to be even less likelihood that such advantages would
apply across the full spread of commercial, voluntary and informal
arrangements for welfare.

So, firstly, is the non-statutory sector cheaper and/or more cost
effective? The answer, in summary, seems to be that it is not

necessarily cheaper or more cost effective. One frequently quoted example that illustrates this point is that of the National Health Service in Britain, which has been favourably compared with the cost of health care in the USA – which is a major policy issue in the USA in the 1990s. There are a range of more specific examples of comparisons between public, private and voluntary-sector provision in the services that have been put out to competitive tender in Britain. Overall the evidence seems to indicate that public organisations have demonstrated they can compete successfully in terms of cost effectiveness. Walker, for instance, has concluded that, overall, the evidence suggests that 'It is at best questionable whether a privatised service is actually more economically efficient or cost effective than a similar one provided publicly' (Walker, 1984, pp. 38–9). More recent evidence supports these reservations. In addition the actual process of contracting incurs costs (including the 'transaction' costs of the tendering process and the cost of monitoring contracted-out services) as well as the 'production' costs of the service in question (Ferris and Graddy, 1992).

But it has also been demonstrated that particular services may indeed be delivered more cheaply, and especially so if the pay and conditions of the service deliverers are significantly reduced. Salaries have been estimated as being between 10 per cent and 29 per cent lower in the voluntary than in the public sector (Lipsky and Smith, 1989–90). Although this does not apply evenly across the sectors, the downgrading of employment conditions is a typical feature of public bidding for competitive contracts in Britain and the USA. The competitive tendering process itself has been associated with downward pressures on pay, on the security or casualisation of employment, and on benefits such as pensions, sick pay, holiday entitlement and trade-union recognition, which in turn has further implications for employees' abilities to protect their pay and conditions, in the future (Whitfield, 1992).

More generally, it has been argued that voluntary bodies are better able to obtain additional resources, whether in terms of voluntary donations or in terms of volunteer labour. In practice however it has also been pointed out that there may be serious limitations on increasing the amounts that can be raised in this way. Brenton pointed out that there were some indications that 'the levels of charitable giving are not keeping pace with the expenditure needs of voluntary agencies at their present levels of operation, let alone those which would be generated by any significant future expansion' (Brenton, 1985, p. 69). Nor does charitable giving in any way correlate with social need. On the contrary, there are popular causes, such as children's charities, and there are unpopular causes, which find it far harder to attract donations. Evidence from Charity Trends in 1991 indicated that the recession had been making an impact on the level of charitable donations in general: 'individual giving may have increased in nominal terms, but it has not matched inflation in the period of recession' (*Charity Trends*, 1991, p. 6). The recession was, perhaps, also beginning to affect corporate giving. (donations from companies declined in relative terms by 3 per cent in 1990–1).

There may well also be severe limitations upon the realistic possibility of increasing the amount of time offered by volunteers. The Charity Household Survey estimated that people gave slightly less time to voluntary activities in 1988–9 than in 1987. This point has been made, for instance, in relation to community care, and especially so in relation to the time constraints on the women who provide so much informal care in the community. Between 1971 and 1990 some three million women entered the labour force, and by the 1990s over half of women were economically active, the second highest proportion in the EC (after Denmark with 60 per cent) (*Social Trends*, 1992). As more and more women undertake paid work there may be fewer and fewer women with time to spare for voluntary labour.

Whilst this view emerged as an explanation for difficulties in recruiting volunteers (for example in some of the cases considered in more detail in Chapter 7), there has also been conflicting evidence. The 1991 National Survey of Voluntary Activity in the UK (Voluntary Action Research, 1991) found that there had actually been an increase in the number of volunteers between 1981 and 1991 (from 44 per cent of the population in 1981 to 51 per cent in 1991) despite the increasing proportion of women in paid employment (a factor which has been particularly significant in view of the fact that women have been rather more likely to volunteer than men, and considerably more likely to perform informal domestic caring tasks such as babysitting or shopping for the elderly). However the National Survey of Voluntary Activity in the UK also found that much of the growth in volunteering during the 1980s was in relation to sports, exercise and environmental issues. 'In contrast, volunteering in the welfare field has remained static. Moreover, there has been an increase in the demand for volunteers in recent years, particularly in the field of welfare provision' (ibid., p. 129).

In any case there are limits to the functions that can be performed effectively by volunteers compared with professionally trained staff. Voluntary labour may indeed provide savings, but not all jobs can be done by volunteers, and even volunteers need to be organised, which typically requires paid organisers. Without adequate organisation volunteers may become disillusioned, leading to them dropping out, which was identified by the National Survey as a particular problem in the field of health and social welfare. The survey concluded that there must be a question mark 'over the capacity of the [voluntary] sector to expand its role in the provision of welfare services' (ibid., p. 133). There was also evidence that about half of those who responded to the survey thought that 'there would be no need for volunteers if the government fulfilled all its responsibilities . . . Volunteering, it could be concluded, is likely to receive wider public support if it is seen to be playing a supportive, supplementary role to the state, rather than acting as a direct replacement for statutory services' (ibid., p. 133).

Finally, as has been pointed out in relation to both Britain and the USA, there may in practice be less, not more, financial accountability in the non-statutory sector, although this is massively and increasingly dependent upon the injection of public funds. Kramer, for instance, has shown how the contracting-out of services to voluntary organisations in the USA can lead to situations where there is ultimately less public accountability in relation to the effective use of public funds (Kramer and Terrell, 1984). Alternatively, however, greater community involvement through voluntary organisations, including self-help and pressure-group organisations, has long been recognised as potentially leading to effective pressure for increased public spending as new needs are identified and gaps in existing service provision are exposed to public debate.

Then what about the argument that the non-state sector provides greater consumer choice in welfare? Again the answer seems to be that this is not necessarily the case. One of the clearest statements against the argument was made by Richard Titmuss (Titmuss, 1968). In the case of health, for example, the patient is typically not in a position to make an effective choice between different types of treatment; and if the patient makes the wrong choice, she or he cannot usually take this back, to be replaced like a faulty supermarket item. Patients tend to believe that the doctor or surgeon knows best (or at least this has tended to be the case in relation to the more specialised, professional areas of knowledge). Titmuss provided a particular example to demonstrate the myth of consumer sovereignty in relation to health; the example of blood for blood transfusions. His comparison of public and commercial markets in blood led him to conclude that 'In commercial blood markets the consumer is not king. He has less freedom to live unharmed; little choice in determining price; is more subject to shortages in supply; is less free from bureaucratization; has fewer opportunities to express altruism; and exercises few checks and controls in relation to consumption, quality and external costs. Far from being sovereign, he is often exploited' (Titmuss, 1970).

In any case, in practice there is evidence that, in practical terms, private health care is not necessarily purchased by individuals exercising rational choice in the market. For example, a survey of 3000 middle-aged men in the more affluent parts of Kent, which is situated in Britain's relatively affluent South East, found that although three out of ten were subscribing to private health-care insurance, most had not personally chosen to do so; the insurance was a managerial perk or a fringe benefit. 'Many said that they would stop subscribing if they left their firms, mainly because of expense or political principle. . . . 'Most respondents did not know the "best buys", and relied on G.P.s' (Calnan, 1991). The report of the survey concluded that using the private sector could enable patients to jump NHS queues; but that overall, 'The major constraints on choice within the private sector suggest that the introduction of market principles into the NHS will do little to enhance choice' (ibid). In any case, it has been suggested that the introduction of internal markets within the NHS has been concerned with the issue of choice and value for money for the purchaser; and the purchasers are typically administrators or doctors who hold their own budgets, not patients.

So what about the voluntary sector? Do voluntary organisations offer greater choice? The broad arguments about the consumer's reliance upon professionals when purchasing services such as health and education apply across the sectors. Nor is it necessarily the case that consumers/clients will have more choice about the way in which services are delivered in the voluntary sector. The more traditional types of charity may be just as patronising as the state sector, and just as likely to believe that they are the best judge of what the consumer really needs. National voluntary organisations have their own policies and priorities which have to be taken into account by both staff and clients at the local level. Even where there is a high level of commitment, in principle, to local involvement and user choice, there may be conflicts of interest. For example the national voluntary agencies that have supported the development of family centres have been identified as experiencing difficulties in relinquishing control to local management groups. As Gibbons' study concluded, being part of a national voluntary agency limited local projects' accountability and their ability to respond to changing local needs (Gibbons, 1990).

Charities that rely upon traditional private-sector funding may also carry the particular agendas of the sponsors in question, agendas which may imply major biases in the type of services that are or are not provided. This may leave even less choice, particularly for less conventionally popular clients, such as unmarried mothers, the long-term unemployed, ex-offenders or drug abusers.

Of course choice within particular services is not the only issue here. More fundamentally, perhaps, the logic of choice would imply that there should be a multiplicity of provision. In a fully developed mixed economy of welfare the client would be able to choose between a range of private, public, voluntary and informal care services. But this is not the reality. Those who can afford to do so can certainly choose to buy private services; a choice that is not available to the rest of the population. But there is not, typically, a range of comparable statutory and voluntary services from which the client can make a rational choice; if there were, there would almost certainly be allegations of duplication and waste, and calls for the services in question to work out appropriate divisions of labour.

Having argued that a mixed economy of welfare does not necessarily offer real choice, however, is not to argue that the issues of choice and accountability are not vitally important ones. On the contrary, debates about ways of promoting greater accountability and choice have been central to discussions about ways of improving welfare-state provision. But these discussions can also be developed, and have been developed, within the context of greater democracy and user involvement within the framework of public-sector provision and public-sector support for voluntary and community-based provision.

This brings us to the next point. State provision has been criticised for being inherently bureaucratic. In contrast it has been argued that the private and voluntary sectors can be more flexible and more innovative in meeting clients' needs. Yet again the evidence would seem to demonstrate that this is not necessarily so.

The term 'bureaucracy' has widely differing meanings (see for example Albrow, 1970, for a more detailed discussion of the different sociological uses of the term). Typically, in everyday usage the word bureaucracy has negative connotations. It is widely used in a pejorative sense to refer to organisational inefficiency, for example, and to 'red tape' and the stifling of creativity. But the founding father sociologist, Weber, developed the concept of bureaucracy in a broader way, posing a more fundamental set of questions about complex organisations in modern industrial society. Weber used the term bureaucracy in relation to the development of rationality in large-scale organisations in both public and private sectors, covering business organisations as well as state organisations, the military, political parties and voluntary and charitable organisations. Bureaucratic forms of organisation, according to Weber, were based upon formal structures with impersonal rules applied by paid officials, 'without hatred or passion', fear or favour.

Overall, Weber argued, bureaucratic forms of organisation were technically superior to traditional forms of organisation in pre-industrial society, which was based upon inherited status and personal loyalty; or who you knew, rather than what you knew. Sociologists have differed as to how far Weber was also aware of the downside, the negative dysfunctions of bureaucracy; he was certainly aware that bureaucratic forms of organisation were potentially very powerful and difficult to control through democratic processes. But functional or dysfunctional, he argued that bureaucratic forms of organisation were fundamentally associated with the development of modern, industrial society.

The key issue then may be more to do with the problems of exerting democratic controls over bureaucracies and minimising their dysfunctions, and less to do with whether or not particular sectors are inherently bureaucratic. By definition, large-scale organisations can be expected to have many if not all of the characteristics identified by Weber, whether these organisations are in the public, private or the voluntary sector. The alternative to formal rules, for instance, would in any case pose further problems, because in the absence of formal rules officials would exercise their discretion according to their own views of the clients in question. Similarly the alternative to formal structures and procedures for the appointment and promotion of officials would be appointment and promotion according to informal networks based upon who you are or who you know. This of course has been the precise criticism of those who have argued for formal structures that would promote equal opportunities in appointments and promotions and thus would break the self-perpetuating charmed circles of powerful, white middle-class men in official positions, be these in the public sector, the private sector or even on boards composed of the 'great and the good, and their wives', who have been said to run the affairs of particular voluntary-sector organisations.

The same applies to the role of professionals within formal organisations, and the issue of how to define and enforce acceptable limits on professional power. Voluntary organisations, and especially the larger, well-established service-delivery organisations, employ professional staff just as public and private-sector organisations do. There are real and important issues about where and how to define the boundaries of professional judgement and discretion, for instance, and about the most appropriate balance to be struck between professionals' accountability to their clients and to the wider community. But these issues are not simply reducible to decisions about where professionals are employed. They cut across sectors, just as the wider issues of bureaucratic organisation do.

So, on balance, are the non-state sectors more flexible, creative and innovative? The answer once again seems to be yes and no; or not necessarily. There are of course excellent examples of innovation and creativity in the voluntary and informal sectors. This seems to have been especially so in particular periods, such as from the mid-1960s, in Britain and the USA when there was some upsurge in innovation, including innovation in meeting needs and innovation amongst self-help and mutual-aid groups. But there are also examples of non-state organisations failing to innovate or respond to changing needs. Crossman's caricature of the voluntary sector as traditional, paternalistic, middle-class do-gooding did not disappear altogether in the postwar period.

There have of course also been examples of relatively traditional policies and practices being dressed up as innovation, because that has often been a funding requirement. In other words funders, be these government funders or private or charitable foundations have tended to emphasise their interest in supporting innovatory projects, but they support them for only a limited time (a feature, for example of the British Urban Programme). This strategy allows sponsors to ration funds, or at least to prevent all their funds from becoming tied up in a limited number of projects; but it places the onus upon the voluntary sector to be constantly devising new ways of presenting projects so that they fit into the latest fashion in grantmanship, whether or not this is really innovatory, or indeed whether innovation is actually what the clients need (they may of course much prefer the continuation of a regular, non-innovatory but essential service, such as a day-care centre, with or without experimentation).

Conversely there have been examples of innovation and change within the state sector. Johnson, for instance, provides examples of innovation in the statutory sector, including the British government's attempts to promote community development and public participation through the Community Development Project. He concluded that 'voluntary organizations do not have a monopoly of pioneering enterprise' (Johnson, 1981, p. 38). Similar points could be made about the attempts by the federal US government to develop new policies and promote citizen participation in the war on poverty in the 1960s (discussed in more detail in Chapter 3).

Perhaps one of the more notable of the relatively recent British examples might be the attempts by some local authorities to promote equal opportunities, both within their own structures and in terms of the services they provided to the public. This latter point does of course raise a further consideration. It could be argued that equal-opportunities policies in the public sector did not arise in a vacuum or even because of the simple benevolence of public-sector organisations. On the contrary, the policies were adopted because there were autonomous movements that were becoming increasingly effective in campaigning against institutional racism and sexism. So innovation and change did, in this wider sense, relate to the existence of voluntary organisations, broadly defined, and to their capacity to bring outside pressure to bear on the public sector. This role of the voluntary sector, as watchdog and source of wider democratic pressure for change, is key to subsequent discussions.

Overall then, the widespread claim that the voluntary sector in particular has some special capacity for flexibility and innovation has to be treated with caution. Despite the literature on the voluntary sector's 'capacity for innovation' (from the Webbs to the Younghusband, Wolfenden and Barclay Reports in Britain), and the very widespread myth that this is the case, Brenton concludes from British and US evidence that 'Voluntary organisations in general cannot then be described as uniquely creative, flexible and innovatory' (Brenton, 1985, p. 184). Brenton goes on to demonstrate that the statutory sector has also been a source of innovation. She quotes for instance from the Barclay Report: 'While much innovation comes from the voluntary sector, there is also clear evidence that innovation is increasingly common in local authority social service departments, though interestingly it was rarely cited in their evidence to us' (ibid., p. 184.)

If the non-statutory sector is in general not necessarily more flexible and innovatory, what about the more specific view that the state-welfare system has been so inherently racist and sexist that it has been unable effectively to tackle institutional discrimination, from within? Or at least not without effective external pressure. Over the 1970s and 1980s there developed a critical literature, that demonstrated just how deeply the welfare state in Britain has been affected by racism and sexism in society as a whole (Wilson, 1977).

More recently Williams has developed this critique of social policy in terms of an integrated analysis of race and gender in relation to social class, an approach which, she argues, has been missing as race and gender have been neglected or marginalised, both in the mainstream and on the left. 'The arguments of the mainstream for redistribution between rich and poor, for universal as against selective welfare provision, for the state and not the market, failed to acknowledge the need for redistribution within families as well as between them, to recognize the specific as well as the general needs of women and Black people' (Williams, 1989, p. 9).

Women and black and ethnic minorities did not just wait, though, until such time as their needs should finally emerge on the social policy agenda. On the contrary, women organised to meet their own needs, for example through developing refuges for battered women and women's community-health projects, such as well-women centres. Women's health-care provision has also been an important issue for women's organisation in the USA (see for example Dale and Foster, 1986; Ruzek, 1978).

In addition women's and black and ethnic-minority groups also organised to put pressure on the mainstream of the public sector to combat institutionalised racism and sexism. This pressure included demands for the public sector to increase the scope of its interventions; for the police to intervene more actively and more sensitively to protect women from domestic violence; for local authorities to provide more child care; for the public sector to combat racism and sexism, within its own ranks through equal opportunities policies, and to exert its influence on the private sector, for example, through including equal-opportunity provisions in public contracts when purchasing goods and services from the private sector (that is, contract compliance).

The point to emphasise here is that whilst the welfare state has been fundamentally criticised for being inherently racist and sexist, neither women's organisations nor black and ethnic-minority organisations have abandoned the public sector as beyond improvement. On the contrary, as Williams for instance demonstrates, there have been significant differences of emphases about strategies and tactics, depending, at least in part, on major differences of theoretical approach and orientation. So liberal feminists, for instance, have been characterised by 'belief in the state as a vehicle for reforms' (Williams, 1989, p. 45), such as maternity leave and state provision of day care, whilst radical feminists have placed more emphasis upon providing 'alternatives to the mainstream forms of state welfare provision', such as women's refuges, and well-women centres (ibid., p. 56). Socialist feminists and black feminists have also differed, both in their analyses of the underlying causes of their oppression and in the most effective strategies to combat this. Women's and black and ethnic-minority groups have gone outside state provision and developed their own forms of welfare provision, either as a matter of choice or simply because self-organisation seemed the only effective way to meet their needs. But this has been taking place within the framework of different strategies, some of which are directed towards combatting racism and sexism in the public sector, and some of which are more geared towards meeting needs through alternative forms of provision; or both. Dale and Foster, for instance, have argued that feminists need to pursue both sets of strategies. Despite the difficulties they maintain that 'feminists must surely keep fighting for reforms to existing welfare institutions' (Dale and Foster, 1986, p. 155) They also argue that feminists should 'put at least some of their efforts into creating and developing alternative forms of welfare provision' (ibid., pp. 171–2) as 'working models of egalitarian, liberating forms of welfare provision' (ibid., p. 172).

It is of course also important to emphasise that racism and sexism are by no means confined to the public sector. Discrimination and oppression have occurred, and do still occur, in the private sector, even when women and black people are prepared to pay privately for services. For example discrimination has taken place in housing finance, with women and black and ethnic minority groups having found it harder to obtain mortgages, and with particular neighbourhoods being 'redlined' or effectively boycotted by savings and loan associations because they were seen as subject to racial change, and therefore not a good credit risk (see, for example, Jean Pogge and David Flax-Hatch, in Nyden and Wiewel, 1991). And the voluntary and informal sectors have their own forms of institutional racism and sexism to combat, which can affect community groups as well as large and well-established voluntary organisations. Black feminists, for example, have pointed to the fact that racism can also affect feminist groups.

The implications of all this are wide reaching. As has already been suggested, organised pressure from women and from black and ethnic minority groups has been central in getting racism and sexism onto the public agenda; but the strategies that have been developed as a consequence, have included strategies for change within the public sector as well as the development of alternative forms of provision. There have also been key demands for the state to play a more active role in promoting equal opportunities within the voluntary and informal sectors (for example through the use of equal opportunities clauses in contracts between local authorities and the voluntary organisations to whom they provide grant aid).

This brings the argument to the final assertion: that voluntary welfare provision and self-help provision have a vital role in promoting active participation and pluralist democracy in society as a whole. This type of approach has been put forward in the British context by Hadley and Hatch (1981). At the simplest level, being a volunteer can be considered a form of participation and active citizenship.

But in itself this is a somewhat limited view of participation. Voluntary organisations are not necessarily more democratically accountable than public bodies, neither do they necessarily involve their staff more actively, let alone their clients. Nor, as has already been suggested, do they necessarily avoid biases of race, gender or class, and these biases also affect the type of voluntary work that people undertake. The 1981 General Household Survey found (perhaps unsurprisingly to many women) that men, especially professional men, were more likely to sit on committees and give advice, whilst women, especially working-class women, were more likely to provide practical help to neighbours or local groups. The 1991 National Survey of Voluntary Activity in the UK provided similar evidence of class biases and gender differences in the pattern of volunteering. For instance men were still rather more likely to be sitting on committees than women, and to be providing information and advice to others, whilst women were rather more likely to be providing direct services, including the provision of informal care. That may still be a very long way away from participation in terms of being involved in key decision-making processes, or participating in decisions concerning the use of significant resources.

So the voluntary sector, even the self-help end of the voluntary sector, does not necessarily involve effective access to participation in decision-making more widely. On the contrary, volunteers can be struggling to provide practical help whilst key decisions over the allocation of vital resources are taken elsewhere, within local and/or, increasingly, central government, or within private-sector organisations.

But this does not of course mean that the public sector would be more democratic and participatory without the voluntary sector. The more traditional do-gooding charities may have done little to promote wider participation and democracy. But that has only been part of the story. The upsurge of new forms of organisation – including self-help and mutual-aid groups, new community and tenants organisations and federations, and other campaigning and advocacy organisations – since the 1960s can be seen as important in their own right as part of an alternative tradition. And they can be seen as important in terms of promoting participation and democracy in a wider sense; as sources of pressure on the public sector. This watchdog and campaigning role for the voluntary sector has been widely recognised as crucial to democracy in the welfare state. As Brenton, for instance, has argued (1985, pp. 220–1) 'If there is one direction in which the voluntary sector could make a significant and valuable contribution to the overall goal of meeting social need, it is that of mounting a watchdog role over the main-line provisions of the welfare state. . . . Such an advocacy function needs to operate at the level of neighbourhood community action, advice and information services, as well as at the national level where the interests of minority, unpopular or neglected groups and causes require social policy and legislative response.' Some of these issues are discussed in more detail in Chapter 6, and in relation to the cases in Chapter 7.

Having reviewed some of the evidence, then, overall it does seem clear that a number of myths have been circulating about the supposed advantages of the non-state sector in the welfare state. The reality would seem to be that there are indeed important functions for the non-state sector, and especially so in relation to the watchdog role to be played by particular types of voluntary organisations. But on the basis of the arguments set out in this chapter, there is no overwhelming case to support any wholesale shift away from the public sector, towards increased private and/or voluntary-sector provision.

In fact there is evidence to suggest that any attempts at wholesale substitution of private-sector services for public-sector services would involve major problems of equity. There are in any case aspects of service provision which have, at least so far, remained relatively unattractive to the private sector because they have relatively low potential in terms of profitability (Whitfield, 1992).

There is also evidence to suggest that attempts at wholesale substitution of voluntary-sector services for public services would be quite unrealistic. The voluntary sector is not in a position to undertake such a major shift, even if voluntary organisations were to choose to go down the path of widespread substitution. Public funds will in any case continue to be necessary for the provision of services in all sectors, as will overall public planning of service provision (Brenton, 1985; Webb and Wistow, 1987). Meanwhile, policies that do attempt to shift the balance of the mixed economy of welfare can be expected to have considerable effects and put considerable strain on the voluntary sector. As Adams, for instance, has argued '[a]lthough the self-help movement has enormous potential, there are inherent dangers' especially if self-help is offered as 'an alternative rather than as a complement, to needed human services. . . . While there is an enormous role for decentralised local participation and small group forms, these must be integrated with changes of national scope. Small is beautiful only if it is part of what is large and functional' (Adams, 1990, p. 122). Subsequent chapters will return to some of these tensions and dilemmas, which voluntary organisations, including self-help community organisations, face when confronted with attempts to change their roles in the shifting balance of the mixed economy of welfare.

Identifying some choices and some alternative implications

So why exactly has there been so much interest in shifting the balance of the mixed economy of welfare? If the logic for such a shift is not straightforwardly and unambiguously compelling in terms of practical social policy and administration, or even in terms of cost effectiveness, then differing political approaches towards the welfare state, and towards the role of the state more generally, need to be examined. This may help to unravel some of the underlying agendas. And it may help, too, in identifying the implications of some of the choices to be made, choices for governments, local authorities and private organisations, and choices for voluntary organisations and local communities, as they develop their own strategies and tactics.

As the Introduction illustrated, the new-right perspectives that were used to justify and explain government policies in Britain and the USA in the 1980s started from the view that the state should play a minimal, residual role. Left to itself the free market would be the most effective mechanism for generating wealth in society (Hayek, 1973, p. 47). State intervention in the economy, and in welfare, must be kept to a minimum if market mechanisms are to succeed. Beyond this minimum provision, welfare should be the responsibility of individuals and their families. For the new right this approach has a moral as well as a political dimension. Murray, for instance, defines the poor not only in terms of their lack of material success; the poor, he argues, are 'defined by their behaviour' (Murray, 1990, p. 1). 'Work', he argues, 'is at the centre of life' and men who do not work do not make good husbands and fathers (ibid., p. 22). Too much state welfare merely reinforces dependency and encourages symptoms of social irresponsibility, such as high rates of illegitimacy and criminal behaviour. Poor communities will be more successful, he argues, if individuals, families and communities take more responsibility for their own welfare. These, then, were the types of political and moral arguments that were used to justify strategies to shift the balance of welfare towards the residual end of the spectrum.

Conversely critics have argued that 'the New Right and business interests are determined to create more favourable conditions for capital accumulation in the 1990s and the twenty-first century. . . . 'Now the "social wage" [health, education, welfare and other services] is being clawed back by capital' (Whitfield, 1992, p. 4). The new right has pursued strategies to fragment welfare state services and undermine the pay, conditions and trade-union organisation of those who have been employed to provide them. 'Rolling back the state', in these terms, has effectively meant that central government has been concerned with undermining as well as directly confronting potential sources of opposition. Local authorities in particular, have been bypassed and marginalised, although they have also been left to cope with frustrated local demands for services such as public housing, demands which local authorities have been increasingly unable to meet.

In contrast reformist approaches to the state have started from the assumption that, within the mixed economy of modern, industrial capitalist societies, the market mechanism is inherently problematic. The market economy has produced economic development, but even within the economic sphere the modern state will typically need to intervene, positively, to plan and to promote further balanced growth. In the process of economic development, meanwhile, new needs have been generated, needs which cannot necessarily be met by individuals and families through traditional mechanisms. The family itself, it is argued, has changed as a result of industrialisation, and this has tended to break down traditional extended family patterns of caring for dependent members. Wilensky and Lebeaux (1965), for instance, set out their account of the growth of public intervention in welfare in the USA in terms of such a perspective. In Britain the Fabian Society, which exerted a key influence on debates on welfare, and especially on the development of the welfare state, since the Second World War has been associated with a similar perspective. Williams, for example, summarises this type of approach to the welfare state, and summarises both its strengths and its limitations (Williams, 1989).

From these perspectives there have been fundamental criticisms of new-right strategies to shift the balance of the mixed economy of welfare away from the state towards the private sector, and towards voluntary-sector and community provision. Whilst not hostile to the private sector per se, reformist perspectives, including reformist perspectives based upon the Fabian tradition, have been firmly convinced of the central role of the state. The potential for increasing the role of the private sector has been seen to be constrained, according to these perspectives, because the requirements of private profitability need to be balanced by state intervention to ensure that goals of social justice and equity are safeguarded, and to ensure that the use of scarce resources is coherently planned. In parallel, reformists have tended to express reservations about the potential for enhancing the role of the voluntary sector and community-based self help, although, as has already been suggested, positions on this have shifted over past decades and few would continue to argue that the voluntary sector either would or should wither away.

The reformist approach came under increasing attack in the 1960s and 1970s, as the new right argued that increasing state intervention was at the roots of the mounting economic difficulties. Increasing state welfare was compounding these economic problems as well as reproducing social dependency and social pathologies according to the new right. In contrast, as has also been suggested, there were criticisms from the left, both from the Marxist left and from the more libertarian left. Marxist approaches to the state have emphasised that, in a capitalist society, the state has not ultimately been neutral. There were inherent limits to the extent to which the state could promote social reform, because the state was itself a capitalist state. Miliband's 1969 study, *The State in Capitalist Society*, represented a classic statement of this approach, along with his debate with Poulanztas on the theoretical nature of the capitalist state. Miliband set out to demonstrate that the state in Western societies was not ultimately impartial; a great weathervane which could be swung in response to different opinions and in response to pressures to meet social needs. Rather Miliband set out to explore the alternative view that the state might be a 'rather special institution, whose main purpose is to defend the predominance of a particular class' (Miliband, 1969, p. 3). Whilst Miliband recognised and analysed important areas where the state could be used to promote social reform and civil liberties, ultimately he saw the possibilities of this as fundamentally limited. Reform was possible, but 'reform always and necessarily falls far short of the promise it was proclaimed to hold: the crusades which were to reach "new frontiers", to create "the great society", to eliminate poverty, to abolish the class struggle, to assure justice for all, etc., etc., – the crusades regularly grind to a halt and the state comes under renewed and increased pressure' (ibid., p. 271). (This perspective may seem more relevant than ever in the light of experiences since the 1960s.)

The implications of this type of analysis of the capitalist state were developed in relation to the welfare state more specifically (for instance, Ginsburg, 1979, Gough, 1979;). The welfare state, according to these types of approaches was seen as fundamentally contradictory; representing real and often important gains for labour, but also performing important functions for capital by assisting in the process of social reproduction, in particular reproducing social relations, installing the work ethic and providing wider legitimacy, making governments credible, and sustaining popular belief in the possibility of achieving social change through the existing social system. Marxists, in general, have therefore tended to be sceptical about the extent to which the welfare state could meet the social needs that were being reproduced in capitalist society, let alone the extent to which the welfare state could lead to wider social equality.

But welfare state gains, however inherently limited according to Marxist perspectives, have still to be defended, both through parliamentary processes and through wider popular pressures. So Marxists have supported both trade-union and community-based campaigns to defend or to improve welfare-state services, and to defend or to improve welfare-state jobs, pay and conditions. In the context of debates with the new right about shifting the boundaries of the mixed economy of welfare, Marxists have argued for transforming rather than undermining public provision. And whilst the logic of this position is to support popular attempts to democratise welfare provision, and to enhance the potential contributions of community and trade union organisations, this has to be achieved in ways which reinforce rather than undermine the framework of public-sector responsibility and public-sector resource provision. There is considerable potential for alliances to be built in practice, between those who support this type of approach on the one hand, and those who support reformist approaches on the other.

There have been potential tensions as well as potential meeting points between reformist and Marxist perspectives on the welfare state, in contrast with libertarian socialist perspectives on the welfare state. For libertarian socialists the state, by definition, represents the key, oppressive force in society. According to this perspective, socialism in general, and welfare more specifically, can only be achieved through small-scale cooperative efforts, based upon mutual aid. Examples of this type of thinking can be found, in the work of Illich on education (Illich, 1973) and the work of Ward on housing (Ward, 1976). Since libertarian socialists share reformist and Marxist objectives of promoting the democratisation of welfare provision through the enhancement of cooperation, participation and community control, there is considerable common ground, and scope for alliances to be built, around the joint defence and improvement of welfare provision.

But there have also been important differences arising from contrasting views on the role of the state, and the ultimate desirability or undesirability of strategies based upon the preservation of the framework of public-sector responsibility underpinned by public-sector resource provision.

Whilst there have been insights to be gained from libertarian approaches and experiences of self-organisation, as will be argued subsequently, there have also been important tensions between these types of approach and those of reformists and Marxists. Without such state support the most vulnerable groups and communities risk finding that, in practice, libertarian socialist freedom to provide welfare within your own community, on the basis of self-help and mutual aid, comes to resemble the freedom of the market, as advocated by the new right.

The argument which is developed in this book is that the goal of achieving greater democratic accountability and pluralism *within* the framework of public-sector responsibility and public-sector provision needs to be contrasted with the new-right approach, in which individual consumer choice is couched in terms of strategies to undermine public-sector responsibility and public-sector provision.

2

The Shifting Concept of Community

It is doubtful whether the concept 'community' refers to a useful abstraction (Stacey, 1969, p. 134).

The term community is used in different senses for different purposes. As used by the sociologist, no one seems to agree on the concept or indeed whether there is any such animal (Community Work and Social Change – a Report on Training, 1968).

There is an issue about whether community is fact or fiction (Cooper, 1989, p. 183).

'When I use a word' Humpty Dumpty said in a rather scornful tone, 'it means just what I choose it to mean – nothing more and nothing less.' 'The question is', said Alice, 'whether you can make things mean so many different things' (Milson, 1974).

The concept of 'community' is notorious for its shiftiness. Beside the term 'community', the myths and ambiguities inherent in some of the notions surrounding 'the mixed economy of welfare could be considered to be relative models of clarity. There is a case to answer as to whether 'community' should actually continue to be used at all.

This chapter explores some of the ambiguous and contradictory uses of the term. Community has been used in different ways over time. And it has been used within the context of alternative sociological approaches and competing political orientations. These fundamental differences are key, it will be argued. It is not just that the term community has been used ambiguously; it has been contested, fought over, and appropriated for different uses and interests to justify different politics, policies and practices. Having looked at some of these competing uses of community, the second part of this chapter looks at some of the contrasting ways in which official policies have been developed to promote community development, community organisation, community participation and community care.

Historical approaches to 'community'

In his critical collection, *Keywords*, Raymond Williams (1976) included an entry on the keyword, 'community', which provides a useful starting point from which to disentangle the history of the term's conflicting uses. Williams pointed out that community has been in the English language since the fourteenth century. Originally it was used to refer to the common people, as opposed to those of rank, or to a state or organised society. Subsequently (by the sixteenth century) the term was used to refer to 'the quality of having something in common' and to 'a sense of common identity and characteristics'. Community also came to be used to refer to a particular quality of relationship, as well as to refer to a distinction between community and civil society on the one hand and the state on the other, and between 'more direct, more total and therefore more significant relationships of community and the more formal, more abstract and more instrumental relationships of state, or of society in its modern sense', as developed in the work of Toennies (1976). From the nineteenth century, then, the term was used to contrast communities and localities with larger, more complex industrial societies.

Williams pointed to further uses, including the notion of community in relation to alternative, often Utopian ways of group living. And he included the use of community in the term community politics, 'which is distinct not only from national politics but from formal local politics and normally involves various kinds of direct action and direct local organisation, "working directly with people", as which it is distinct from "service to the community", which has an older sense of voluntary work supplementary to official provision or paid service' (Williams, 1976, p. 65).

Williams concluded that there is a common thread in these different uses, in that community tends to be used as a 'warmly persuasive word' whether this is to describe an existing set of relationships or an alternative set of relationships. Unlike all other terms of social organisation, he argues, 'it seems never to be used unfavourably, and never to be given any positive opposing or distinguishing term' (ibid., pp. 65–6). This stakes out a useful agenda for reviewing the use of the term 'community.' The final point, however, about the predominance of warm and favourable connotations turns out to be more problematic than Williams seems to have recognised.

William's approach in *Keywords* has provided a starting point for further historical anaylsis. Eileen and Stephen Yeo's survey of the use of community pick out three different and competing aspects and meanings. They start from the sixteenth-century usage of community as 'holding something in common, a feeling of common identity and, most positively of all, a quality of mutual caring in human relations' (Yeo and Yeo, 1988, p. 231), the type of community envisaged, for instance by the Diggers in the seventeenth century and by socialists such as Robert Owen and William Morris in the nineteenth century. This community of mutual caring – a community 'made by people for themselves', (ibid., p. 231), community as a 'vision of a fully liberated humanity living in supportive social relations' (ibid., p. 232) – is contrasted with two alternative approaches: community as service and community as the state.

Community as service, it was argued, was developed in the nineteenth century as a middle-class ideal of service to the poor, in place of working-class mutuality and community. University settlements, for example, provided vehicles for middle-class philanthropy in 'suitable centres of a strong community life' (ibid., p. 239). This middle-class approach to community, the Yeos argue, 'with its stress on service within formal organisations tended to restrict working class women and to displace their communities' (ibid., p. 241). And it tended to be invoked 'in and against situations of working class militancy' (ibid., p. 242).

Following on from this, they argue, 'community as the state' refers to a usage which sets out 'the community' and community interests as interpreted by the state, in opposition to independent working-class action. They suggest that the term has been increasingly hijacked for this type of more coercive use, during the twentieth century. In 1925 Stanley Baldwin when commenting on the miners, said: 'If the will to strike should overcome the will to peace temporarily . . . let me say that no minority in a free country has ever yet coerced a whole community. The community will always protect itself' (p. 247). This use of community may be found more recently of course, and once again in relation to the miners, who were defined in terms of the community's 'enemy within' in the strike of 1984–5 (Samuel *et al.*, 1985).

Sociological approaches to 'community'

Sociological approaches to the concept of community provide another way into the contradictory and conflicting usages of the word. Bulmer's 1987 study *The Social Basis of Community Care*, unpacks some of the most frequently used bowdlerised versions of sociological ideas and studies. Community, as Bulmer illustrates, can be defined in terms of people who live in a common geographical area. Or it can be defined in terms of common interests, interests which may be as diverse as 'ethnic origin, religion, politics, occupation, leisure pursuits or sexual propensity, as in the Jewish community . . . the occupational community of the police' or the 'gay community' (Willmott, 1984, p. 5) 'The two types of community are not mutually exclusive – quite small areas may have different interest communities within them – but they tend to point in rather different directions' (ibid.). As Bulmer points out, such diverse uses can cover a very wide range of meanings. As he went on to demonstrate, in an article back in 1955 Hillery found ninety-four sociological definitions, and all that they had in common was that they dealt with people. Similarly Bulmer quoted Halsey's conclusion that the term has so many meanings as to be meaningless (Bulmer, 1987, p. 28). Such a wide-ranging description describes everything and therefore nothing.

So does it help, to unpack the term further, to investigate community's relationship with different sociological approaches in more analytical terms in order to analyse the nature of social relations and social change more generally?

In classic sociological usage, Toennies' terms of *gemeinschaft* and *gesellchaft*, approximately translated as 'community' and 'association', relate to a particular sociological approach to the interpretation of social change. According to this approach, earlier stages of social development tended to be characterised by social relationships that were small-scale and personal; community ties based upon the family and traditional community ties, Toennies argued. In contrast, industrialised, urban societies tended to be characterised by 'individualism, contractualism and the rational pursuit of interest' in an abstract, impersonal city (although Toennies was also concerned with the possibility of reintroducing traditional personal ties within modern society) (Toennies, 1957, p. 42). The disintegration of primary groups, the decline of 'community' and the development of more impersonal social relations in complex, urban, industrial societies have featured in the work of a number of the founding fathers of sociology.

As Bell explained, 'Behind such theories – whether of the left or the right – lay a 'romantic notion of the past that sees society as having once been made up of small "organic" communities that were shattered by industrialism and modern life, and replaced by an "atomistic" society which is unable to provide the basic gratifications and call forth the loyalties that the older communities knew' (Bell, 1956, p. 77). Community is seen in these terms as idealised, a lost world which may or may not be recoverable; a nostalgic approach which has nevertheless had considerable influence in sociological debates. This has also been the starting point for a range of empirical studies that have set out to explore how far this 'lost community' relates to the reality of particular communities. Such an approach has interest in its own right. And it is clearly highly relevant in policy terms for community care to know to what extent community ties still persist, or could at least be revived, to provide informal caring (whether or not such a revival of traditional neighbourhoods would be desirable, in any case, marked as such neighbourhoods were by insecurity and constraints, as well as by solidarity and mutual support).

The empirical evidence for the community-lost theory does not, Bulmer argues, turn out to be overwhelming. People in cities tend to draw upon the same sources of support as people in rural areas: kin, neighbours and friends. This seems to have been found in both British and US studies. On the basis of such studies, Bulmer (1987) concluded that there was little empirical evidence for the 'community-lost' thesis that urban residents lacked sources of support in comparison with rural residents.

Conversely, however, the alternative thesis of 'community saved' is not clearly documented either. Studies such as Young and Willmott in Britain (Young and Willmott, 1957) and Gans in the USA, (Gans, 1962) have identified the continuing existence of communities of urban 'villages' with strong social ties within particular neighbourhoods. But Bulmer argues that it is essential to consider the total picture of these residents' social networks. Typically the locality was an important source of networks in these studies, but so too were wider, external networks. Focusing on the neighbourhood provided only part of the total picture.

As an alternative then, Bulmer considers the value of Wellman's term 'community liberated', an approach which takes account of this wider framework of networks where ties of kin, work and residence are not necessarily combined. This approach 'frees the concept of community from its purely local roots and allows for informal ties in terms of social networks' (Wellman, 1979). This takes the concept of community back to some combination of community in terms of locality, and community in terms of shared interests, but with the major focus on the networks and ties of individuals and their families.

The empirical reality, then, does not neatly fit with the traditional nostalgia of the community-lost approach. Such an approach to the explanation of social change, and the development of modern, urban, industrial society, has been subjected to criticism, too, on more theoretical grounds. In particular, Marxist sociologists have argued that such an approach obscures the nature of the capitalist class relations which actually divide communities, within both urban and rural areas, in modern industrial societies. Castells, for instance, in his earlier work criticised the very notion of 'urbanism', as developed by Wirth and others in the Chicago school of urban sociology, as an ideological approach that obscures the underlying importance of capital, and capitalist social relations which underpin both urban and other social relations (Castells, 1977). In his subsequent work, however, he also reintroduced the term community in relation to his reconsideration of the positive potential of new social movements (Castells, 1983, Lowe, 1986).

Without dismissing the term community altogether, other Marxists have also emphasised the importance of unpacking the term and disentangling the different implications for different social classes. Harvey, for instance, argues that 'Different classes construct their sense of territory and community in radically different ways' (Harvey, 1989 p. 265). 'Low income populations, usually lacking the means to overcome and hence command space, find themselves for the most part trapped in space. . . In this space, the community can be positive, in terms of mutual aid and defence, but conversely, for the poor, the community can be limiting, and can lead to mutual predation, with tight but often highly conflictual interpersonal social bonding in both private and public spaces' (ibid., p. 267). These negative aspects of community for those on low income are increasing, Harvey argues, with the processes of impoverishment, more generally, and with the spread of informalisation (by which he is referring to the increasing spread of the informal economy as a means of survival in poor areas, together with the increasing casualisation of formal employment in the wake of economic restructuring). This leads to increasing racial tension (and black and ethnic minority communities are, in any case, disproportionately at risk here). Restructuring has increased the incidence of poverty and unemployment in US cities, he argues, whilst neo-conservative policies have undercut the flow of public services, 'and hence the life-support mechanisms for the mass of the unemployed and the poor. . . The balance between competition, mutual predation and mutual aid has consequently shifted within low income populations' (ibid.). In the USA, he argues, as in Europe, there has been a dramatic rise in for instance, drug trafficking and prostitution, as well as in legal forms of the informal economy.

Conversely the term community has very different connotations for the affluent. For them, Harvey argues, the construction of community relates to the preservation of privilege: community organisations are formed, for instance, in order to maintain the 'tone' of the community, to maintain property values and to keep 'undesirables' out. The affluent are in any case more mobile, with wider choices altogether, and they have greater access to power and can therefore influence the use of wider resources; a point which has of course been noted widely, and not just by Marxists.

For Harvey, however, there are positives as well as negatives in the 'post-modern' city. He sees a role for campaigns for community control, to be waged as part of wider struggles for decentralised socialist solutions. 'True empowerment', he argues, 'must be won by struggle from below and not given out of largesse from above', and community struggles have a role, alongside class struggles, in this scenario (ibid.).

At this point it might be useful to pause briefly and draw attention to some of the differing ways in which the term 'empowerment' is used. Here Harvey is using this term within the context of the wider changes that will be required if the powerless in society are to gain power. The term empowerment is often used far more loosely however, almost as if empowerment were a technique that individuals or communities could acquire in order to gain power. Logically such an approach would imply that power in society is there for the taking; you just need to learn how to do it, to be more assertive or whatever.

If power were, in reality, equally accessible to all, in a truly pluralist, democratic society such a view would reasonably follow. But alternatively, if power is conceived in terms of its relationships with other interests in society, such as major economic interests, as Marxists for instance would argue, then power is not simply there for the taking because the powerful have vested interests in defending their power. According to this type of analysis empowerment is a key concept, but this is in the more specific and limited terms of enabling people and organisations to use most effectively the power that they do have, whether to press for immediate improvements and/or to press for longer-term goals of social change (the sense in which Harvey is using the term).

In addition to his focus on class relations, Harvey also considers the implications of polarisation and impoverishment for women in the community. Poverty has been feminised, and women have been particularly vulnerable to the processes of restructuring and informalisation, although women have also devised mechanisms for survival within this informal economy, including homeworking and informal childcare. Women have been particularly trapped within these low-income communities, although community organisations have also played a key role in their survival.

This ambivalence about the community, for women, has been considered from a number of perspectives. Bulmer, for instance, considers ways in which community can be oppressive for women. In particular community care, as a number of authors have pointed out, typically implies care by women (Finch and Groves, 1983; Ungerson, 1987; Baldwin and Twigg, 1991). Caring responsibilities, whether for children or for elderly or handicapped relatives are an important enough issue in their own right. And caring responsibilities effectively bind women to particular localities and limit their search for work, their opportunities for education and training, their social and leisure activities and their scope for wider political involvement. The community can be a prison as well as a source of mutual aid and collective solidarity. Similarly, official programmes for community intervention, whether in the form of projects to promote community care in the First World or to promote community development in the Third World, have been criticised by feminists on the grounds that such projects may add to women's existing burdens of domestic work and waged labour without empowering them to participate in developing their own alternative solutions, unless male power structures are explicitly and effectively challenged. Some of these points are picked up in Chapter 5. The very factors that tie women in the community, then, make them particularly vulnerable in official community intervention projects.

Finally, it has been pointed out that communities' own definitions of themselves may be changing and dynamic rather than constant and static. Whilst such changes may be related to wider processes of change (such as the effects of industrial restructuring, over time, in older industrial areas), particular events and crises such as the impact of a major strike may also act as catalysts. For example, in the aftermath of the 1984–5 miners' strike in Britain, a study of community, continuity and change found that some observers in one of the mining communities in the study believed that the experience of the strike had actually improved collective morale in what was already a united community where the strike had been solid. Conversely, others referred to the divisive effects of the strike, in terms of conflicts between those who remained on strike and those who broke the strike and worked where the strike had *not* been solid. In one of the communities in the study, where there were already divisions between long-established and more recent immigrants, these divisions were exacerbated by the experiences of the strike. As one miner in this area commented, 'The strike never died. That animosity with fellows is still there. When you go the club, they don't speak to each other' (Waddington, Wykes and Critcher, 1991, p. 98).

Similarly, women's active involvement in their communities was also dynamic and variable, rather than static or one-dimensional. Some women reported that their involvement in supporting the strike had resulted in long-term changes in their horizons. Being active in the strike was reported to have made many women 'very independent, it made them realise there was another life outside their home . . . a lot of them were surprised at the amount of things they could do' (ibid., p. 87). Conversely, others pointed out that women in mining villages had in any case traditionally been concerned with community issues. During the strike, women's organising around community issues such as soup kitchens and collecting money came to the fore. Whilst some women had clearly broadened the range of their experiences – and their horizons – during the strike, once the strike was over the pressure on them to revert to more traditional roles was considered to have been powerful. Some of these dynamic processes of community identification and involvement, both for women and for men, emerge again in relation to some of the case studies considered in Chapter 7, together with some of the potential implications for community work practice.

Before moving on to look at official approaches to community in terms of public policy interventions to promote community development, community organisation, community participation and community care, it might be useful to summarise the argument so far. From both historical and sociological evidence, the meaning of the term community emerges as a slippery one. It has been used in inherently ambiguous and contradictory ways. Typically community refers to geographically defined social groupings and to groupings with shared interests, although these two usages do not necessarily coincide. But it is not just the term that ambiguous; community, as a concept has been actively contested over time. As Williams argued, community is a 'warmly persuasive word'. This word has been used to try to build credence for fundamentally different projects, projects which may be inherently controlling for oppressed groups, and projects which may be liberating, conjuring up images of mutuality, and mutual caring in human relationships. More specifically, community may be used in the context of community politics, as contrasted with formal politics, and community may be set up in opposition to class and class politics. Or community struggles may be seen in the context of wider alliances (alliances which relate to class politics) to promote the empowerment of the disempowered to take more control over their own destinies (Williams, 1976, pp. 65–6).

Community and community politics

For the political left these latter aspects of debates about community took on particular significance, in the context of the relative revival of interest in Marxist perspectives, from the late 1960s, and early 1970s, followed by subsequent challenges to that interest. Community politics has featured in these debates, alongside debates about 'new social movements' in general, a term which has been used to include such diverse movements as the students' movement, the civil rights movement, the women's movement, gay liberation, the peace movement and the green movement, along with urban social movements, including residents' and tenants' movements. Broadly defined as representing shared interests as well as or in place of shared localities, each of these could just about fit into the most elastic definition of communities of interest.

For the left there have been broad questions about the nature of the relationships between these movements, with left-wing explanations and left-wing political strategies. For sections of the traditional left, and for the structuralist left, at least some of these movements were seen initially as a form of diversion and confusion, a distraction from the serious business of class politics. Initially, feminism was criticised, for instance, as a middle-class women's preoccupation, substituting gender politics for class politics. From this perspective, feminism was seen as potentially divisive by the labour movement, reinforcing divisions between working-class women and working-class men.

Alternatively, another left-wing perspective on the new social movements was that they were inherently reformist. At best, some critics argued, community politics, for instance in the form of urban social movements, could parallel the reformism of the trade-union movement, bargaining around issues of social consumption such as housing, just as the trade unions were bargaining around wages and conditions in the sphere of production, without offering any basic challenge to the rules of the game within which they were bargaining. But outside the framework of revolutionary politics such movements could not lead to any more fundamental social change. Castells, for example, referred to various urban protest movements as a form of 'urban trade unionism' (Castells, 1978, p. 171), although he also referred to their potential for playing a strategic role in wider political processes, an emphasis which he developed in his subsequent work.

Others on the left have taken up this latter view, seeing the new social movements as representing a significant way forward and offering new and more fundamental challenges to a post-industrial, or post-Fordist, form of capitalism. What, if anything, does this mean, and how, if at all, does this relate to the reality of community politics, or to local and national politics more widely?

Touraine used the term 'post-industrial society' to refer to a new type of society in which the changing forms of technology, and the changing role of knowledge and creativity, called for new forms of resistance. Whilst he did not argue that capitalist and socialist forms of society would become identical, or that the working class would become irrelevant in this new technocratic, programmed society, he did argue that the 'Working class is no longer a privileged historical agent' (Touraine, 1974, p. 17), as it had been in classical Marxist theory. By this he meant that the working class and working-class politics were no longer key to the movement for socialism. In contrast, in the aftermath of the student movement in France in May 1968, Touraine placed particular emphasis on the progressive potential of the student movement and upon the significance of cultural issues and struggles for greater participation, more generally (Touraine, 1974).

Subsequent approaches have picked up these themes and developed related and alternative arguments about the changing nature of capitalism, whether in terms of the role of knowledge and technology in production, in terms of increasing problems of legitimation and motivation in late capitalism (Habermas, 1980) or in terms of the development of post-Fordism, in which flexible specialisation and small-scale production runs were supposed to be increasingly replacing the old mass-production methods (Murray, 1988). Taken together these types of arguments have been developed to imply that, since capitalism has changed so significantly, late twentieth-century capitalism can no longer be challenged effectively by traditional working class movements or strategies. Instead new and more flexible forms of resistance are required, relating to locality and identity, and these will need to replace the older and more formal forms of organisation at national level.

As capitalism develops greater control mechanism, and intrudes further and further into people's personal lives, it has been argued, so new social movements have developed, raising demands about participation and personal autonomy, lifestyle and values, demands which involve the democratisation of everyday life. So, in the womens' movement the personal is political in a very fundamental way, which goes beyond the specifics of any traditional party programme. What is being demanded here, is a total transformation of social relations (see for example Melucci, 1988).

Taken together the new social movements have been seen, then, as posing a radically new and fundamentally more transformative type of politics, making demands for changes 'which cannot be accommodated within industrial society' (Scott, 1990, p. 153). This type of theme is picked up in Castells' work after he had rejected Marxist structuralism and moved on to see the new urban social movements as potential embryos of future societies, with the 'alternative city' as a network of self-managed, 'culturally meaningful' communities (Lowe, 1986, p. 193). This takes the argument back, perhaps, to one of Raymond Williams' definitions of community that is couched in terms of experiments in alternative types of living.

But whether the new social movements do have any such fundamentally transformative potential remains highly debatable. As Scott, for instance, has pointed out, the apparently non-negotiable nature of some of their demands may actually reflect their relative newness, rather than their ultimate nature; before it has crystallised, any movement may at first make wide demands, but then engage in the wider political process by pursuing and negotiating around more specific demands. Once the issues are successfully placed upon the political agenda, as in the case of green issues, then new tensions may be generated within the movement as more specific bargaining actually begins. Whilst these movements have tended to emphasise participation and democracy, Scott has also questioned how far they have actually pursued totally different organisational styles based upon spontaneity; in fact he refers to the existence of high levels of organisation within black churches, for example, and within the NAACP (National Association for the Advancement of Colored People) in the USA.

Nor is it easy to see the different new social movements coalescing to form a unified movement for social transformation. The previous chapter has already referred to some of the important differences of perspective within feminism, for example between liberal, reformist and socialist feminists (Williams, 1989). As Segal, for instance, has demonstrated, far from coming together by the late 1980s the women's movement had become, if anything, more fragmented (Segal, 1987). Similar points could be made in relation to black and ethnic-minority organisations, and to the green movement.

Differences between the different movements have also become clearer over time. Of course there have been links, and there have been successful alliances built between them. There have also been important historical and theoretical connections, as well as personal links (with key individuals from the civil-rights movement in the USA, for instance, going on to play key roles in the students' movement, the women's movement, and in community politics more generally. (Doug McAdam's 1988 follow-up study of the 1000 or so volunteers who went to Mississippi to register black voters in 1964 provides illustrations of these trends in terms of the subsequent life-stories of some of the individuals concerned.) But there have also been important tensions and differences. One obvious example, is the issue of identity politics and the women's movement. In both Britain and the USA black feminists have made important criticisms of the women's movement, insofar as white women have failed to recognise the importance of racial discrimination and oppression, or to understand the importance of black women's need to define their own oppressions and their own demands (Carby, 1982; hooks, 1982). White women have also attempted to grapple with some of these issues (Barrett and McIntosh, 1985). The difficulties inherent in working through these different identity politics, and developing united positions on issues of common concern have been more easily recognised than resolved.

More generally, the fragmentation of the British left in the Thatcher years was not compensated for by any major upsurge or coming together of the new social movements. In practice social movements and organisations, like labour organisations, have needed to relate to the wider political process in order to make significant practical gains. And in the 1980s, this was difficult to achieve, whatever the sphere; whether the issue concerned production or consumption there were no easy alternatives. Similar points have been made about the difficulties of building links and making connections between progressive movements and between cities and regions in the USA. It has, in fact, been argued that far from coming together to press for more radical social change, during the 1970s and 1980s, the reverse was happening, at least in some US cities. Fainstein and Fainstein, for instance, have argued that since the late 1960s 'community groups have become part of regular urban politics, routinely consulted but rarely pressing for large-scale transformation. Contemporary grass-roots activism is better captured by the term community politics than the term social movement, as urban groups have become more modest in their aims and less threatening to established power' (Fainstein and Fainstein, 1991, p. 135).

Arguing against depicting the new social movements as holding the key to social development and social transformation is not at all to deny them any positive role, however. On the contrary, in this book it will be argued that the new social movements do have a vital role to play.

This is a key point for democracy, and participation, both in the context of contemporary capitalist states and in relation to the development of socialism. As Meikins Wood argues, 'The socialist project should be *enriched* by the resources and insights of the new social movements'. But, she argues, the new social movements, and their diversity, should not be substituted for the wider struggle against capitalism (Meikins Wood, 1988, p. 80). There are parallels here with Offe's view of the role of the new social movements in terms of their contribution to building a democratic, participatory socialist society (Keane, 1984). Equally clearly, as the previous discussion of the new social movements has pointed out, there is nothing automatic about such a result. Alliances do not just happen, let alone alliances committed to building a democratic socialist society; alliances have to be painstakingly constructed by social actors, women and men. Nor is there anything inherently socialist about the new social movements. Like the term community, new social movements embody differing and often contradictory tendencies.

Official definitions and community intervention

These differing and contradictory aspects to the term community have also run through official interventions in the community. Typically, it will be suggested, governments and other official agencies have intervened to promote communities and enhance community spirit for differing and often conflicting purposes. Some of these relate to goals such as citizen participation in economic and social development, community education and social reform, and some of them relate to efforts to mobilise self-help, especially in the form of unpaid labour, whether this is unpaid labour to promote economic development or unpaid labour to provide social services, and especially to provide social care. Not infrequently such programmes have contained strong ideological and/or political agendas, starting with the British colonial policy goal of safeguarding the colonies from the fear of communist influence, post-independence, and building popular support for the legitimacy of existing economic and social relations, within the mixed economy. Of course there have been examples of programmes that have contained elements of more direct coercion, but typically, it will be suggested, the blend has been more ambiguous, closer perhaps to the carrot than to the stick.

This is not, however, to underestimate the importance of the fact that different social groups have been affected by official community-intervention programmes in different ways, and that programmes directed towards communities, as undifferentiated wholes, without taking adequate account of the social stratification patterns of those communities have tended to benefit the richer and more powerful members of those communities, often to the detriment of the poorer and less powerful. And the powerful have tended to be disproportionately male, and the less powerful to be disproportionately female. This issue has been widely identified and not only on the left. In a World Bank report on the role of community participation in development planning and project management, for instance, it was argued that community participation can be a 'two-edged sword . . . as there is a danger of the project being coopted by the politically powerful with the result that certain groups have much less access than they would have had were the project to have been administered without any community involvement' (Bamberger, 1988, p. 10).

The two-edged sword is an image which can be more widely applied. As Cary has argued, 'Community development can be viewed as both a radical and a conservative process. It is radical to the extent that, in calling for greater citizen participation, it creates new groupings and patterns of decision makers', but 'Community development can also be seen as a conservative process' by keeping issues defined, in local terms, within broadly existing social arrangements (Cary, 1970, p. 5).

From the Second World War the British government developed an interest in community development as part of the concern to promote 'the development of political institutions and political power until the day arrives when the people can become effectively self-governing, (Colonial Office, 1943). 'Mass education was seen as key in promoting the general well-being and prosperity of the community, and ensuring that true democracy could function. 'The explosive temper which may result from such a change [rapid economic and social change] can only be controlled and guided by wisely directed mass education with particular stress on the development of social and civic responsibility' (ibid., p. 7).

These, then, were some of the roots of mass-education programmes that were the forerunners of community-development programmes in the British colonies. These programmes did contain ideological and political objectives. And they contained a basic commitment to self-help to promote development, a commitment which typically involved unpaid labour. But the programmes also contained commitments to popular participation. Community development was defined as a 'movement designed to promote better living for the whole community with the active participation and on the initiative of the community' (report of the Ashridge Conference, 1954, quoted in Du Sautoy, 1958, p. 2; see Du Sautoy, 1958, for accounts of such programmes, especially in Africa). A similar commitment to community development, as a bottom upwards, rather than a top downwards approach to development, was expressed by Nehru in relation to the Indian community-development programmes. 'The initiative for the Community Projects', he argued, 'should come, wherever possible, from the people who are most affected by them' (Nehru, 1957, p. 8).

The reality, it has been argued, was somewhat different. The British colonial approach has been criticised for being essentially paternalistic. Whatever the formal commitment to participation, the focus was upon getting 'backward people in the right frame of mind', which meant providing unpaid labour for development projects (the benefits of which were disproportionately appropriated by the already powerful), and more generally in persuading them to accept the legitimacy of existing social relationships. Manhgezi, for example, has argued that such an approach had no relevance for the development needs and requirements of the underdeveloped states of tropical Africa (Manghezi, 1976).

Community development has gained such a paternalistic reputation in the Third World that the term has been effectively abandoned, in some circles, in favour of alternatives, such as community participation. (Despite this, however, the term is still used in other contexts, and so it will reappear, in this and other chapters, in spite of these understandable attempts to kill it off.) The World Bank workshop on this, in 1986, accepted a definition of community participation which was, in fact, reminiscent of the earlier definitions of community development. 'In the context of development, community participation refers to an active process whereby beneficiaries influence the direction and execution of development projects rather than merely receive a share of project benefits' (S. Paul, quoted in Bamberger, 1988). The World Bank Workshop also accepted that community participation in development projects should be seen as an evolutionary process leading to increased participation in development at local, regional or national levels. The World Bank report saw community participation as concerning economic development *and* empowerment and social justice. Community participation could lead to greater project efficiency and local resource mobilisation (especially the mobilisation of unpaid labour). Conversely it could lead to local communities making increased demands for more services. It could lead to a more equitable distribution of project benefits, or conversely to the cooption of the project by certain groups. Overall, however, despite these differing approaches and possible outcomes, the consensus was that community participation should be promoted more actively.

There are strong parallels with the more recent history of community development and community participation programmes, both in Britain, and in USA. Although there are variations in terminology, similar ranges of objectives can be identified, and a parallel diversity, in terms of the outcomes.

Before coming on to these official initiatives, however, a comment on terminology may be helpful here. In USA the terms 'community organisation' and 'community action' have been used to include official programmes that support community participation. In Britain, in contrast, community organisation has often been applied to working with agencies to develop social planning, whilst community action has been used, to refer to an approach which starts from the powerlessness of local groups and welfare publics and that seeks to mobilise them 'for the representation and promotion of their collective interests' (Bryant, 1972, p. 206). Community action in Britain has sometimes been loosely associated with conflict strategies, in contrast with consensus strategies, although Bryant himself pointed out that in reality community groups actually use bargaining and negotiating strategies as well as confrontation (Bryant, 1972, p. 208) For this discussion, then, it may be more helpful not to use the term community action in this latter sense, and to leave the term community organisation on one side.

There have of course been direct attempts to transfer programmes and approaches across the Atlantic, attempts which were particularly marked in the development of the British Community Development Project at the end of the 1960s. US experts were invited to a conference at Ditchley to pass on the lessons of the US 'War on Poverty', although when they offered some negative lessons and warnings this was not altogether appreciated by their British hosts. (See for example Loney, 1983.) Chapter 3 discusses some of these issues in more detail in relation to employment and training in both Britain and the USA.

Overall, it has been argued, community-development programmes of this type could not substitute for the wider resources that were really required to tackle poverty; but such programmes could have important benefits – including the benefits of increased organisation, self-confidence and assertiveness – in low income communities, which were disproportionately black and ethnic-minority communities (Kramer, 1969).

Such a view of the impact of community-action programmes links into a longer radical strand within the US tradition, a strand with its key focus on the empowerment of the powerless as the ultimate goal of community action. Alinsky's *Rules for Radicals* provides an explicit statement of this approach. 'In this book', Alinsky explains, 'we are concerned with how to create mass organisations to seize power and give it to the people; to realize the democratic dream of equality, justice, peace, cooperation, equal and full opportunities for education, full and useful employment, health, and the creation of those circumstances in which man [sic] can have the chance to live by values that give meaning to life' (Alinsky, 1971, p. 1). It should perhaps be noted that Alinsky was not organising with government funds, and he was himself deeply sceptical about the possibilities of the federal government's War on Poverty (although it should perhaps also be noted that Alinsky was proposing to work for the empowerment of the powerless within rather than beyond the framework of existing socio-economic relations.)

More recently, in Britain, community development has been predominantly of interest (insofar as it has been of official interest at all) to local authorities (see for example Association of Metropolitan Authorities, 1989), whilst central government has been more concerned with 'community' in relation to the promotion of community care. The emphasis has returned to the promotion of self-help, and especially of unpaid labour to provide informal care in the community for those who might otherwise need institutional care, for example in a hospital or a residential home for the elderly. The government commissioned-report by Sir Roy Griffiths (Griffiths, 1988) set out key areas for policy development in relation to community care, starting with the objective of supporting the provision of care by families, friends, neighbours and other local people, and where possible strengthening the network of care. Publicly provided community-care services would fill in the gaps left when informal care was unable to meet the needs identified. The legislation that was passed to implement community care policies, within the context of wider changes in health-service provision (The NHS and Community Care Act, 1990), reinforced this emphasis on the role of informal and community-based caring, together with increased emphasis upon the role of the voluntary and the private sectors.

Earlier in this chapter some of the potential limitations to this type of approach were discussed. There are serious questions about the extent to which such community networks currently exist, or could be developed, or indeed about who is actually going to be available to provide this care. Such scepticism is not at all to deny that many, if not most, people would prefer to remain in their own homes, with the support of informal and publicly provided community-care services, rather than go into residential care. Nor is it to imply that a wide range of community organisations are not concerned to offer unpaid labour to provide care. They do. There is widespread practical recognition of the importance of community care.

The point that is important here is the issue of balance. Are governments so concerned with the need to develop community care (and especially so as the proportion of the very elderly increases) that official support for community development becomes reduced to official support for the promotion of community care? As it was suggested in Chapter 1, there are serious dangers inherent in attempts to shift the balance of care significantly away from public towards voluntary and informal provision, and especially so in the absence of major resourcing for the voluntary and informal sectors that are supposed to play an enhanced role as service providers. Without this the policy risks being self-defeating. There are, in addition, serious problems for community organisations in attempting to take on such responsibilities, and especially so as they become involved in contracting relationships as 'providers' for local authority 'purchasers', becoming employers and taking on the management of buildings, for instance. As subsequent chapters will illustrate, community groups can be overwhelmed by such responsibilities in the absence of adequate training and support.

The point of raising these wider approaches to community development is in no way to pose them as straightforward alternatives. Nor is it in any way to negate the criticisms of previous programmes, or to underestimate the difficulties of professional community workers if they do attempt to empower the powerless whilst employed by statutory authorities. (Subsequent chapters will look in detail at some of these issues and possible ways forward.) Rather the point is simply to illustrate that official approaches to the community do not need to be confined to the promotion of community care. There is a wider tradition and an alternative set of definitions to be recaptured. Despite all the ambiguities and contradictions inherent in the very concept of community, and in policies to promote community development, there remain strands that have continuing relevance in developing more democratic approaches to welfare, and to social planning in general.

3

Policies for Jobs and Training: Community Development and Local Economic Development

This chapter sets out to consider debates about the scope and importance of policies for jobs and training in relation to community development strategies within the mixed economy of welfare. How have these debates developed over time and in different contexts? And what are the major implications for community organisations, women and black and ethnic-minority groups who are concerned to improve their opportunities for jobs and training within the framework of the mixed economy of welfare?

Economic and social planning, and community development in Third-World countries, in the south

In the previous chapter it was suggested that community-development programmes were devised and promoted in British colonies, in the postwar period in particular, for a number of reasons, including political reasons. The British government was concerned to develop adult education, and specifically mass literacy, as part of wider strategies to secure a democratic transition to self-government. Community-development programmes were also typically linked to strategies for economic development. These links were direct and explicit, for example in the case of road construction and irrigation projects, and programmes to increase agricultural productivity and promote income-generation projects.

There were also indirect links, as in the case of projects to improve the basic health, education, welfare and productivity of rural populations. T. R. Batten for instance, writing in 1957, included within the remit of community development the teaching and stimulation of new methods and skills to grow more food, have better health and possess more material goods through economic development, whilst ensuring that the 'feeling or spirit of community is not destroyed' (Batten, 1957, pp. 5, 6). Development was broadly defined, and included both economic and social objectives.

It is in no way being suggested that community-development strategies and programmes, per se, *have* necessarily provided economic development alongside goals of social justice. The reality is more complex, and far less satisfactory. All that is being suggested is that from the outset these goals of linked economic and social development were firmly placed upon the agenda for community development in the Third World.

Jobs, training and community development in Britain and the USA

In the USA jobs and training issues have been clearly on the agenda for community development, too. The Poverty Programme, which was provided with federal financial backing in 1965, had a major focus on economic issues. In fact the programme was run from the Office of Economic Opportunity. What this actually meant, in practice, however, was more contentious. (see for instance Marris and Rein, 1972). The point being made here, however, is simply that, in whatever form and from whichever perspective, the issues of jobs, training and economic opportunity more generally were at least on the agenda, just as they had been, in the Third-World context.

In contrast with the USA, and with policy for community development in British colonies, the British government's first foray into officially sponsored community development in the metropolis at the end of the 1960s, had narrower objectives by far. The government's Community Development Project (CDP) started quite explicitly from the view that economic development was not the issue. Overall, it was suggested, the mixed economy was providing economic growth that was benefiting the majority of the population.

There was some recognition of the need to improve and coordinate service delivery, as well as to tackle the pathology of deprived communities. But the need to integrate these policies with regional economic and employment policy was not addressed. In this the British programme differed from the US experience, despite the fact that British civil servants made conscious efforts to learn from their US counterparts. In 1969 Martin Rein, one of the US experts invited to comment on plans for CDP programmes, made precisely this criticism. As the Home Office account explains, 'his own conclusion [Rein's] after studying CDP was that it was likely to suffer from being planned separately from regional economic and employment policy', and that improving service provision would be inadequate, unless job opportunities were also improved (in Loney, 1983, p. 51).

This was also the view of a number of the staff who came to work in the CDP. As the different CDP teams analysed the causes of deprivation in the twelve project areas in question, a number came to the conclusion that the 'problems in their areas reflected structural changes in the economy outside the control of the local community' (Butcher *et al.*, 1990, p. 98). The implication of this view was that community development could achieve only limited gains at the neighbourhood level. Wider economic and social-planning policies were also required, at both national and regional level, if the older industrial areas were to be protected from bearing disproportionate costs of social change in terms of unemployment and poverty. More could be achieved locally, too, if community groups built alliances with 'the wider organisations of the working class, such as progressive sections of the trade union movement and political organisations' (Craig, 1989, p. 11). 'Community struggles' according to this view, 'were an important focus for change in their own right but they were also to be seen as one dimension of a broader struggle' (ibid.).

This structuralist approach was not, however, the only perspective within CDP, or, more generally on the issue of economic planning and the importance of jobs and training issues, for communities in deprived areas such as inner cities. On the contrary, the Inner Area Studies, which were sponsored by the Department of the Environment and had a less open-ended brief than the CDPs, came to similar conclusions, although from a different perspective (which was by no stretch of the imagination Marxist). By the end of the 1970s, it has been argued, the centrality of economic issues had been firmly recognised. Butcher and others argue that Peter Shore's

White Paper in 1977 'marked a sea-change in official thinking. The inner-city problem was now perceived as essentially an economic problem' (Butcher *et al.*, 1990, p. 198). The official solutions being put forward at that time included partnerships between central and local government within the framework of the mixed economy. The Urban Programme of government support for deprived areas was expanded to provide increased although still totally inadequate resources (a point made at the time by the opposition Conservative Party spokesman, Michael Heseltine) (Loney, 1983, p. 165; Smith, 1990, p. 254). But local communities were notably absent as partners, let alone as participants in broader campaigns for economic and social change.

As the next section will argue in more detail, there was a period in the early 1980s when a number of local authorities in Britain did attempt to pursue radical economic and social policies, in partnership with local communities and with women's groups and black and ethnic-minority groups. But since then there have been powerful pressures to revert to far more limited policies for local economic development. Policies have been increasingly defined by central government, and there has been pressure to work in partnerships where the interests of the private sector rather than those of the local community organisations predominate. These policies have faced increasing criticism, and by the beginning of the 1990s there was some evidence that, whether or not the substance was changing, 'the harsh language of the enterprise culture is now being tempered by softer references to the "community" and "partnership" between government, business and the local people' (Robinson and Shaw, 1991).

Jobs, training and community development; from the 1980s to the 1990s and beyond

In Britain, in the early 1980s, it has been argued, policies for jobs, training and community development became sharply polarised. The Conservative government had espoused new right economic policies that were applied to deprived areas in the form of policy instruments such as urban development corporations (UDCs) and enterprise zones (EZs). These initiatives were specifically intended to promote private-sector investment in economic regeneration by removing planning and other controls that were believed to be interfering with the operations of the free market, and by bypassing local authorities, who were believed to be bureaucratic, inflexible and too tied into the interests of their own workforces and their own constituencies (that is local communities) to respond effectively to the requirements of private capital. Whilst the language was that of the free market, it has been pointed out that UDCs and EZs actually provided public subsidies to private investors, so that the reality behind the rhetoric was not laissez faire at all but straightforward subsidy (Massey, 1982; Shutt, 1984), an issue which has been picked up and developed in subsequent criticisms of this approach.

Meanwhile, the Labour Party made gains in local elections in 1980 and 1981. In a number of areas, Labour controlled local authorities set out to find ways to counter the effects of rising unemployment, on local communities in their areas. In some areas, such as Greater London, jobs and training became key issues in the development of a political counteroffensive: the 'municipal socialism' of groupings that have been described as the new urban left (for example Boddy and Fudge, 1984; Gyford, 1985). One interpretation of this growth of municipal socialism was that, in the face of electoral defeat, nationally, the new urban left began to rethink previous policies, moving in the direction of policies for 'a far more decentralized, consumer-oriented socialism as opposed to the hitherto prevailing centralized state socialism associated with post-war Labour governments' (Butcher *et al.*, 1990, p. 100).

In reality there was continuity as well as change here. Some of the Labour councils concerned had histories of municipal socialism which provided the basis for the 'new' approaches (for example Sheffield). Nor was it the case that the municipal socialists were united in posing municipal socialism as an *alternative* to socialism at state level. On the contrary, in fact Boddy quotes David Blunkett, the then leader of Sheffield City Council, as arguing that 'If we genuinely believe in social ownership and democratic control of economic and industrial activity through direct intervention, then logically local government as well as, and not instead of central government should be a vital tool in this process. . . . Anything done at local level should not be seen as an alternative to bringing about a dramatic shift towards democratic socialist change at national level' (Boddy and Fudge, 1984, pp. 177–8).

But the new urban left was strongly committed, not only to the role of local government, but also to the active participation of local communities in local economic strategies for jobs and training. Blunkett and Jackson have described this commitment to active participation in democratic planning in the following terms: 'It [democratic planning, based upon new relationships between local authorities and local people] involves combining activities in many areas of the local economy: the spreading of economic information and analysis beyond elite policy makers; bringing voluntary groups and local communities into the economic debate; enabling workers to contribute imaginatively to the development of their industry or service; providing opportunities, support, education and training to local small businesses and cooperative enterprises in a framework of planned investment, and bringing the knowledge of what needs doing as expressed directly by those who want it closer together with those who want it done' (Blunkett and Jackson, 1987, p. 141). Mackintosh and Wainwright, in their study of the Greater London Council (GLC), set out a similar commitment to 'an innovatory method of making economic policy. It was to be developed with the participation of working people. It aimed to strengthen the control of working class Londoners over resources and policy' (Mackintosh and Wainwright, 1987, p. 2).

In addition to this commitment to community participation, a number of authorities were also committed to the development of equal opportunities, both in terms of jobs and training and in terms of services and service delivery. The importance of local authorities' potential role in promoting equal opportunities was recognised far more widely than that of the municipal socialists in the mid-1980s. For example CIPFA (the Chartered Institute of Public Finance and Accountancy) spelt out the importance of local authorities intervening to ensure access for 'disadvantaged groups eg. – ethnic minorities, women, the disabled, ex-offenders etc., to quality training opportunities which will allow them to compete on equal terms in the labour market.' Without such intervention, the CIPFA paper argued, there were dangers that 'members of these groups may be relegated to second class training schemes, which may do little more than keep them off the unemployment register' (CIPFA, 1985, p. 72).

The municipal socialists were also committed to equal opportunities as part of a wider commitment to social justice. In addition to the arguments about social justice it was also argued that unless disadvantaged groups in the labour force were supported by policies to enhance their pay, working conditions and job prospects, then it would be correspondingly difficult to implement wider, progressive policies 'to regenerate the British economy and break with its role as a low-wage and low-productivity economy' (Costello, Michie and Milne, 1989). Otherwise such attempts to break out of the low-wage, low-productivity cycle would be undermined by employers who were able to undercut pay and conditions by exploiting the vulnerability of the most disadvantaged. Finally, there were also political considerations here, with some of the relevant politicians committed to the development of a 'rainbow coalition' to build a wide base of support, especially in areas where the traditional working class vote was seen to be declining as manufacturing and transport jobs were disappearing.

So what did these new approaches to local economic strategies actually mean in practice? For the purposes of this chapter, three separate, although related, aspects of policy will be considered. Firstly, there were policies to intervene in the restructuring process in the private sector to safeguard existing jobs and promote new ones, whether this intervention took the form of investment or other forms of direct intervention, or whether it took the form of indirect intervention, for example through land-use planning policies and/or the provision of sites and premises. In the GLC's London Industrial Strategy these policies were described as 'restructuring for labour', meaning that public policy would be concerned that any public resources for the private sector should be matched by safeguards for the interests of labour, in terms of appropriate jobs for local communities allocated on the basis of equal opportunities, with reasonable pay and conditions. In principle this was to involve significant levels of active participation both from the workforces and from local communities.

The second major policy area concerned the role of the public sector itself, as a direct employer and as a source of contracts, as well as a provider of local services, including local education and training. Given the decline of private manufacturing, 'The local authority is often the largest single employer in a particular area, and thus its own manpower policies can have a significant impact' (CIPFA, 1985, p. 70). This aspect of policy development drew heavily upon US experiences, especially in relation to 'contract compliance', or the use of the local authorities' own purchasing power to persuade contractors to comply with equal opportunities policies and with other requirements on pay and conditions, such as health and safety regulations and minimum-wage legislation.

The third policy area concerned the direct support of community initiatives around employment and training. For example there were programmes of grants for community groups, women's organisations and black and ethnic-minority communities to develop their own income-generation projects, including cooperative ventures, community enterprise schemes and community training projects. This fitted into wider programmes of support and grant aid for the voluntary sector, and for community groups, women's groups and black and ethnic minority groups in particular (Blunkett and Jackson, 1987, pp. 89–107).

The effectiveness of the policies in practice?

The whole notion of restructuring for labour has been the subject of critical debate (for example Gough, 1986). Certainly, in practice social objectives for the quality of employment have proved elusive. Butcher and others have argued that the evidence from Mackintosh and Wainwright's study was that, 'Market constraints have limited the scope for local planning agreements, and even fundamental requirements on fair wages and conditions of employment have had to be sacrificed in the interests of commercial survival' (Butcher *et al.*, 1990, p. 105). This also applied to requirements for equal-opportunities policies.

Nevertheless, with all these important caveats, there were some, albeit limited, achievements. In Sheffield, for example, Duncan and Goodwin commented that as a result of these initiatives, a thousand jobs were created in a three-year period (Duncan and Goodwin, 1988). Some thirty cooperative ventures were developed, making modest contributions to local employment: one strand rather than a significant thread in tacking joblessness, and poor pay and conditions. And, however modest these contributions were, it is worth noting that the cost per job was far less than the comparable cost of job creation in government sponsored schemes, such as enterprise zones.

Since the early 1980s the scope has narrowed further for a number of reasons, including the tightening of central-government control on local-authority finances, increasing financial difficulties in local government more generally and further legislative restrictions on their role in relation to the private sector (the 1989 Local Government and Housing Act defined local authorities' role in local economic strategies, although in practice these changes were not fully implemented), not to mention the abolition of the GLC and the metropolitan counties in 1986.

There were also important lessons to be learnt in terms of community participation in economic and social planning. Mackintosh and Wainwright (1987) provide a number of examples of very active community participation in economic and social planning, of which one of the better known examples was the alternative development plan – the 'People's Plan' – put forward by a local community, with GLC support, to counteract the proposal to build a 'Stolport' airport in the Royal Docks area, in East London (although in the event the planned airport still went ahead).

In other areas, such as Coin Street, local community groups proved more successful in actually implementing alternative community-based plans for jobs as well as homes and community facilities. 'Coin Street is a 13 acre site on the River Thames near Waterloo Bridge which was originally planned by the GLC in the early 1970s for offices and hotels. But after a series of public inquiries and persistent community action backed by the local authorities, Coin Street was bought by the GLC in 1986 just before abolition and was then sold to a local trust, the Coin Street Community Builders. . . . Coin Street is an example of a local initiative, not between local authorities and property companies, but between local authorities and the community, where they are the joint developers' (Colenutt, 1988, pp. 124–5).

The continuing relevance of community participation in economic and social planning, such as Coin Street, has in some ways become easier rather than harder to argue. This is because some of the deficiencies of the market-led approach have become increasingly the subject of public debate, as even considerable public investment has failed to alleviate local community needs and there has been growing recognition of the need for a softer, more community-concerned public face. So even urban development corporations, such as the Tyne and Wear Development Corporation were, towards the end of the 1980s, commenting that 'involvement with the local community is vital' (Tyne and Wear Development Corporation, 1988, p. 24), whatever this may have actually meant in practice.

Meanwhile the second strand of municipal policies in the 1980s – developing the role of the public sector as a source of jobs and contracts as well as the provider of services – has also become increasingly problematic, although once again in some contradictory ways. In the early to mid-1980s, this policy area was perhaps the least contentious because it was, by definition, more predictable than.the more problematic attempts to influence the private sector. One view (Butcher *et al.*, 1990). was that in face of the difficulties encountered in attempting to intervene in private firms, local authorities such as Sheffield and Manchester turned increasingly towards saving and creating jobs within their own workforces, and opening these jobs up to those who had previously been discriminated against in the labour force – women and black and ethnic minorities. In terms of the number of jobs concerned, this was a key policy area (see for example Centre for Local Economic Strategies, 1987).

In the event this policy was severely curtailed – the Conservatives won a further term of office in 1987 and tighter constraints were put upon local-authority spending. In addition, legislation to promote compulsory competitive tendering (Local Government Act, 1988) meant that a number of local-authority services had to be opened up to competition from private contractors. There were constraints upon requirements that could be held to be anticompetitive in market terms, including the types of requirements that had formed major parts of contract-compliance strategies (such as the requirements for contractors to comply with equal-opportunities policies and to promote local training opportunities). In order to compete and so keep the work 'in-house', local authorities were increasingly forced to act like private employers, which has actually led to constraints upon the pay and conditions of the workforces concerned. Unsurprisingly, low-paid women workers, such as cleaners and catering staff, have been disproportionately affected (see for example Whitfield, 1992).

Amongst the many casualties of these processes of change was a project on school meals in the London borough of Haringey. This project was developed by the Haringey Women's Employment

Project, a women's community employment and training project that was funded by the GLC and the local council. The aim was to demonstrate that public services such as school meals could compete most effectively with private competition, not by price cutting, but by improving the quality of the service and making it more relevant to local community needs. The project worked with the council, the trade union concerned (National Union of Public Employees – NUPE) and local,teachers, parents and community groups to work out a food policy, the School Meals Charter.

As one of the project's initiators, Ursula Murray, commented, 'The School Meals Project in its own way refreshed and renewed the links needed between individual interest and collective action. It demonstrated how community interests can work with trade unions and local authorities to shape society, protect and create jobs and improve services to local communities' (Murray, 1989).

School Meals were subjected to drastic cuts in Haringey in 1991, and the Haringey Women's Employment Project was wound up. This represented a major defeat in terms of the initiatives concerned, although not necessarily such a total defeat for some of the project's ideas. More generally, for instance, there has increasing interest in the issue of quality in the public sector, with both Labour and Conservative Parties committed to the promotion of quality assurance in public services (Gaster, 1991). So far, however, this discussion of quality assurance has focused around guarantees to the individual rather than around guarantees to local communities, at least as far as the Citizen's Charter has been concerned.

The third strand in jobs and training strategies was the support of local community initiatives to run their own schemes directly. This strand featured in a range of authorities, just as it had, in government supported programmes to deal with the effects of unemployment, and the need for (re)training (through the Manpower Services Commission). In terms of numbers of jobs and training places, this area of policy has been small scale, especially when compared with the number of jobs and training places involved directly in the public sector, or in the planning and investment decisions of major private employers. Community schemes have nevertheless been seen as important, because they have had the potential to reach groups and communities who might otherwise have been bypassed by new developments and because they have been seen as having the potential to develop new approaches to jobs and training. Local authorities provided support for such projects, including cooperative ventures, community enterprises and community-based training schemes.

Such schemes have been criticised for being so small scale and for being vulnerable to the very market pressures that they were set up to circumvent (so that cooperative projects, for instance, may survive only at the price of paying very low wages in order to remain competitive). As Newman argues in her review of the experiences of local job-creation projects, 'Low capitalisation often results in poor working conditions. . . . Nor do local projects necessarily tackle issues of equal opportunities' (Newman, 1989). Despite these caveats, however, Newman concludes that where such projects are well supported and well-run, they can play a valuable and exemplary, if somewhat marginal, role. In areas of particularly high unemployment, such as Northern Ireland, such projects can become proportionately even more significant in view of the relative dearth of alternative sources of jobs, training or community services. In Northern Ireland, for example, a whole range of key community initiatives relating to jobs and training schemes depend upon local, government and/or European funding.

Nevertheless running local projects tends to be very labour intensive and energy absorbing; it is difficult enough for community groups to find the resources and skills to do this successfully, let alone to have the resources and energy left for wider participation and campaigning work. These types of tensions seem to be increasing, within community work more generally, as community groups come under growing pressure to focus on running community services themselves in response to policies for community care adopted by 'enabling' local authority in the 1990s. Some of these pressures, together with their impact on community groups, are considered in more detail in Chapter 7.

Before coming to summarise aspects of the situation in the 1990s, however, there are some parallels to be drawn between British and US experiences from the early to the late 1980s. There were conscious attempts to draw on such lessons by both the right and the left of the political spectrum, just as there had been in the earlier phases of the War on Poverty. And once again there were also lessons that were not drawn on or were misapplied.

Some recent parallels with US experiences

'The US has served as the model for many of the economic and political policies of British government since the 1960s', stated Meyer and Kraushaar in a comparison of local economic development and community development strategies in Britain and the US (Meyer and Kraushaar, 1989, pp. 95–100). Amongst the better-known examples of transatlantic imports were the Urban Development Corporations, which, according to Meyer and Kraushaar, were 'conscious imitations of such US models as the Baltimore Inner Harbor, Boston Waterfront, and Pittsburgh Golden Triangle projects'. These were examples of 'growth coalition' approaches to urban regeneration; projects that were based upon public-sector priming for private-property-development-led initiatives to promote the physical renewal of inner-city areas, typically involving commercial and tourist developments together with up-market housing. This was the model developed, for instance, by the London Docklands Development Corporation. The other example of US exports identified by Meyer and Kraushaar was the Urban Development Grant, broadly modelled on the US Urban Development Action Grant, which again used public (in this case federal) funds to promote private investment in property development. Both initiatives fit into the wider framework of Reagan's policies in the 1980s, to promote private, market-led solutions (policies which in the Introduction) were outlined and compared with British policies under the Thatcher government of the same period).

Despite the 1980s rhetoric of rolling back the state, on both sides of the Atlantic, central government in Britain retained and even strengthened central controls on local government powers and spending, whilst this did not occur in the same way in the USA. As a result, cities and other local authorities in the USA have retained greater autonomy, with wider scope to develop policies and raise taxes to finance local economic development. Potentially this has meant that there has been scope for local experimentation. Meyer and Kraushaar also suggest that the decentralised approach of the USA is of particular importance for local communities, and for black and ethnic minority groups, because 'the American model permits somewhat easier access into the local political system by disadvantaged and minority groups' (ibid., p. 99).

Before looking at some examples where US community and minority groups have made positive use of these opportunities, however, some of the negative aspects need to be summarised. Meyer and Kraushaar entitle their article, 'The Grass is always Greener', pointing to the fact that local authorities and local communities in Britain may find the relative powers of US local government attractive in comparison with their own situations. But they also point to the fact that local powers to intervene in the local economy are, by definition, limited by the wider processes of international capital restructuring. Unable to control these wider forces, local authorities risk becoming caught up in competition with each other as one area tries to outbid another in competing to lure private investors into their areas (although this particular criticism has also been applied to local authorities in Britain, despite their relatively reduced powers and resources to outbid each other in this way). And in any case, it has been argued, in practice local economic development in many US cities has actually been dominated by local business interests, who have been more effective than local communities in working together with professionals on planning and decision making. It has been argued that, in reality, local efforts tend to promote restructuring in the interests of capital rather than of labour.

In a review of the US experience Hambleton points to evidence that 'economic development has become firmly established as a top priority for city governments' (Hambleton, 1989, p. 17). with goals of job retention and job creation, the expansion of the tax base and the promotion of downtown development. Typically, local economic development strategies were based upon public/private organisations, and 'deal making' was key. But, Hambleton argues, the evidence is that 'Only a small proportion of the cities – less than 10 per cent in both these surveys [that is, surveys of local economic development activity] – view it as important to channel economic benefits to the poorer areas of their city or to focus efforts on the needs of the economically disadvantaged residents'. Strategies were not typically geared to developing community skills, or to assisting community-based economic-development organisations and retraining workers whose jobs had been eliminated. Far from the benefits of such market-led growth strategies trickling down, in cities such as Baltimore, Hambleton argued, 'figures on poverty and unemployment rates show that conditions in most of Baltimore's neighbourhoods became worse during the "renaissance years" (ibid., p. 73).

In a separate article on the experience of Houston, Texas, Hambleton concluded that unless there is strong public-sector intervention to safeguard the wider community interests, unbridled private-sector development can lead to chaos, and to unacceptable social costs on the population (ibid., pp. 273–8). It is worth emphasising at this point that Hambleton was not arguing against the involvement of the private sector per se, whether on traditional socialist grounds or on any other ideological grounds. On the contrary, he argued that 'It is, in my view, very important to strengthen private sector involvement in inner city areas. Indeed, I was among those advocating the need for more inventive forms of public/private sector collaboration in urban areas some years ago' (ibid., p. 277). The points he was emphasising were rather about the form of such collaborations, and the extent to which social and community interests were able to be safeguarded.

Before considering some of the implications of these types of criticism to Britain in the 1990s, however, there are alternative strategies and case studies to compare and contrast. In the 1970s and 1980s, there were also instances of progressive strategies that were linked to community participation in planning and local economic development, in US cities. Chicago, under Mayor Washington between 1983 and 1987, provided, it has been argued, 'a unique test case for an investigation of the opportunities and constraints for progressive economic development in the United States, as well as local economic development generally' (Wiewel, 1990, p. 307). In 1983 Harold Washington, a respected black state legislator and US congressman, was elected mayor with the support of a coalition of blacks, Hispanics and other minority groups, white progressives, and community organisations. Prior to Washington's election, Chicago's economic development strategy had been dominated by a 'growth machine' of private-sector interests with public-sector support and the focus was on property-led strategies for service-sector development and middle-class housing, rather than on low-income housing or attempting to preserve a balance between manufacturing and service-sector jobs in order to meet the employment needs of low-income residents.

The neighbourhood movement in Chicago had roots going back to before the Second World War. Wiewel referred to the continuing influence of Saul Alinsky's work in Chicago, with its strong and broad-based neighbourhood coalitions with a tradition of combative politics. Effective community organisations had a long history and the War on Poverty also contributed, albeit in different ways, to increased community expertise (Gills in Clavel and Wiewel, 1991). In the late 1970s, and early 1980s, interest in developing local economic policies in opposition to the growth-machine approach had grown with the development of organisations such as the Community Workshop on Economic Development. The main feature of these alternative approaches was an emphasis on jobs for Chicagoans and 'balanced development', by which, Wiewel summarises, was meant 'increased support for small and minority businesses; for development projects outside the central business district; and an emphasis on manufacturing firms' (Wiewel, 1990, p. 311). Business retention was emphasised rather than simply bidding for new investment, manufacturing as well as rather than instead of services, job creation rather than property development, neighbourhoods rather than downtown, and community participation in development rather than business control, with more open and accessible forms of local government. In no way was this an ideologically based socialist programme. There are practical parallels, but there are also clear political differences between this and some of the objectives of British municipal socialists. But it was the programme of a progressive coalition, with specific goals for local economic development to benefit local communities.

The case of Chicago has been quoted as a positive example in a number of studies, including Hambleton's. Commentators who were directly involved have tended to be modest in their evaluation of Washington's actual achievements, before his untimely death from a heart attack in 1987. In practice, it has been argued, property development in the downtown area proceeded in similar ways as before. But there were more significant shifts, it has been argued, in the city's own workforce and in the use of public-sector contracts to promote local jobs and training, including jobs and training in not-for-profit community-based organisations. Whilst contracting out of services has been widely seen as privatisation, Wiewel argued – in a separate evaluation of the Chicago experience – under certain circumstances contracting out can bring real benefits to neighbourhood organisations (Wiewel, 1989, p. 118). More directly, although the number of city employees was actually contained, the percentages of women and minority employees increased. Less directly, many neighbourhood organisations received contracts to provide services such as job training, housing rehabilitation and neighbourhood revitalisation. And the power of public support to the private sector, including the power of direct purchasing (contract compliance) was used to persuade firms to provide jobs and training to local people, including women and minorities.

In addition there was greater scope for community participation. 'Although it is too soon to be sure', Wiewel argued, 'there is general agreement that the level of expectations, and acceptance, regarding participation in the policy process by representatives of neighbourhoods and minorities has been greatly increased and cannot be turned back' (Wiewel, 1990, p. 315). That remains to be proved, of course. Some of the participants in the experience have also expressed reservations, including reservations about the fragility of Mayor Washington's progressive coalition between black, Hispanic and white working-class and progressive groupings. The possibility of community organisations and their leaders being coopted by city hall was clearly recognised, as was the fact that some of Chicago's self-proclaimed community leaders' were actually unaccountable to the communities they were claiming to represent (Brehm, 1991; Gills, 1991, pp. 57–9). But even amongst these critics there was also agreement that, overall, the election of Mayor Washington was a 'magic moment' (Gills, 1991, p. 59). which offered new possibilities.

Strategies for the 1990s and beyond

Some of the criticisms of the growth-coalition, market-led approach of the 1980s have been applied across both sides of the Atlantic. As has already been suggested, these criticisms have come from expected quarters; but they have certainly not been confined to the ideological and political critics of the Thatcher/Reagan approach to urban regeneration. In Britain the government's own watchdog, the National Audit Office, has been critical of the urban development corporations (Audit Commission, 1989).

As Robinson and Shaw have argued, 'it is now not only acceptable but even politically expedient to "bring the community back in". . . . As with poverty in the 1960s, those people who live in the inner cities have been apparently "rediscovered". Indeed, no self-respecting urban development corporation (UDC) would now dare leave out reference to the community in their public pronouncement' (Robinson and Shaw, 1991, p. 62).

Robinson and Shaw in no way exaggerate the actual effects of such a shift in rhetoric. 'For all the talk', they suggest, 'real power remains firmly in the hands of central government supported by a sympathetic business elite' in areas such as the North-East. But they do argue that a reevaluation of policy really does need to take place. This would be to develop policies and practices that meet the needs of the residents of disadvantaged communities. And it would also be for the more pragmatic reason that the collapse of the property market by the early 1990s cast serious doubts on the continuing potential of property-led initiatives. Alternatively, they argue that community participation will be vital in giving legitimacy to regeneration, ensuring creativity, and meeting local needs for jobs, training and services. As Shutt has argued, much more could be achieved, and 'Community economic development initiatives could play a much greater role in tackling racial inequalities and deep-seated unemployment problems in the inner cities and outer estates' if funding for social projects were increased and the 'inter-relationship between social and economic objectives given greater recognition' (Shutt, in Henderson, 1991). Whilst this will not by itself achieve major change, local authorities will, at least, have to submit their economic development plans for review and consultation (following the 1989 Local Government and Housing Act), and such consultations could provide opportunities for community organisations to raise these issues more publicly and to press for change, if only at the local level (although the legal requirement is only to consult the business community).

Even in the cold climate of the early 1990s, there are, in any case, still relevant examples of local economic strategies that are geared to provide tangible benefits in terms of jobs and training, whilst linking into wider strategies for empowerment and equal opportunities. Newman provides a case study of just such a local-authority strategy in Harlow. Harlow's strategy recognises the limitations of local-authority intervention to influence private investment decisions. But the strategy does emphasise the potential for improving the position of and empowering the more disadvantaged in the labour market, especially through the provision of quality training to women and other disadvantaged groups and through strategies to improve the quality of jobs at the same time as improving the quality of public services. Harlow is attempting to walk a political tightrope, collaborating with the private sector on areas of common interest, such as the provision of training or specific joint-funded initiatives such as an employment service for people with disabilities, whilst retaining a separate and progressive stance on issues of potential conflict, such as working conditions in both public and private sectors, and the provision of resources for social objectives. Overall the economic strategy in Harlow is linked to anti-poverty strategies, such as support for credit unions and for cooperatives that meet social needs, such as a bus cooperative and a nursery cooperative. (Newman, 1991).

Local authorities such as Harlow can expect major changes in the context for local economic strategies in the 1990s. Quite apart from whatever changes can be anticipated in underlying economic trends, major changes can also be anticipated in relation to the impact of European integration and to the development of unitary authorities for local government in Britain.

Some of the changes that can be anticipated in relation to European integration are discussed more fully in Chapter 4. The importance of European integration has been increasingly (if somewhat belatedly in some cases) recognised both by local authorities and by local community organisations. As the guide, *Signposts to Community Economic Development* (Henderson, 1991). points out, 'The introduction in 1992 of the Single European Market, and the overhaul of the European Community's Structural Funds, will present both challenges and opportunities to those involved in community economic development, and it seems clear that UK organisations will need to become more familiar with the experiences of local employment initiatives and related forms of community enterprise which have sprung up across Europe (Henderson, 1991, p. 3). As this guide also pointed out, the European Commission launched a programme of support for Local Employment Development Action (LEDA). in 1986, and the European Network on Local Development and Local Employment Initiatives (ELISE). was launched by Directorate-General V to provide information on local employment initiatives and to stimulate networking between them. The Commission's ERGO Action Programme is also concerned to promote dialogue and collaboration 'between existing actors in the field of long-term unemployment initiatives' (ibid., p. 24). Overall then, the EC has been seen as giving greater priority to supporting the 'social economy' sector.

Other changes have already taken place, including the creation of Training and Enterprise Councils (TECs), a development which has diverted major responsibilities for training away from local authorities. Local authorities stand to lose further responsibilities for training with the shift of responsibility for further education away from local education authorities under the Further and Higher Education Act, 1992. Taken together, it can be expected that key aspects of education and training for young people and adults will be removed from direct public-sector control altogether, at both local and regional level. In particular areas local communities have been developing ways of interacting with organisations such as TECs, however, to try to ensure that local training needs are tackled.

Elsewhere in this chapter it has already been argued that local community initiatives have clear limitations. Local cooperatives, for example, do not and cannot by themselves solve unemployment or meet training needs on a wide scale. But they do meet the immediate needs of some of those who have been most disadvantaged, whilst potentially raising wider issues about alternative ways of meeting employment and social needs. As such, local initiatives may play a useful role within the framework of wider regional and national economic strategies. The public sector has a key role here, because such initiatives require considerable and often continuing support.

Similarly the contract culture tends to discriminate against rather than bring significant benefits to small local-community groups. But contracting out, for instance in the field of community care, could also be developed in radically different ways, enabling community groups, women's groups and minority groups to run certain services and to employ local people in more locally relevant ways whilst still providing quality employment and training opportunities. Some of these issues are considered in more detail in Chapter 6, and Chapter 7 provides specific examples through case studies. Once again, however, significant public-sector support will be required if these potential opportunities are to be realised, and realised without simply further undermining public-sector jobs and services.

Finally, active community participation will also need continuing public support. As Byrne has argued, from the experience of community participation in the North-East, public support, including community-work support for poor people's organisations, is actually a relatively cheap activity, although it is essential for active citizen participation (Byrne, 1989, p. 165). Of course, by itself even the most active workplace community participation will not necessarily lead to the provision of locally relevant jobs and training opportunities. The scope for community participation is just as limited by the interests of private capital as is the scope for local-authority local economic strategies. But without such active participation, linked to strategies and structures to promote equal opportunities, there is even less chance that local economic development will actually benefit the groups and communities with the greatest need for jobs, training and services.

4

Some International Comparisons from the North

Earlier chapters have identified a number of common trends in debates around the mixed economy of welfare, and the boundaries between public-, private- and voluntary-sector provision.

As previous chapters have also argued, whilst there have been common pressures and recognisably parallel debates around the mixed economy of welfare in a range of countries, there have, however, been important differences too. As Mishra has argued, 'The intriguing problem of the dialectic between general models and the uniqueness of nation-states is highlighted in the case of the economic crisis of the 1970s and its effect on different nation-states' (Mishra, 1990, p. 6). 'A nation has its history – economic, political and social. At any given moment in time it also has a set of institutions through which it regulates production and distribution, manages conflict, and, more generally, makes societal decisions and maintains social values. The "crisis" of capitalism therefore takes on a specific form as it impacts on nation-states at different points in the trajectory of their history and development' (ibid., p. 7).

One set of differences arises from the different starting points, in specific countries, in relation to the different balances that exist between the public, private and voluntary sectors (for a variety of historical, economic, social and political reasons) (Room, 1990). Comparisons between new-right policies as applied in Britain and the USA in the 1980s, for example, have to take account of these key differences. So do comparisons between Britain and some of the more recent Mediterranean members of the European Community, with different histories of state welfare provision.

The second set of differences arises because governments can and do reach widely differing conclusions about the most effective and the most politically acceptable ways of tackling similar problems. So there have been widely differing government responses to increasing economic difficulties, just as there have been widely differing responses to accusations that public welfare provision is too bureaucratic and too controlling. Despite common challenges to the 'neo-Keynsian orthodoxy of the post-war years', it has been argued, this 'has not been replaced thus far by a new orthodoxy – whether of the right, centre or left. No new "settlement" or even its lineaments, are in sight' (Mishra, 1990, p. 2). And governments can and do change, within any one particular state, whether as a result of party-political changes through general elections, for instance, or whether as a result of internal strategic shifts, within the same political party, over time. The implication of this view is that there generally *is* at least *one* if not more alternative strategy/strategies that could be pursued, even in the face of increasingly common problems.

So far, many of the comparisons between Britain and elsewhere have concentrated on the USA. Whilst Britain and the USA have had important historical differences in terms of the structures of their welfare systems, they have also had important points of comparison, it has been suggested, and especially so in relation to the promotion of liberal, free-market type strategies since the 1980s. On the basis of such similarities, Esping-Andersen has characterised both Britain and the USA as falling within the liberal, market-oriented type of regime (although Britain also has a legacy of policies based upon universalism and decommodification). In contrast, Esping-Andersen has identified two other models of welfare, the conservative, corporatist-statist type regimes of countries with histories such as those of Germany, France and Italy (which have been developed on the basis of strong state involvement, typically backed by the church, with an emphasis upon the role of the family and paternalistic social obligations within the existing social order) and the social-democratic type regimes of countries such as Norway and Sweden (Esping-Andersen, 1990).

This chapter is concerned to identify both similarities and contrasts in state responses to the increasingly shared dilemmas of the 1980s and 1990s and the shifting boundaries of the mixed economy of welfare across these varying models of welfare state.

After a brief review of some aspects of the US experience, this chapter looks at some experiences in Central, Eastern and Western Europe (including Germany, as an example of a state with a conservative, corporatist–statist type welfare history, and Sweden, as an example of a state with a social-democratic type welfare history). In the final part of this chapter the focus shifts to the European Community itself. There has been growing concern with the effects as well as with the processes of increasing integration. Major economic and social changes have been predicted, changes which may, increasingly, be met by policy initiatives at EC level rather than at the level of national governments. In response to this potential shift in the locus of decision making, there are a number of initiatives across national boundaries, including the formation of networks between voluntary organisations, to attempt to increase their effectiveness at European level in the post-1992 scenario.

Some common patterns and pressures

Strategies to contain public expenditure on welfare have been widespread, along with strategies to privatise services, typically in the expectation, if not always the reality, of achieving significant savings as a result. The promotion of the voluntary sector in general and self-help in particular has also been widespread, although client and community participation has been promoted too as part of fundamentally different strategies.

Examples from the USA have already been quoted. The Reagan administration's attempts to contain federal welfare spending in the 1980s have been justified as essential to the new-right's strategy for wider recovery. Alternatively this approach has been described as being effectively a declaration of 'a new class war on the unemployed, the unemployable, and the working poor' (Fox Piven and Cloward, 1982, p. 1). Fox Piven and Cloward argued that although Reagan had not in fact been elected on a specific mandate to cut welfare, it was politically easier to reduce welfare spending for vulnerable groups than it was to reduce public expenditure in areas where there were powerful vested interests, such as in the case of defence expenditure. In addition, they argued, reductions in welfare would reduce workers' bargaining power more generally; coupled with compulsion for the poor to work, for example through

Workfare schemes, the effect would be to force labour to accept lower paid jobs, thereby preserving profitability for employers but at the expense of the lower paid. Such a view fits into the analysis of Harrison and Bluestone, in which 'zapping labor' and reducing welfare provision form part of the new-right's strategy for economic restructuring for capital – at the expense of labour (Harrison and Bluestone, 1988).

Reductions in planned federal spending on social programmes were related to shifts in overall responsibility, with states and local authorities increasingly being expected to cope (see for example Jacobs, 1992). This was part of the wider retreat of federal government (apart from federal defence expenditure) that was noted in Chapter 3, both in relation to social programmes and in relation to support for local economic development (Meyer and Kraushaar, 1989). Similar federal/central government strategies towards local authorities have been identified in a number of countries. Meanwhile, in the USA privatisation and the contracting out of service provision to voluntary organisations were already firmly established. Ironically, in fact, it has been argued that from the 1960s the federal government had actually promoted contracting out/purchase of services, for different reasons, as part of strategies to *increase* federal support to states in the area of social-service provision. In contrast, contracting out was being advocated in Britain in the 1980s as part of the reverse strategy.

In evaluating the lessons of this earlier US experience for Britain in 1981, a report for the National Council for Voluntary Organisations concluded that it was not at all clear that contracting out was ultimately significantly cheaper than direct service provision (a point that was raised in Chapter 1). In many instances the public sector effectively had little or no choice of which agency to use anyhow (for example, large and well-established voluntary agencies dominated provision in particular areas, such as Massachussetts, where the Massachussetts Society for the Prevention of Cruelty to Children had 75 per cent of contracts for protective programmes). Meanwhile agencies were involved in constant pressures to achieve readily measurable results, such as the number of clients seen, which also tended to militate against quality rather than quantity provision (Lanning, 1981). There have also been increasing pressures on agencies to become more commercialised in this changing climate (Jacobs, 1992). These are precisely the type of dilemmas and criticisms that have been identified and applied to more recent experiences, both in the USA and more widely (AMA, 1990).

Alternatively, however, there have also been references to very different types of experiences within particular US cities and local authorities. Chapter 3 included examples of contracting out that were used in response to pressures for change, pressures which came from self-help groups, community organisations and neighbourhood movements. These initiatives were part of positive and equal-opportunities strategies to promote jobs and training in cooperatives and small businesses. In addition to these examples around jobs and training, Clavel's study of progressive cities provides other types of examples of contracting out, including examples concerned with providing community services in new ways. In Hartford, for instance, the city council began to 'encourage citizen participation, not just in policy decisions, but in performance – in the actual delivery of services to residents' (Clavel, 1986). In recreation provision, for example, a neighbourhood incentive programme was set up so that groups of adults could plan and organise their own adult-education activities. Clavel argues that 'This system involved far more people and offered a greater variety of recreational activities than the former, more traditional program had' (ibid., p. 41). The range of activities was wide, demonstrating a variety of ways in which the public sector could develop new forms of partnership with community organisations, partnerships which included community and cooperative forms of service provision, as well as community participation in public planning policies.

Within Europe there have been comparable challenges from the new right to the 'truce' around welfare-state provision, as well as challenges and alternative strategies from the left. Room, for instance, argues that although the welfare state in the postwar period developed in different ways, building upon varying national traditions and depending upon a range of specific factors within each particular state, there have also been some common patterns in the responses from the 1970s and 1980s. As the economic climate became less favourable, restructuring was accompanied by significant increases in the number of people living in poverty as a result of unemployment and low wages, whilst demographic change and changing family patterns simultaneously increased the number of those in poverty through old age or single parenthood. Room refers to an estimated 38.6 million living in poverty across the

European Community in 1975. By 1980 this figure had reached 39.5 million, and by 1985 the figure was 43.9 million (with one estimate putting the figure as high as 49.7 million in 1985) (quoted in Baine, Benington and Russell, 1992, p. 72). The EC had expanded its membership over this period, so these figures are not comparable; but even so they still represent a significant increase, even when that factor is taken into account (Room, 1990). In some EC countries, this expansion of poverty has been described in terms of the 'new poverty', referring to those who have been thrown out of the labour force through the restructuring process (whether from manual jobs or, increasingly, from middle-class jobs), as well as referring to those who have become poor through changing family patterns (including the growing number of single parents who are trying to raise their children on inadequate benefits).

In response to these pressures, Room identified a number of recurrent themes. There were moves to reorganise welfare provision and to control the overall pressure on public expenditure. For example, this was the pattern in Denmark, from 1982, and in West Germany. There were also pressures for more means testing to reduce public welfare to a more residual, less universalist basis. In several countries, including France (despite a government of the left, with a different rhetoric) and the Netherlands (with a well-developed tradition of support for preventative approaches including community development), there were increases in emergency-type responses to need, responses which included the provision of benefits in kind, such as food, provided in soup kitchens, and temporary shelter for the homeless. Room contrasts such traditional, charitable (and often church-based) approaches with alternative, social democratic-approaches to welfare, on the basis of public provision that is available as of right to all citizens (the approach, for example, of Denmark under social-democratic governments up to 1982). Over the same period community-care policies were widely developed (for example in Italy) for a range of reasons, including the expectation that community care would prove cheaper than institutional care. But typically, Room argues, community-care policies were effectively hampered, in practice, by inadequate funding. Conversely, too, in the 1970s and 1980s he identifies the growth of alternative responses, including the growth of cooperatives and self-help groups – amongst the poor as well as amongst wider sections of the population – as a result of dissatisfaction with bureaucratic and authoritarian forms of state provision, from a left-wing, rather than a right-wing perspective.

Each of these tendencies can be identified, for example, in the case of (then West) Germany, which has already been discussed in terms of having been typified as representing the conservative, corporatist–statist tradition of welfare (Esping-Andersen, 1990). There was a change of government, from Socialist–Liberal (SPD–FDP) to Christian Democrat–Liberal (CDU–FDP), with debate in 1983 concentrating on issues of public expenditure in general, and social spending more specifically. The CDU–FDP government argued that in order to revitalise the economy it was necessary to shift expenditure from consumption to investment, and that this entailed containing increases in social expenditure, policies which included a long-term restructuring of social security. In response, critics from the social democrats and the trade unions have argued that the government was effectively 'waging class struggle from above' (Wolfgang Zapf sets out this view, and contrasts it with the government's justifications, in Zapf, 1986, p. 139). Critics argued that the government's response to the economic situation was to promote restructuring, to shift the burden onto labour, and to put pressure onto the labour force more generally, for instance through wage cuts in the public sector.

In (West) Germany, as elsewhere, debates on the future of welfare have also been concerned with the mixed economy of welfare and its potentially changing boundaries. Zapf, for instance, considers that a new theory of welfare production is evolving that allows for a more thorough-going analysis of the production of private and public goods, an analysis which takes fuller account of the role of associations and households, as well as the role of the public sector. He calls for a new balance in welfare provision that would recognize and support 'the needs for smaller units, more individual care and more creative self-realization', within the mixed economy of welfare (Zapf, 1986, p. 141). The implications of such an approach, he argues, are that decentralisation, increased innovation and creativity can be promoted through increasing the role of voluntary organisations and supporting self-help initiatives. Whilst he supports this, however, he argues that such an approach should be complementary to, rather than a substitute for, the functions of the state and the market. 'We must be careful', he concludes, 'not to overrate the potential of associations and primary groups' (ibid.,

p. 150). 'The new needs and demands cannot be satisfied simply in the small is beautiful worlds of associations and primary groups. On the other hand, an increased role for those associations and primary groups seems inevitable, because the new differentiated needs and pluralized life-styles are clashing with the trends towards further standardization, bureaucratization and anonymity' (ibid., p. 152).

Brauns and Kramer point to similar conclusions about the nature of shifts in debates about the welfare state and the boundaries of the mixed economy of welfare in (West) Germany. They also identify the growth of questioning of the previous consensus as economic difficulties and unemployment grew from the mid-1970s. And they identify a convergence of criticisms from both the far right and the far left about the bureaucratic and authoritarian nature of public welfare provision. In the 1980s in Berlin, for instance, they identified some support from the right for self-help groups, although these included self-help groups that were concerned with alternative life-styles (a concern which had been seen as more characteristic of the libertarian left) (Brauns and Kramer, 1989). Room identified similar contradictions in the criticisms made by the CDU of social-insurance provision, which had traditionally been supported by the Social Democrats and the trade unions; the CDU arguing that this had benefited the organised working class but not the marginals and the poor. Such criticisms were consistent too with more traditional responses to the poor that were based upon charitable approaches, including those of church-based charities such as those organised by both Catholic and Lutheran churches (both of which were identified as still significant, at least outside the city states of Berlin, Bremen and Hamburg, despite the length of the rather different tradition of earnings-related social insurance in (West) Germany). Matzat has identified support for self-help right across these different perspectives. 'In West Germany today [1989] there is almost no politically relevant grouping which does not – with more or less volume – sing the praises of self-help or include supportive statements in its manifesto. Conservatives refer to personal responsibility for individual well-being and to traditional Christian charity; Social Democrats reiterate the old principle of solidarity; the Green Party assumes that self-help belongs to the same alternative grass-root movement from which the party itself originates. Only the trade unions remain reserved and suspicious, fearing a loss of jobs in the health and welfare sector' (Matzat, 1989, p. 11).

In contrast with the more traditional critics of state welfare provision, Brauns and Kramer identified 'so-called self-help groups', which, they argued, 'have grown substantially both in number and significance. Many of these groups originally grew out of the student movement', they suggest, 'or other reform movements since then' (Brauns and Kramer, p. 133). Estimates of the number of these organisations vary from between 20 000 and 40 000. Such groups have often been small. Their concerns have varied, covering, for example, housing, including squatting, as well as health, together with life-style and environmental issues.

West Germany has provided a number of examples of self-help in housing, including the case of Berlin. In 1977 the Berlin Senat, inspired, it has been suggested, by urban homesteading programmes in the USA, proposed to turn over run-down houses to resident cooperatives for renovation. There was widespread interest from residents and a scheme was eventually agreed. Since then, it has been argued, renovation schemes carried out through resident coopera-tives, have demonstrated their value, the cooperative approach having led to savings of some 15 per cent of construction costs because residents contributed labour for the less skilled tasks. In addition, it has been argued, 'the identification of the people with their houses is very high. . . . In short, with regard to cost, effectiveness and acceptance the dual way [ie public sector/ cooperative partnership] in these cases is cheaper, better and more popular' (Evers, Nowotny and Wintersberger, 1987, p. 213). Whilst it has been argued that such schemes have also contributed to the legitimacy of those public authorities who are prepared to work within such partnerships, self-help, in the form of squatting for instance, has also been explicitly linked to alternative and consciously anti-state perspectives more characteristic of the libertarian left. As Grunow, has argued, self-help movements have included 'very diverse perspectives and goals' (Grunow, 1986, p. 199).

Despite the widespread nature of support for self-help from such different political quarters, the movement was still extremely small. It has been estimated that only 3 per cent of the population of West Germany were members of self-help groups in the mid-1980s. But a 1986 survey reported that up to a third of the population said that they were interested and might become members of such groups (Grunow, 1986).

Examples of self-help and participation have also been identified in what was previously the German Democratic Republic (GDR), under fundamentally different structures. Chamberlayne has argued that prior to 1989 there were 'vigorous forms of participation in the workplace and the community' (Chamberlayne, 1990, p. 145). For example tenants' associations contributed directly to repairs and cleaning, receiving payment for part of their time and for materials. Self-help projects also carried out activities such as renovating old people's flats and maintaining playgrounds.

Critics and sceptics argued that citizen participation of this type simply represented a form of 'citizen exploitation' (ibid., p. 145) as the state was using citizen participation to extract unpaid labour and/or using neighbourhood committees as vehicles for social control. But others argued that citizen participation raised the potential of developing more far-reaching changes. This latter trend was identified, she argued, with reform communists and intellectuals who in the 1980s had been concerned to promote more democratic and decentralised structures. She concluded that the experiences of tenants and neighbourhood committees, together with other civic committees, were potentially significant factors that should be taken into account when considering the future potential for developing democratic local structures.

Both parallels and contrasts have emerged in relation the more-recently established welfare democracies in Portugal and Spain. In both these countries public welfare provision differed prior to their becoming multi-party democracies in the 1970s. Following the death of Franco in 1975 in Spain, in the late 1970s and 1980s, Rubiol argued, 'criticism of the supposed faults and inadequacies of the Welfare State was not welcome since we ourselves were trying to attain such a system' (that is, comprehensive social security and health and welfare provision) (Rubiol, 1990). Whilst improvements were made at national level, she argued, self-help in the Spanish context could still effectively mean family provision and charity of a traditional kind, 'charity giving instead of promoting individual and group development (ibid., p. 37). A similar view of the predominance of private and charitable approaches to welfare, in Franco's Spain is set out by Rossell and Rimbau (1989). Like Rubiol they argue that despite subsequent attempts to develop public provision, these attempts have not kept pace with the growth in social needs, including the growth in needs arising from unemployment. As a result new initiatives to promote decentralisation, participation and self-help in some regions and cities, (such as Barcelona) were joined onto a more traditional voluntary sector that is centred around the family and church-based charity organisations. 'Spain has had to join the rush into welfare pluralism as a means of coping with the inevitable constraints on public spending on welfare' (Rossell and Rimbau, 1989, p. 122). Community-development initiatives have supported local participation schemes, for example in urban renewal in Zaragoza and Aragon, and around health, for instance in Barcelona, initiatives which coexist with Catholic and other traditional charitable approaches to self-help.

In contrast, Eastern and Central Europe have been viewed as having been at the other end of the spectrum with regard to direct state involvement in welfare provision. The state planned and the state provided. However it has also been argued that there were times in the former East Germany and Soviet Union when more active participation was both permitted and actively promoted (George and Manning, 1980). Participation through trade unions was key to the provision of health and welfare more generally as well as to health and safety at work and trade unions also had a role in the allocation of housing and nursery places. Overall however, social organisations operated within clearly defined parameters set out by the state and operated through the party: a permit was necessary to set up a social organisation in the USSR in the pre-glasnost and perestroika period (Hegelson, 1989). Similar trends have been identified elsewhere in Eastern and Central Europe. In Hungary, for instance, it has been suggested that there had been a range of civil associations in the prewar period. In the postwar period, however most of these were dissolved and informal gatherings were viewed as potentially politically subversive. The effect of this, Tausz argued, was that local communities were 'rendered incompetent in taking decisions related to their own social conditions. . . . The energies of local communities remained suppressed' (Tausz, 1990, p. 302).

Meanwhile, for a variety of economic, political and social reasons, it was becoming increasingly evident that there were pressures for change. There were moves to shift away from central planning, with an expanding role for private market mechanisms, both in production and in welfare provision. Hungary was in the forefront of these developments in East and Central Europe, well before Gorbachev launched perestroika and glasnost in the Soviet Union. There had been increasing use of market mechanisms since the end of the 1960s, and from the mid-1980s, the use of market mechanisms spread into housing, for example, with an extension of private housing provision.

But economic liberalisation began to be accompanied by increasing social polarisation, with market mechanisms benefiting some sections, but disadvantaging others. Since then poverty, unemployment and homelessness have gained recognition as public issues. This has been increasingly marked since the fall of the Communist government in 1989. As Ferge argued in 1990, 'The economic situation did not ameliorate last year', and the state's reform package resulted in a 'shift of the burdens of the crisis on the shoulders of the population, and more specifically on its weakest groups' (Ferge, 1990, p. 107).

Social needs increased as a result of economic restructuring. Rapidly rising inflation (offically estimated at 26 per cent in 1990 and unofficially at 40 per cent) exacerbated these problems for all those on fixed incomes and wages. There was greater public recognition of social problems and social polarisation. And poverty had also been 'rediscovered', with an estimated 30 per cent of the population falling below the poverty line. Ferge, for instance, has argued that 'poverty is rapidly increasing, hitting by now about one third of families' (ibid.). Tausz (1990) has described some of the initiatives that were launched at the end of the 1970s and early 1980s as intellectuals and professionals discovered poverty and home-lessness and began to organise to address these problems. The Foundation Supporting the Poor (SZETA), for instance, worked with the poor, the homeless, the unemployed and gypsies in Budapest.

Whilst some of these initiatives began by organising immediate relief for pressing social problems (the distribution of clothes, for example, and the provision of shelter and refuges for the homeless) there were also efforts to move towards more active community participation. In 1989 the Hungarian Association of Community Development was formed to promote such developments through networking, publishing papers and organising training courses. The association was established in response to a range of experiences in Hungary, in both urban and rural areas, during the 1980s (Varga and Vercseg, 1992), and it has actively pursued ways of networking with academics and practitioners in Western Europe, as they face increasingly similar problems.

This increasing interest in establishing wider dialogues has also been identified, more generally, in the sphere of social policy. There have been a number of international conferences, aimed at generating a new East–West dialogue (Deacon and Szalai, 1990, p. 2). Deacon has identified a number of different approaches within this international dialogue, with a range of strategies drawing on different models and experiences. Models that attracted particular attention (both in Eastern and Central Europe and in Third-World countries) were those of the Scandinavian countries, especially that of Sweden. Ferge, for instance, argued that the Swedish model might be adapted to the different situation and the different history of the state's role in Hungary to provide a fourth road, based upon a pluralist social market economy with a strong non-market sector with its own values and mechanisms (Ferge, 1990, p. 113). As suggested earlier in this chapter, Sweden has been held up as an example of the social-democratic model of welfare within the mixed economy (Esping-Andersen, 1990), a model which had, at least until 1990, resisted major inroads from the new right. Sweden (together with Austria) had refused 'to abandon the goals of the welfare state, notably full employment, economic growth and social welfare' (Mishra, 1990, p. 2).

There would seem to be widespread agreement that in Sweden (at least until the early 1990s) the social-democratic mixed economy succeeded in maintaining relatively high levels of employment, with a strongly developed welfare state, providing welfare benefits, as of right, to citizens (for example Castles, 1978). Social democrats have argued that the Swedish experience demonstrates the potential for democratic social reform, and feminists have drawn from the Swedish experience, in arguing for the potential value of democratic state intervention to promote women's equality in the workplace and in society. But the social-democratic welfare state in Sweden has not gone uncontested (for example Parkin, 1972). The Swedish system has provided benefits for both capital and labour. This coalition of interests working together under conditions of growth, came under increasing pressure, however, from the mid-1970s. Even those, (like Mishra) who noted Sweden's relative success in 'bucking the trend' in the 1980s, accepted that there was nothing inevitable about the continuation of this version of welfare. Sweden weathered the storms of the 1970s and 1980s, Mishra argued, 'without sacrificing economic effectiveness and social justice. But it would be foolish to claim historical inevitability for either its continuation [that is, Sweden's policies] or its decline and fall' (Mishra, 1990, p. 66). Sweden was not insulated from wider economic pressures and, as elsewhere, the changing economic climate from the mid-1970s did lead to increasing questioning and challenges, such as arguments for reducing the role of the state in welfare by promoting more choice (Wilson, 1979). For instance, a report prepared for the Swedish Secretariat for Futures Studies argued in 1982 that Sweden could not afford to continue to increase public expenditure on jobs and welfare, and that other forms of care should in any case be investigated because citizens must assume more responsibility for caring for each other in cooperative ways. The same report argued for a greater role for the voluntary sector, and for more active citizen participation (although still within the framework of national provision).

In Sweden, state welfare provision has been criticised for being too controlling, and these criticisms have been voiced both by the right and by the left. Whilst recognising positive achievements, Gould (1988) has summarised some of the major criticisms of Swedish neo-Marxists, such as Sjostrom, who argued that policies for child care and for the treatment of alcoholism, for instance, were excessively controlling, and especially so as they were applied to the working class. In the mid-1980s, anarchists such as Ronnby expressed even stronger views on the controlling nature of the welfare state in Sweden, which was, he argued, tending to make everyone completely dependent on the state. Ronnby's alternative was for a more communal approach, based upon self-help and mutual aid. In relation to Sweden, as elsewhere, this libertarian left-wing critique had points in common with the views of the new right. Gould cites Shenfield's study of Sweden as a case in the failure of socialism, from this perspective, a case study which includes criticisms of Swedish social policy on the grounds that it involved excessive compulsion. Gould also demonstrates the development of 'softer', more liberal approaches during the 1980s, with less emphasis on 'harder' forms of coercion, shifts in emphasis which cut across left–right political divides (Gould, 1988).

In Sweden, public policy solutions to these types of criticisms of the welfare state did not simply follow patterns developed elsewhere;

just as debates about strategies to cope with increasing economic difficulties did not simply result in the development of economic and social policies that had been promoted more widely elsewhere. For example there were efforts to promote change and improve accountability, flexibility, client participation and choice within the public sector itself. Within the social services, one example would be the development of committees within residential homes, so that key decisions about the running of the homes could be taken by the residents themselves. Another example would be the more flexible use of different public-sector workers to maintain contact with the vulnerable and to identify their needs; for example, from the end of the 1960s, local authorities, with the participation of postmen, actively sought out information on the social needs of groups such as the elderly living alone in rural areas (Kohn, 1977).

In 1984 Sweden embarked upon an experiment to develop new approaches to decentralisation and local democracy through the 'free communes' scheme. Within the experimental free communes (comprising nine municipalities and three county councils), local government could experiment with whatever new approaches they chose in order to find ways of improving the quality and relevance of service provision, and to decentralise power, to provide greater participation and democracy. There were basic guarantees, including guarantees that overall standards would not be reduced in key areas, and that the interests of disadvantaged groups would be protected. Beyond that, local authorities could experiment as they saw fit, and pass on their recommendations for change to central government. Services were to be developed in ways which ensured equivalence rather than uniformity, recognising the need for diversity and flexibility. And local government employees as well as users and community organisations were to be directly involved in working on new approaches. 'One does not have to privatise things in order to create alternatives, diversity and variety. Change and renewal can be achieved within the public sector' it was argued (Nygren, 1989, p. 12).

The overall conclusion of the Swedish experience reinforces Mishra's view that whilst different states may have been subjected to similar pressures and even to similar arguments in policy debates, there have been important differences in the strategies that were developed in response. The future, though, offers no guarantees that these differences will persist. Meanwhile, integration at European level is increasing, and potential members of the EC, whether from east, north or south, can expect to be increasingly affected by these common trends.

The EC and increasing European integration

Increasing economic and social integration has been taking place in Europe, a trend which was expected to be strengthened following the formal commencement of the single European market in 1992. The European Commission has identified some of the challenges that this process of integration can be expected to reinforce, as restructuring eliminates over-capacity in the more open market (*Social Europe*: European Economy Special Edition, 1990). Broadly, through processes of takeover, merger, joint venture and the relocation or closure of firms, it has been argued, 'investment and employment in key sectors is becoming more concentrated in the hands of a smaller number of larger, more powerful transnational firms, aiming to reap the benefits of economies of scale, which may come from mass production for mass markets' (Benington, 1991, p. 87). The results of these processes, in social terms, are unclear. The European Commission's own estimates in 1989 suggested that up to half of industrial jobs in the EC may be in sectors that will be affected by this process of concentration, although the Commission believed that subsequent job gains will offset any initial job losses. However it has been predicted that there will be overall losers as well as winners (Rajan, 1990), and certain regions are likely to be particular losers, with Britain and Italy suffering the worst job losses, in the short term, and the lowest job gain, according to EC predictions, with an even worse outlook for Britain predicted by others (for example Neuberger, 1989). Polarisation is anticipated, with growing poverty accompanying unemployment and increasing social need being concentrated in particular regions.

The EC itself has shown increasing awareness of these potentially growing problems. European social policy has, it has been argued, concentrated on labour-market policies to facilitate economic objectives, with the development of policies for training for example (through the European Social Fund), and for the promotion of labour mobility more generally. Over time, however, there has been more concern for a wider focus on social issues. Part of this concern, it has been argued, stems from economic interests, including the fear of 'social dumping', meaning that employers who have offered relatively decent wages have become concerned that they may be undercut by competition from the lower-wage areas of more peripheral Europe, or by transnationals unfairly competing by shifting production to such areas (Baine *et al.*, 1992; Lodge, 1989). This concern to prevent social dumping forms part of the context for the EC's increasing interest in promoting positive social and labour policies with the development of the Social Charter of 'Fundamental Social Rights'. The Social Charter goes beyond previous concerns to facilitate labour mobility within the EC; so there is a guarantee for freedom of movement but there is also provision for the right to a decent wage, social protection (that is, social security), freedom of association and collective bargaining, vocational training, equal treatment for women, information and workers' participation, protection of health and safety, protection of children and adolescents, rights for the elderly for retirement, and rights for the disabled.

Ratification of the Social Charter was up held up by objections from Britain, with the Thatcher government arguing that implementation of the charter would increase the role of the EC and interfere with market mechanisms, just as Britain was attempting to roll back the state and free up the market, (objections which continued, despite the generally modified style of her successor's approach to the EC). But this view of the Social Charter, like the issue of Europe more generally, has been contested in Britain from different perspectives. Some have seen the charter as protecting the interests of rational employers and potentially offering some protection from social dumping, which, if not contained, could reinforce Britain's problems as a low-investment, low-productivity low-wage economy. Whilst it has been criticised for its potential limitations, it has also been seen, overall, as relevant to the interests of labour as well as capital (Grahl and Teague, 1990). Others, on the left, have been far more sceptical about the charter leading to significant improvements for labour, and consider that it lacks effective enforcement mechanisms. According to this view the charter is seen as something of an irrelevance, in practice; although the Social Charter has been presented as having some significance, according to this perspective, as part of wider attempts to promote a more caring, and so more acceptable, legitimate image for the EC, more generally.

Meanwhile, even those who have been more enthusiastic about European integration have accepted that there have also been political, social and ideological factors behind this increasing concern with social policy at European level. Lodge refers to the view of Jacques Delors, the French socialist who became president of the European Commission, that 'Each and every Community citizen needs to feel bound by the links which unite European society' (Lodge, 1989, p. 309). The EC was demonstrating interest in developing a human face in order to build legitimacy, a human face based on notions of dialogue between employers and trade unions, with concern for the new poor and for social justice. This type of approach seemed closer to social democratic traditions, mixed with Christian democracy, rather than to the new right (the parliament of the European Community gained a socialist majority in 1989). But similar perspectives can be traced to earlier times, for instance the European poverty programmes became increasingly concerned to tackle the problems of the 'new poor', who were suffering from structural unemployment, as well tackling the problems of other groups, including the increasing number of elderly poor, single parents and the marginalised.

The European poverty programmes have been minuscule in comparison with the scale of the problems and in comparison with other areas of EC spending. Although the entire social budget grew in absolute terms from the mid-1970s to the 1980s, even by the end of the 1980s, it was only 7.2 per cent of the EC budget, whilst unemployment doubled over the same period. Funds for the third programme, the 70 million allocated in 1989 for a five-year programme, were, however, double the amount agreed for the second programme, although as critics pointed out, even this sum (which came under pressure itself) was still roughly equivalent to the social services budget for just one English local authority for one year.

Whatever their other limitations, however, each of these programmes did provide some services that would otherwise not have been provided. They also included some commitment to the active participation of the poor themselves. And there is some evidence that, at least in some cases, the recipients *did* participate. Reporting on the first programme, Dennett, *et al.*, concluded that although few of the projects achieved mass participation (those at Marolles and Craigmillar were the exceptions here, and both projects had already been operating for nearly twenty years), 'nearly all the projects succeeded in mobilising groups of local people around particular issues, as co-operatives, claimants' unions, tenants' associations and the like. . . . In summary, the many forms of participation and self-help developed in the European Programme not only fulfil the Council criteria but are one of the programme's most important achievements' (Dennett *et al.*, 1982, p. 233). An evaluation of the community resource centres that were funded in Britain as part of this programme came to similar conclusions about the significance of the community participation that did take place, even within the constraints of the poverty programme (Lees and Mayo, 1984). In evaluating the second programme, from 1985–8, the EC placed considerable value on the continuation of this strand of community participation. In his comments on the second programme in *Social Europe* in January 1989, for instance, Jean-Paul Tricert specifically commended 'those experiments which encourage participation by and mobilization of the groups concerned, for example by setting up cooperatives, subcontracting firms or self-help and mutual aid networks'. The third programme, 'for an economic and social integration of the least-favoured groups', has been presented as fitting within such an approach (although it was not called a poverty programme, the British government having objected) (Tricert, 1989).

Meanwhile, at European level there has been some wider (if little publicised) recognition of the importance of community development. In 1989 a resolution was passed by the Council of Europe that endorsed community development and called for increased support of community-development programmes by local authorities and others, and 'for a greater promotion of the principles and practice of community development throughout Member States' (McConnell, 1990, p. 2). The Standing Conference of Local and Regional Authorities of Europe resolved (Resolution 208 1989) that self-help and community development 'should be high on the list of political options of local and regional government in Europe', as the authorities believed that 'community development can offer important lessons and inspirations for government and public authorities'. So local and regional authorities should draw upon the experiences of international organisations (EEC, OECD and the

UN) and other official promoters of community development to provide support, including financial resources and support for those taking 'initiatives aimed at improving their community by their own work'. The Standing Conference resolution also included support for the creation of a European association for community development.

In response to these processes at European level, voluntary and community organisations, including women's organisations and black and ethnic-minority groups, have begun to organise themselves. There has been increasing concern about the possible impact of the single market on certain groups, and this has been particularly marked in relation to its possible impact on black and ethnic-minority groups in Britain. For example the London Research Centre produced an information pack, drawing upon a conference to consider the possible effects of the single market on black people, who feared that 1992 would facilitate the free movement of European nationals at the expense of non-EC nationals, especially black and other minority-group workers who risked becoming even more marginalised and oppressed. The information pack included a much quoted article by Sivanandan, who argued that 'we are moving from an ethnocentric to a Eurocentric racism – and 1992 won't help' (Sivanandan, 1988). Similar points were argued by Conroy, in a critical review of integration and change in Western Europe, in terms of the notion of fortress Europe. Conroy argued that 'The rights of migrants to Europe after 1992 are likely to be severely curtailed as access to one Member State will endow the entrant with freedom of movement of the twelve. . . . 'But how to distinguish', Conroy asked, if this were to be pursued 'between a recently arrived Kurd and a resident second generation Turk? A possible answer is by accelerated street controls of identity cards and passports of all non-whites. This will and does foster tension and racism' (Conroy , 1990, p. 297).

The activities of women's organisations, meanwhile, have also included lobbying at European level. Whilst the EC has offered important protection to women, for instance in terms of equal pay for equal-value work, maternity rights, and training, women wish 'to preserve their recent hard-won rights' and to ensure that social legislation is harmonised upwards, that is to the most progressive standards, rather than downwards to the lowest common denominator (European Women's Lobby, November 1989, background paper no. 6). As there was increasing evidence that recession was affecting women particularly seriously, these concerns to protect previous gains, and to make equality a reality in fact as well as in law, took on even greater relevance.

Similarly networks have been developed to enable voluntary groups to operate more effectively at the increasingly important EC level. Eurolink Age is a network of organisations concerned with older people and ageing. The Euro Citizen Action Service was launched in 1990 to provide a service to the voluntary sector that would enable voluntary organisations to find their way around EC decision-making processes and be more effective in representing their particular interests at EC level. In 1991 one source identified some 60 such networks, and the number was increasing (quoted in Baine *et al.*, 1992, p. 38).

The Combined Bureau for Social Development in The Hague was established in 1990 to 'form an institutional relationship between Community Development agencies, so that we can operate as a collective on the European stage to promote community development – to put it on the agenda of the EC as a strategy for tackling social and economic problems and for extending participatory democracy' (Thomas, 1990, p. 48). 'It is time, in a word', Thomas argued when explaining this initiative, 'that community development came out of the closet, as far as the EC is concerned'.

There have, in addition, been efforts to build networks between community organisations across Europe, including the networks developed through the poverty programmes. This has been seen as increasingly important as alternative scenarios for the future of Europe are contested. Benington, for instance, has argued that there are competing approaches, for a 'competitive European market, with an enhanced role for consumers, and, on the other hand, a caring European community, with strengthened rights of citizenship. . . . Voluntary and community organisations can play an important part in helping to shape the scenarios for the future of Europe. The slogan "Think Global; Act Local" has never been more relevant', he concludes (Benington, 1991, p. 95). Anyone who has worked to support community organisations in building effective networks across cities, let alone wider regions, however, will be only too aware of some of the practical difficulties in achieving these objectives. However sceptical community organisations might be, though, there does seem to be increasing recognition that, like it or loathe it, 1992 has arrived in some form or other, and that this is a reality which community organisations ignore at their peril.

5

Some International Comparisons from the South

As the previous chapter argued, international forces and the policies of international agencies have become more important than ever before in determining the context for community development at the local level. There are increasing parallels as well as contrasts to be drawn. There are lessons too, for the First World to draw from the experiences of the Third World, and especially so in relation to community participation and community development, an important point to emphasise given that Western social policy analysis has been criticised for being Eurocentrist or Western-centred in tending to assume that comparative social-policy learning is predominantly a one-way process, with the Third World doing the learning, whilst for the First World 'the experience(s) of developing countries are irrelevant' (MacPherson 1987, pp. 215–217).

As has already been suggested, European integration has been more clearly recognised as having key implications for community development within the EC, but it has potential implications, too, for community development, in the Third World. This chapter considers some of the wider forces and agencies that have been affecting community development in Third-World countries. The first part of the chapter summarises a range of developing policies and practices in relation to the role of international agencies. The competing policies and practices of non-governmental agencies, both international 'NGOs' and local voluntary self-help organisations, are compared and contrasted. The chapter concludes with specific cases that illustrate some of the complexities, and some of the competing and contrasting possibilities, of these different approaches.

As was suggested in Chapter 2, despite having been extensively criticised for its colonialist and paternalistic connotations, in the 1950s and 1960s community development seems to have made some form of come-back in the Third World (although typically under slightly different nomenclature, such as 'community participation'). Writing in the mid-1980s, Midgley argued that 'Community participation is a new catchword in development studies and particularly in the field of social development. Popularised by the United Nations and other official bodies, it now permeates the literature on the subject . . . in addition to the United Nations, community participation ideals have been enthusiastically endorsed by officials at the World Health Organisation and at UNICEF. They have also been championed by non-governmental development organisations and by academics at universities in both developing and industrial countries' (Midgely *et al.*, 1986, p. 14). So what was going on? Why was a relatively discredited notion suddenly so apparently popular again?

Midgley suggested that in the mid-1980s 'it may be argued that community participation principles are a primary expression of populist ideals in the Third World today. As in populism, current community participation theory suggests that ordinary people have been exploited by politicians and bureaucrats and that they have been excluded not only from political affairs but from the development process in general. By organising local people and making them aware of their situation, community participation provides a mechanism for the mobilization of the masses and a collective means of redress' (ibid., p. 16).

Meanwhile alternative explanations for community development programmes' hitherto relative lack of success in promoting development and tackling poverty in Third-World countries have concentrated on more structural arguments. Programmes have been criticised, for instance, for failing to take adequate account of – let alone to combat – the structural inequalities of class and caste, and for failing to challenge vested interests, including vested interests in land ownership and the provision of credit. So programmes provided disproportionate benefits to the relatively few, benefits which failed to trickle down to the poor, despite the fact that it was they who had provided most of the unpaid labour that built the community schools and the local roads for the carts of the better off to transport their produce to market.

From the 1960s and 1970s there was increasing discussion, too, of the international dimensions of structural inequalities. The failure of development strategies and the underdevelopment of the Third World was related to the development of the First, industrialised world. As MacPherson argued, criticisms of community development were linked to 'the growing awareness that the development strategies imposed on Third World countries were not bringing "development" but were entrenching the process of undedevelopment' (MacPherson, 1982, p. 168). One of the key figures in this debate was Andre Gunder Frank, who published a book outlining his theory of underdevelopment in 1969. Frank argued that Third-World countries, such as the countries of Latin America, suffered as a result *of* the processes of development of capitalist relations, and the exploitative relations between First and Third World. Theories of underdevelopment have been contentious, not least within the left, and Frank has subsequently revised his approach to take account of criticisms raised in these debates. The variation in patterns of development in Third-World countries has also required further explanation, including the growth experienced in newly industrialising countries on the Pacific rim and elsewhere. The point here is not that there were definitive answers, simply that there was renewed questioning of development strategies in the light of debates about structural inequalities, both nationally and internationally.

A third aspect of criticisms of community development and community participation focused upon the role of women in development. From the mid-1970s feminists were increasingly challenging the gender-blind assumptions of development strategies and community-development programmes. Women's specific contributions to development have all too often been ignored in programmes that have taken as given that farmers or householders are male, with women in subsidiary roles as wives and mothers, a model which fails to take account of the reality of so many women's lives in the Third World as well as the First (and especially so where men have been drawn into migrant wage labour, leaving the women behind to grow the food and care for the children and the elderly). Women have been ignored in the development process; or they have been reinforced in traditional roles (Afshar, 1991). Increasingly women have also been drawn into international production processes and exploited in the lowest waged work, including the most exploited work in enterprise zones (Mitter, 1986; Nash and Fernandez Kelly,

1983). Furthermore they have been overburdened as they have been expected to take on community development roles and tasks in addition to their economic roles and domestic responsibilities (Moser, 1989).

The Decade for Women (1976–85) signified a growing awareness that there were key issues around women and development. Once again there were alternative approaches. There were feminists who challenged traditional male approaches and called for development strategies that would give greater power to women (for example Development Dialogue 1–2, 1982, 'Another Development with Women'). And there were more pragmatic approaches which recognised the validity of some of these criticisms; that development strategies which ignored the interests and contributions of half the population would be correspondingly less effective, even in their own terms, and that models of the family based upon middle-class European myths were particularly inappropriate for Third-World realities.

Traditional approaches to community development have needed to take account of each of these major areas of criticism. (See for example Dore and Mar (eds), 1981, for an analysis of these criticisms of traditional approaches.) Meanwhile, community participation entered the international agenda and in the 1970s gained official recognition. For example, in 1976 the ILO, at the World Employment Conference, identified the crucial role played by participation in the implementation of basic-needs strategies. In the same year, in its Nairobi General Conference, UNESCO pointed to the relevance of adult education, not only for its contribution to enriching the knowledge and skills of individuals but also for its contribution to promoting participation in social, economic and cultural development. And in 1978, at Alma Ata, the World Health Organisation and the United Nations Children's Fund sponsored a conference that emphasised the importance of community participation. More recent examples include the 1990 conference sponsored by the United Nations Economic Commission for Africa, together with a number of citizens' associations, which adopted the 'African Charter for Popular Participation in Development and Transformation'. This charter called for governments and international organisations to create the necessary conditions for community empowerment and popular participation in development strategies to tackle the economic and social crisis that was so tragically manifest in 'the suffering, hardship and impoverishment of the vast majority of African people' (ifda, 1990, p. 3).

So how were these international agencies' commitments to community participation going to take account of past criticisms? And how did they intend to relate to the changing global circumstances of the mid-1970s, through to the 1980s and 1990s and beyond? Clearly a change of name, from community development to community participation, would not of itself be sufficient to redress the inadequacies or the paternalism of the legacy of the past, although changes in terminology have been seen as symbolic of wider changes. As Chapter 2 pointed out, like community development, the term community participation has been used in fundamentally differing ways. Community participation can be used to refer to empowerment as part of radical social change, and community participation can be used to refer to methods for increasing project effectiveness, whilst reducing costs to the public sector. Community participation can be promoted to increase the legitimacy of official structures and organisations, demonstrating their concern for the poor, and it can be promoted to preempt arguments about the need for more fundamental forms of social change (Moser, 1989).

Meanwhile community participation has also fitted into the logic of self-help, in the context of major shifts in official thinking about the role of the state. This has been increasingly marked, both at national and at international level, since the mid-1970s. As was suggested in the Introduction, from the mid-1970s, there were increasing economic difficulties and increasing pressures for restructuring to cope with recession, pressures which affected Third-World countries, and especially Sub-Saharan Africa and Latin American countries, particularly seriously. These pressures were in many cases compounded by the oil crisis. The response of international agencies to this global situation, was to argue for the merits of a more market-led approach to development, with increased reliance on the private sector, a reduction in the role of government, and a reduced public sector, including the public service sector. This was the logic of Reaganomics and Thatcherism, applied this time to the Third World. Structural adjustment programmes to carry out such strategies were prerequisites for loans from international agencies.

Structural adjustment has typically involved reductions in public subsidies, including subsidies for basic foodstuffs (which had helped to maintain nutritional levels, and so the basic health of the poor, in a number of countries). In addition, structural adjustment has involved attempts to hold down spending on social services such as health and education. In some cases this has been achieved through cuts, but there have also been pressures for privatisation/contracting out of services with the objective of achieving savings. And there have been pressures to increase charges to service users (including, for example, charges such as school fees). Just as in Britain, privatisation and cuts can take more than one form. And just as in Britain, and elsewhere in the West, reductions in the role of the state can be accompanied by efforts to increase the role of the voluntary sector and community self-help.

In a number of cases, structural adjustment packages have been associated with popular unrest. 'IMF' riots and/or strikes have occurred in some cases, including for example, in Bolivia, Jamaica, Peru and the Sudan. The fear of such upheavals has been identified as an additional factor in increasing international agencies' interest in finding alternative, less disruptive approaches to development, increasing the legitimacy of existing arrangements and demonstrating that international agencies, too, may have a human face. When these factors are added to international agencies' interest in promoting self-help and mutual aid to reduce public responsibility and public expenditure, the relative popularity of community participation may become more readily explicable.

One conclusion to be drawn from this discussion is that community-participation programmes may have been promoted for a variety of often conflicting reasons, typically recognisably similar to some, at least, of the reasons for the promotion of the community development approaches that community participation was supposed to move beyond. To argue along these lines, however, is absolutely not to argue that international support for community participation simply represents some form of global conspiracy against the poor. That in effect would be to revert to approaches based upon over-deterministic functionalism; with community-participation schemes merely performing functions for international capital. Whereas the reality, it is being argued, is more complex, with outcomes representing the results of competition between conflicting interests, within and between different institutions, governments and local communities.

It is not being suggested here that the different actors have equal chances of influencing the outcome; on the contrary there are powerful structural disadvantages for the poor, minority groups and women in the Third World, just as there are in the First. But that is not to argue that they have had nothing to gain from community participation, at least as far as some of the more favourable situations have been concerned (see for example Thomas, 1985, on Women in Kenya).

Can communities derive significant benefits from these official strategies to promote self-help? The case of self-help housing in the Third World

Community participation in housing, and more specifically self-help/self-build housing schemes, was placed on the official international agenda in the mid-1970s. The UN Habitat Conference endorsed the notion in 1976, and at the same time the World Bank began to put resources into such schemes. Self-build housing may be built or improved by the occupants themselves, or the occupants may pay others to carry out all or part of the construction work. Projects may be implemented by individuals or families, or by community organisations working cooperatively.

Community participation in housing, and particularly self-build approaches, acquired widespread support in the 1970s for a number of reasons. Housing needs were growing in expanding Third-World cities far more rapidly than the provision of affordable housing to meet these needs (Skinner and Rodell, 1983). Publicly provided housing had concentrated on meeting the needs of public servants and those who could afford to pay rent. Meanwhile the poor, and migrants coming to cities to seek work, squatted in makeshift shacks. Government responses to such squatter settlements were initially typically negative: to bulldoze the settlements and get rid of the eye-sores. But this did nothing to meet the housing needs of the urban poor, and squatting continued to increase. By the end of the 1980s, it was estimated that around half of the residents of Third-World cities were living in some kind of squatter area (Schlyter, 1988, p. 11).

By the early 1970s official approaches to squatting were being challenged and alternatives were being proposed. One of the best-known advocates of the alternative of self-build was Turner, a libertarian socialist who argued that squatter settlements were far from being totally negative solutions to the housing crisis in Third-World cities; on the contrary they demonstrated dynamism, community self-organisation and self-help. Turner and others concluded that when 'dwellers control the major decisions and are free to make their own contributions in the design, construction or management of their housing' the process stimulated individual and social well-being, as well as producing cheaper and more appropriate housing to meet their needs (Turner and Fichter, 1972).

Participation, self-help and self-build schemes were proposed, then, to improve existing squatter settlements and to provide add-itional accommodation. Broadly the role of international agencies and governments would be to facilitate these schemes, for example through providing credit to buy building materials, and by ensuring legal access to land and to basic amenities such as piped water. Individuals, families and communities were to provide the rest.

This approach has been subjected to major criticisms. Ward, for example, has argued that the antistatism implicit in many such schemes can be used by governments to evade their responsibilities (Ward, 1982). Instead, individual responsibility and the value of individual home ownership would be reinforced, a point which has been related to wider concerns about political stability and the defusing of potential urban conflict. Moser, for example, argued that one of the objectives of USAID Alliance for Progress projects to tackle urban marginality had been to head off any possible replication of the 'Cuba/Che Guevara shock' (Moser, 1989, p. 91), although in the event the residents of the slums of Latin America were not as revolutionary as had been feared at the time. Not that home ownership has necessarily produced the desired ideological or political effects either, a point which has been argued in relation to Britain, (for example Marshall *et al.*, 1988) as well as to Third-World countries (for example Schlyter, 1984).

Critics have argued that the World Bank has supported such projects as part of wider strategies to enhance the legitimacy of the existing order, presenting an image of caring, in an increasingly unequal global order. From a Marxist perspective, Burgess criticised self-help approaches to Third-World housing as providing housing on the cheap in order to keep employers' labour costs down at the expense of the poor, who had to pay for everything they received and/or provide unpaid labour (Burgess, 1982). Any effects on the costs of labour could, however, be difficult to ascertain, especially in view of the extent to which the poor, and particularly women, in Third-World cities have survived through informal rather than formal work (in the George area of Lusaka, for instance, only 33 per cent of women were classified as economically active, a figure which Schlyter regarded as a vast underestimate because it took no account of informal, and often illegal trading, beer brewing and so on).

In any case, in unequal societies benefits from such schemes may be disproportionately appropriated by the better off, and these tendencies may be exacerbated where there is a private market in land (because any improvements may simply push up the value of the properties, and this in turn puts pressure on the poorest to sell to those who can afford to pay more). Poorer squatters may simply be unable to afford any improvements, or private ownership of land may rule out such schemes in the first place if private landowners prefer to develop the land for alternative, more profitable uses (Dwyer, 1975). Ward's 1989 study, *Corruption, Development and Inequality*, provides evidence of the ways in which such schemes disproportionately benefit local leaders and reinforce their power. Women also tend to benefit less from such schemes as they find it harder to obtain credit or provide the necessary labour, even though women-headed households are likely to be amongst the poorest and in the greatest housing need.

In practice, however, there do seem to have been cases where self-help housing schemes have provided real benefits, even to the poorer sections of local communities. And there are cases where women's participation has been successfully supported. These cases deserve attention, if only because of the view that in reality, at least in the current context, the poor in Third-World cities are not likely to be provided with an adequate supply of acceptable alternatives – such as affordable public housing if this were to be their preferred choice (Moser and Peake, 1987).

One of the World Bank's early self-build schemes (agreed in 1973) was in Lusaka, Zambia. Despite government attempts to clear the squatters, at the beginning of the 1970s, over a third of the population of Lusaka were squatting. The World Bank provided funding towards the upgrading and servicing of some 17 000 dwellings and the preparation and servicing of some 7000 plots in overspill areas (to make room for roads and other improvements). Loans were provided for building materials, to be drawn in cash or materials, and residents could either provide the labour themselves or pay others to do all or part of it on their behalf. Community participation was built into the scheme, both in terms of participation in planning decisions such as where roads, schools, clinics and community centres should be sited, and in terms of participation in the building process itself. Training was also provided, through the Zambian government, including training workshops to support residents in developing their own skills and organisations.

So how successful was the scheme? Overall it resulted in higher levels of improvement than had been anticipated. The poorer residents did benefit, as well as the better-off ones, although there was evidence that they found it increasingly difficult to pay off their loans, especially as food prices were soaring faster than incomes by the end of the 1970s. However the poorest were not pressured into selling because the land was publicly owned and leased back (although there was some evidence of rooms being sublet, despite the fact that this was not officially supposed to happen because the scheme was not intended to promote private landlordism). Women, who headed nearly a fifth of urban households, benefited proportionately less than men, and women tended to drop out faster than men; but it has been argued that those women who did stay with the scheme, put more into their house improvements than the men (Schlyter, 1988).

Evaluation studies demonstrated that there was considerable satisfaction with the scheme, despite some differences of view, for example over the siting of schools. And there was more active participation than was the norm in other Zambian official projects. The actual process of participation was, however, closely linked to the United National Independence Party (UNIP). During this period the party was strongly organised in the locality, and participation focused around party leaders. The negative side of this was that other groups and interests were less well represented. For example, professional project workers had felt the need to intervene to ensure that the minority group of Jehovah's witnesses were not actively discriminated against (by having roads run through their homes). And Schlyter's study found that women felt that they had attended more meetings but had been less effectively represented on powerful committees than the men. One effect of this relative lack of powerful participation by women was that the layout of the improved housing was criticised as unsuited to women's needs. For example, the traditional layout of housing compounds had been circular, which meant that women had been able to supervise each other's children whilst performing their own domestic tasks, which made it easier for women to leave the home to engage in other activities (such as petty trading). The new grid layout made this impossible (Moser and Peake, 1987).

So, there *was* community participation in the Lusaka scheme, both in planning and implementing the project. But more could have been achieved, and especially so in relation to ensuring that women's participation was powerful and effective. Since then, however, the situation deteriorated. Increasing economic difficulties affected the provision of resources, including building supplies. The Zambian government decentralised responsibility but failed to provide accompanying resources to district councils, and local residents became increasingly unable or unwilling to keep up repayments on the deteriorating scheme, let alone to invest in additional improvements.

Nicaragua has provided examples of community participation in housing that were successful in overcoming some of the shortcomings identified in schemes like the one in Lusaka. However they were not able to withstand wider pressures either; in this case pressures that resulted from the war and the economic difficulties of the late 1980s.

Following the growth of Managua in the Somoza period, and the destruction of 75 per cent of buildings in the earthquake of 1972, the Sandinista regime faced a major housing crisis, with a shortage of some 240 000 units. After some initial public building proved relatively expensive, and not altogether popular with residents (because even relatively low-rise flats lacked small garden plots, so that tenants were unable to grow vegetables or keep livestock, as many wished), from 1981–2 the government shifted its attention to self-build schemes. The Ministry of Housing and Human Settlements (MINVAH) provided technical support and building materials at controlled prices, whilst local neighbourhood committees, the Sandinista Defence Committees (CDS), organised community participation on a collective basis. Community participation was a major feature of government policy, and the CDS committees had already worked on other aspects of community participation, for example health care and adult literacy.

The resulting homes were the subject of criticism, for example from professional architects who thought that they were ugly. And some professionals believed that building resources could actually have been used more effectively through public building schemes (Darke *et al.*). Self-help schemes are not necessarily cheaper in the long run. But the housing was relatively cheap for the residents, and it was evidently popular in terms of meeting popular aspirations (Massey, 1987). This positive view was shared beyond the confines of those who might have been expected to have taken a positive view, for ideological or other reasons. A UN study of self-help housing, which examined a number of schemes, concluded in 1989 that the Nicaraguan schemes had been particularly successful (UN Centre for Human Settlements, 1989). In addition, the Nicaraguan self-help housing schemes were collectively organised, and within the Nicaraguan experiences there were examples of successful efforts to overcome the barriers to women's effective participation. A case study that illustrates this latter point was the San Judas scheme in a low-income area in Managua. Here the women, including women who were single parents, *did* succeed in overcoming major obstacles. And these women *did* acquire the necessary construction skills to go on to complete their own homes.

The Nicaraguan schemes were no more able to survive external pressures than the Zambian scheme had been, however. The impact of the war affected resources, including building supplies, as well as morale. There was no way in which community participation could compensate for the lack of basic inputs from the state. Once again there may be relevant parallels to be drawn between the experiences of community participation in the Third World and the West. Whilst self-build schemes have been relatively rare in the West (with some significant exceptions), tenant participation schemes have been more common; but here again community participation cannot be expected to compensate if basic support is not forthcoming from the public sector. Chapter 7 raises some of these issues in the British context.

From international agencies and national governments to the role of non-governmental organisations (NGOs)

So far the discussion of policies and experiences in Third-World countries has concentrated on the aims and objectives of international agencies, together with the aims and objectives of national governments. This leaves the discussion of the various aims and objectives of non-governmental organisations, the NGOs, which are also relevant, and particularly so in considering debates about changes within the mixed economy of welfare. Like the voluntary sector within nation states, however, the NGOs are by no means a unified sector. There are major variations between NGOs, despite the fact that they may be linked together as one sector for the purposes of particular arguments.

NGOs have been held up as representing potential alternative approaches to development, approaches which transcend the limitations of traditional approaches to community development. In a much quoted chapter, Marsden and Oakley argued, at the beginning of the 1980s, that NGOs had undergone major changes and had gained the potential to reach the poorest sections of society in the Third World and to work with them, in new ways, to increase their participation in decision-making and to promote their empowerment. Until the 1970s, Marsden and Oakley argued, 'the major role of most NGOs, including relief agencies and international voluntary organisations, mirrored the earlier charitable foundations in the West, being concerned mainly with disaster relief and with provision for "outcasts" – the physically and mentally handicapped who still remain the primary objects of many government welfare programmes in Third World countries' (Marsden and Oakley, 1982, p. 156). Since then, they argued, NGOs have expanded their work and, significantly, developed alternative approaches, based upon notions of empowerment, to enable the poor to understand the nature and causes of international inequality and poverty and to develop non-exploitative strategies for development.

Marsden and Oakley provided examples to illustrate the growing potential for alternative approaches through NGOs. They drew upon case material from the Bhoomi Sena movement in Maharastra State in India (which developed through the activities of student volunteers from Bombay University who contributed to adult education and community-action initiatives in small projects throughout the state), and from the Fishermen's Movement in north-east Brazil, which drew its inspiration from the radical ideas of Paolo Freire and those within the Catholic church who espoused liberation theology. The authors concluded by contrasting these radical approaches with government community-development schemes, which, they argued were typically 'fettered by an elaborate and often "corrupt" bureaucracy, supporting a system of privilege and nepotism which, at least in part, such non-governmental initiatives are able to bypass through their associations with international aid agencies' (ibid., p. 161). Similarly positive conclusions have been drawn about the Bhoomi Sena movement, for example, by Md Anisur Rahman, who has described the movement in terms of its achievements in enhancing human dignity through liberation from bonded labour, and in terms of struggling for land rights and implementation of the minimum-wage law, as steps towards self-development and self-determination (Rahman, 1990).

Since then a number of accounts have put forward the positive case for the contribution NGOs can make to development, based upon strategies to reach those in greatest need and upon people-to-people aid rather than upon official approaches to development in which benefits tend to be siphoned off by elites, rather than trickling down as free market theorists have argued that they would (for example Holloway, 1989).

However others have been more sceptical, arguing that there is also a downside to NGOs. Midgley, for example, has pointed to the paternalism that can pervade voluntary as well as statutory organisations. 'Many [voluntary organisations] are run by middle-class individuals whose views are liberal and paternalistic rather than radically egalitarian' (Midgely *et al.*, p. 155). And he has pointed out that NGOs, too, typically require external sources of support, whether from governments or from international agencies or whatever, so that even apparently relatively spontaneous forms of community organisation may be crucially linked into formal organisations and external interests. This point applied, he argued, to the Bhoomi Sena movement in India that was mentioned above (ibid., p. 153). And in Third-World countries, as well as in the West, voluntary effort may result in a lack of coordination and duplication of services. Midgley concluded that it was questionable 'whether the voluntary sector is any more able to promote authentic participation than the state' (ibid., p. 157). The limits of both needed to be recognised. Community participation and voluntary effort both have a contribution to make, but 'If the critical problems of mass poverty and deprivation in the Third World are to be dealt with, concerted action by the state will be needed' (ibid., p. 158).

Part of the differences between these alternative approaches to the role of NGOs in Third-World development can be more clearly understood if the range of different types of NGOs is set out. The term has been applied to international agencies for charitable relief, and to those international agencies, Oxfam for instance, which have combined relief work with longer-term development work (including support for local NGOs) and with campaigning against the structural roots of global poverty and deprivation. Similarly, within Third-World countries NGOs' increasing work ranges from the most traditional and consensual forms of charitable relief through to consciousness raising and political as well as community-based action. Since the late 1960s, the role of student movements, intellectuals and professionals in promoting the latter type of activity seems to have been a feature of NGOs in Third-World countries, as well as in the West.

Analysing the limits and possibilities of NGOs in development in the Philippines at the end of the 1980s, Constantino-David (1990) identified seven broad types within the plethora of more than 16 000 registered NGOs in the country. Within the first two types (people's organisation and cooperatives, and social development agencies) which were the major focus of her study, Constantino-David further distinguished between NGOs in terms of size and funding sources and in terms of orientation. NGOs varied in size from the very small to those big organisations with over a hundred employees, the 'BINGOs'. Those NGOs which, she argued, had effectively settled for being apologists for the government rather than empowering the people, were designated as government-run/ inspired NGOs, or 'GRINGOS'. Those NGOs which tried to remain neutral or 'apolitical' were described as traditional NGOs or 'TANGOs', whilst business-organised NGOs were described as 'BONGOs'.

Constantino-David also set out the views of those NGOs who perceived the Aquino regime as 'simply a dog with a new collar' (Constantino-David, 1990, p. 5). Such NGOs emphasised the importance of conscientisation, mobilisation and advocacy if people were to be empowered to promote more fundamental change and democratic development. She argued that NGOs in the Philippines had developed 'a vast reservoir of expertise in dealing with people's problems' with creativity and dynamism (ibid., p. 6). Whilst there were difficulties and dilemmas, she saw people's organisations and social development agencies as the potential bearers of an alternative future 'through a process that places emphasis on people's empowerment, that is, the ability of communities and sectors to define their own problems, decide on their options and determine their own future' (ibid., p. 14). She also recognised these organisations' need of additional support, however, including support from academics, who could provide help with 'theory, skills, technology, documentation and popularization as fellow-travellers on the road towards people's empowerment' (ibid., p. 14).

This brings the argument back to the connection between local NGOs and other local forms of support, as well as between international NGOs and international agencies more generally. Whilst NGOs have developed their range and scope to include programmes to promote empowerment as well as those to provide relief and welfare, that development in itself poses further questions, it has been argued, questions which include the relationship between micro issues in the Third World and macro issues in the West (Boyer, 1990). Clearly there have been changes in the patterns of international/northern NGO operations over the past two decades or so. And clearly there have been major developments in the spread and range of NGO activities within Third-World countries, in India and the Philippines for example, developments which have important implications for international/northern-based NGOs (Burnell, 1992). But, as soon as projects move beyond the smallest self-help initiative, NGOs enter the wider arena of competing interests at national and then at international level. Moser concluded her review of community participation in urban projects in the Third World by commenting that 'While the constraints affecting different implementing agencies vary, nevertheless this review shows that they also share a number in common. In reality international donor agencies and small NGOs may be less apart than they often think in terms of current preoccupations concerning community participation', a comment which has both positive and negative aspects, depending upon the perspective adopted (Moser, 1989, p. 130).

Community action and community development in the 'First World in the Third World': The case of South Africa

Having summarised some of the trends in international and national governments, together with the changing roles of NGOs, in relation to community development and community participation in the Third World, this chapter concludes with a very specific case, the case of South Africa. In South Africa First-World and Third-World conditions coexist within one state, if not exactly cheek by jowl. The two worlds were set apart by the structures of apartheid, and the term 'community' was used as a euphemism to obscure racial and other divisions in the context of extreme racial inequalities (Lund, 1991). Despite its relative isolation, at least until the beginning of the 1990s, the South African government nevertheless developed policies to cope with some of the pressures resulting from these extreme inequalities, policies which actually had strong parallels (as well as important differences) with similar policies being developed elsewhere for the mixed economy of welfare.

For the black majority meanwhile, community action became a key ingredient in popular struggles against apartheid. Unsurprisingly, demands for improved health, education, housing and social welfare provision (up to the standard enjoyed by whites) have been high on the black agenda.

Faced with these aspirations during the 1980s the apartheid state sought to find a way of preempting further popular discontent by improving welfare, whilst containing public expenditure in a period of increasing financial difficulty. The South African government's responses to these conflicting pressures included types of policies which have already been identified and discussed in widely differing contexts. These policies included the privatisation of particular public services and increased charges for those who afford to pay. For example public housing units were sold off and hospital charges were increased (South African Institute of Race Relations, 1988).

Another major element in the government's social policies was the promotion of decentralisation and self-help. However in the context of apartheid, this meant that government-supported local authorities in the 'homelands' and black townships were to be, as far as possible, self sufficient, bearing the cost of their own inadequate services themselves, whilst whites continued to enjoy vastly superior services in their separate areas. It was argued, as Botha and

Kaplinsky have explained, that 'if black townships wanted self-government, they must also be self-financing' (Botha and Kaplinsky, 1989, p. 11). This strategy meant that 'In order to survive the [local community] Councils had to increase rents to levels beyond the reach of ordinary people. This put them in a collision course with the communities. The civic associations which proliferated in the late 1970s and early 1980s became the main opposition force to the Community councils [government-sanctioned black local authorities]. challenging them at every level' (ibid., p. 11).

Black activists organised to make this strategy inoperable. From the late 1970s there had been a proliferation of independent community organisations throughout the country, in parallel with and linked to the mobilisation of trade-union organisations. Matiwana and Walters (1986) for instance have traced a connection between the growth of student radicalism in the 1970s, and the commitment of groups of radical students to organising, including community organising. These student activists were, they argued, influenced by a range of ideas from Britain and the US, including the work of Alinsky and the experiences of the CDPs in Britain; they were also influenced by other Third-World writers and experiences, including the work of Freire (Matiwana and Walters, 1986, p. 54). At first, in the late 1970s, issues relating to squatting were central, (with resistance to the forcible removal of squatter settlements). By the early 1980s, black community activists began to organise resistance to the decentralisation plans of the Apartheid State. Local community organisations worked together in wider groupings of civic associations in the different townships. Tactics included rent boycotts, which undermined local authorities' potential for achieving the type of economic self-sufficiency that the central government had in mind, and challenged the legitimacy of those black councillors who were seen to be collaborating with the regime. Apartheid decentralisation was rendered widely inoperable.

In the period of sharper repression which followed in the mid-1980s, it became increasingly difficult for community organisations to function effectively, despite the skills that had been developed in working 'underground'. But civic and community organisations did manage to survive, and they linked up with trade-union organisations under the umbrella of the United Democratic Front, (formed in 1983) which united political opposition inside South Africa with the exiled African National Congress.

Having played key roles in organising resistance to apartheid, community organisations were faced with new challenges when talks began, to negotiate a democratic settlement in South Africa. Whilst in the past the major focus had been on resistance, community organisations had also been involved in welfare functions (in South Africa, as elsewhere, there had actually been a wide range of voluntary and community organisations, including church organisations, and mutual-aid and savings clubs). Some community organisations had also been involved in developing alternative social policies (for example, working on the development of alternative, non-racial schools and teaching materials in response to the widespread boycott of schools by young black people in the mid-1980s (see for example Muller, 1987). The involvement of community organisations in developing alternatives for the future was clearly on the agenda. (see for example Report on the ANC National Consultative Conference on Local government, 1990, p. 38). It was believed that civics should continue to play an active role in improving the quality of community life, which could include welfare functions.

Academics also recognised that, given the fact that resources would be limited, even in a post apartheid state, it was of vital importance that the effectiveness of community organisations be maximised. This in turn involved recognition of the importance of the contribution of the voluntary sector, both formal and informal. Lund, for example, raised the importance of providing training and support systems for community-based carers (who were actually key in caring for black elderly people in both rural and urban areas) and doing so without reinforcing women carers in gender-stereotyped roles (Lund, 1991). Lund was also clear that, as the British experience had demonstrated, community care, and voluntary effort more generally, depended for their effectiveness upon the bedrock of state support (Lund, 1990).

This brings the argument back to some of the implications of case material from the previous sections. In South Africa, as elsewhere, community participation, community development and self-help strategies may have potential relevance in the future, both for communities and for governments and international agencies (albeit for varying and often conflicting purposes). But none of these purposes is likely to be achieved spontaneously; community initiatives need to be provided with regular public financing, together with education and training, including training for equal opportunities and community work support.

6

The Changing Role and Potential of the Non-Statutory Community Sector in Britain

Chapter 1 set out some of the different factors involved in governments' interests in shifting the balance of welfare provision away from the statutory sector with a greater role for the voluntary sector as well as for private provision. Chapter 1 also commented on the growth of particular types of voluntary and community activities, including advocacy, mutual aid and self-help activities. Similar ranges of trends were identified, both in terms of governments' interests and in terms of the growth of self-help and mutual-aid activities, in developed countries (Chapter 4) and in relation to the Third World (Chapter 5).

This chapter focuses on the impact of these different processes on the voluntary sector, and especially on the impact of self-help, mutual-aid and community organisations in Britain. Self-help, mutual aid and community activity more generally have been considered to have developed for a number of reasons, in Britain as elsewhere, since the 1960s. Governments have viewed these developments with increasing ambivalence. The role of the voluntary sector has been given more prominence, but resources for community organising have been increasingly constrained. Typically, local authorities have been at the sharp end of some of these financial pressures, with spending constraints from central government on the one hand and increasing demands for resources, including resources to support voluntary and community activities, on the other. Over the same period, a number of local authorities came to support community development principles as the basis for developing their strategies towards the voluntary sector, strategies which in the early 1990s faced mounting financial difficulties because of the recession. Faced with these different pressures and possibilities, the voluntary sector in general, and community organisations more specifically, have attempted to voice their common interests and anxieties more effectively, both at local-government level and, increasingly, at national level and beyond.

Growth and change in the non-statutory community sector

There seems to be widespread agreement that from the 1960s, and 1970s the nature of the voluntary sector changed. There was an upsurge of self-help, mutual aid and community activity, and the growth of a range of new organisations (Brenton, 1985; Wann, 1992). The Caloustie Gulbenkian Foundation Study Group (writing in 1973) attempted to explain this upsurge of interest in a number of ways, pointing to the increasing complexity and fragmentation of life, which led to new efforts to achieve effective participation. 'Citizens' rights groups, consumer groups, tenants' associations or shop floor groups are a few examples of community efforts through which people seek more control over their lives' (Caloustie Gulbenkian Foundation, 1973, p. 10). In addition to increasing government interest, which included an interest in making services more effective and in promoting the use of volunteers, the group also identified the growth of 'a number of spontaneous self-help and community action groups and of co-operation among voluntary agencies' (ibid., p. 11). A study by the Community Association movement in Britain similarly identified an upsurge of new types of alternative neighbourhood and community organisation and provision in this period, including the growth of large numbers of tenants' associations, which came together in the National Tenants' Organisation in 1977. 'In the 1960's amenity and environmental societies began to emerge in considerable numbers while self-help groups, often with a major interest in some particular aspect of health, housing or welfare rights appeared in many neighbourhoods also among black populations' (Clarke, 1990, p. 77).

In addition to some of the reasons put forward by the Gulbenkian Group to explain these changes, there have been explanations focusing on other processes of change during this period. These include the effects of the student movement and a wider questioning of traditional approaches to official and professional decision making and service delivery. The Introduction and Chapter 1 have already discussed some of the ideological and political roots of this questioning, including, but by no means exclusively, socialist, libertarian socialist and feminist roots. These fitted into wider trends and more general tendencies away from centralism and towards a belief in ordinary people, as the Barclay Report summarised in the early 1980s (Barclay, 1982). Similar trends were identified, for example, in Chapters 4 and 5, in connection with the growth of self-help and mutual aid in parts of Europe and in particular Third-World countries.

The result was that the voluntary sector, which was already varied, became even more diffuse. There were clearly identifiable sub-sectors within the voluntary sector. The new trends had some impact, too, upon the more established parts of the voluntary sector. As the study *Enterprising Neighbours* demonstrated, well-established community associations decided that they needed to take account of these changes if they were to survive into the twenty-first century (Clarke, 1990).

There have been a number of different approaches to characterising the different and developing elements within the voluntary sector, as Chapter 1 illustrated. Johnson, for instance, divided organisations into service-providing organisations, self-help groups and pressure groups (Johnson, 1981), whilst Murray (Murray, 1969) also included resource organisations and coordinat-ing organisations, pointing out that particular organisations may perform more than one of these different functions. Chanan developed these approaches further (in order to demonstrate some different points about the voluntary sector, and public support for it) and categorised the voluntary sector in the following way.

1. Independent local groups.
2. Professionally-run or nationally-standardised organisations which have local branches using volunteer labour, such as the Citizens' Advice Bureau, the Women's Royal Voluntary Service and the Red Cross.
3. Umbrella groups or interventionist projects, such as Councils of Voluntary Service, community development projects or resource

centres, which stimulate, support or coordinate other local organisations.

4. Professional non-profit organisations which provide a specific service for a fee, such as most housing associations and training schemes. These often use mainly paid staff' (Chanan, 1991, p. 8).

Chanan then went on to profile community activity of all kinds in particular localities as follows:

A Personal and household activity
B Informal community activity
C Independent local groups
D Professionally-run volunteer-using organisations
E Umbrella groups and support projects
F Professional non-profit organisations (ibid., p. 9).

The point of looking at the voluntary sector in this way is that it allowed Chanan to emphasise the importance of the level of informal activity, the volume of activity under category A, in any particular community, followed by B, and steeply declining through to F. In contrast Chanan argued that the weight of public funding to the voluntary sector would be almost inverse, with the greatest funding going to F – professional non-profit organisations – and the least funding going to support A – personal and household activities. There were a number of reasons for this mismatch, including, Chanan pointed out, the 'massive neglect of most forms of unpaid work in society' (ibid., p. 9). This neglect has had crucial gender implications because women are disproportionately likely to be performing undervalued, unpaid work. And there have been class implications too, as Chanan also pointed out. Formal volunteering has been associated with those who organise volunteers to provide services for the other part of the population, the passive, 'inactive' recipients of volunteering. The fact that much research on volunteering has excluded help given to family and friends has led to the reinforcement of these biases, in Chanan's view, rendering virtually invisible the contributions of many working-class people, and women particularly.

These biases need to be borne in mind when attempting to evaluate the growth of self-help, mutual aid and community activity from the 1960s and 1970s. This is in no way to deny that there were processes of growth and change; but the extent of these changes may have been more variable than has sometimes been supposed, and there may also have been more elements of continuity than have typically been recognised, and ebbs and flows rather than simple patterns of growth, especially amongst the more informal types of organisation and activity.

Estimates of the extent of self-help, mutual aid and community activity are, then, particularly problematic. On the basis of the General Household Survey study in 1981 (considered in Chapter 1), excluding help to immediate family and friends, it was estimated that 23 per cent of those aged sixteen and over had done some voluntary work in the previous twelve months. A national survey in 1987 estimated the far higher figure of 44 per cent for those who had done some voluntary work within the previous month, and the 1991 National Survey of Voluntary Activity in the UK concluded that about half of adults (51 per cent) in Britain had been involved in formal voluntary activity over the past twelve months, with a further third having taken part in informal voluntary activity. Even these figures may be missing important aspects of community activity. For instance, some community activities have become formalised and registered as charitable organisations; but charitable efforts also include a far wider range of less formalised activities and organisations. The National Council for Voluntary Organisations (NCVO) estimated that there were twice as many organisations, (including community organisations) that were *not* registered as charities as the 160 000 organisations that *were* registered at the beginning of the 1990s (quoted in Chanan, 1991, p. 6). Similarly, in his study of community initiatives at the end of the 1980s, Willmott estimated that there were some 2000 tenants' organisations active in Britain at that time, together with 1200 community organisations and 18 500 play organisations that were affiliated to national bodies. But of course this still did not account for all those local organisations that were not affiliated to national organisations (Willmott, 1989).

Further local studies may provide a more comprehensive picture. In the absence of more recent comprehensive data, Willmott writing in 1989, still found it useful to refer to the study of self-help carried out in two inner-city areas of London by Knight and Hayes in 1981 (see Knight and Hayes, 1981). In these two areas, covering populations of 8000 and 5000 respectively, Knight and Hayes identified eighteen groups in all (twelve groups in the larger area and six groups in the smaller area). Of these eighteen groups, eight were part of borough-wide groupings, seven were purely local groups and three spanned both local and borough-wide interests and activities. The range included pensioners' groups, women's aid, black self-help, tenants' and community-centre associations and community arts. Of the eighteen it was estimated that two had been set up by the people concerned compared with four set up by community workers, four by clergy and eight by community activists, who were described as being typically young, well educated, middle class and socially and politically committed.

How far such a picture was typical, even in 1981, is inevitably problematic, given the lack of comparative data. But there would seem to be widespread agreement that community activity, including self-help and mutual aid, has not simply arisen spontaneously. Both professionals and activists have played key roles in raising questions about needs and how far these are, or are not, being met, and in stimulating alternative forms of activity, including collective action, and collective forms of provision. For example the local authorities who produced the paper, *Community Development, the Local Authority Role*, in 1989, argued that 'the conventional wisdom is that somehow schemes such as tenant co-operatives, neighbourhood playschemes, community care and so on must arise in some spontaneous way from the "bottom up". But, in reality, they argued, 'Many community-based projects originate in discussions around ideas between community workers, other professionals working in the community, local people, and community activists' (AMA, 1989, p. 15).

There would seem, then, to have been different strands and influences at work rather than any simple spontaneous upsurge in community activity in this period. Amongst some of the concerned professionals and activists there were attempts to develop alternative approaches and practices which challenged traditions of professionally dominated, hierarchical, controlling and/or white middle-class-male approaches to social planning and service delivery. In addition there was a tradition of working-class self-help, from the trade unions and friendly societies through to community and tenants' organisations. Whilst these had their own history and traditions they did not exist in a vacuum, and were in turn affected by, as well as affecting other approaches. And finally, both of these strands have been affected in different ways by wider official influences, including influences from both central and local government.

The first strand could be illustrated by the growth of self-help organisations, in the specific sense in which self-help has been used in relation to health and related social-service issues. Self-help groups, in this sense of self-help have, it has been argued, 'burgeoned in recent years (that is in the late 1970s and early 1980s), taking on not only common and familiar problems but also those of a much rarer nature' (Richardson, 1984). In addition to well-established organisations for people with disabilities such as deafness and blindness, there was an expansion of national and local groups concerned with a wide range of health and related issues. A publication on local initiatives in Britain in 1982 listed some 140 self-help organisations, ranging from well-established organisations such as The Royal National Institute for the Deaf, and the Royal National Institute for the Blind, through to Anorexic Aid, Depressives Anonymous, Women's Aid Federation, Rape Crisis Centre and Gingerbread. Typically, Richardson argued, in contrast with some of the older established organisations, self-help groups were based upon principles of mutual support amongst those directly affected, whether as patients or as carers of patients. This mutual support would include information sharing, for instance, together with practical mutual aid such as shared transport to visit hospitals. In addition self-help groups typically included some pressure-group activity to improve health and welfare services, to challenge traditional and hierarchical professional practices and to make professionals, and services, more responsive to the needs of the group in question. This latter point included combatting institutionalised racism and sexism (as expressed, for instance in the underdevelopment of care for conditions such as sickle-cell anaemia, or in the lack of choice for women in maternity services). By the mid-1980s, there was a national network of self-help groups in Britain. 'Action for Health', for example, provides a useful account of the growth of the community-health movement in Britain, explaining the links between self-help and community-development work to support collective approaches to positive community health, and providing examples of collective approaches and projects to counter racism and sexism and other forms of institutionalised discrimination and disadvantage (CPF, 1988).

Similarly, self-help became recognised as an increasingly important phenomenon in the USA. Estimates of the membership of such groups varied, at the beginning of the 1990s, from six million to fifteen million (Powell, 1990). Self-help in the USA has similarly been linked to the movements of the 1960s, particularly the civil and human-rights movements. Despite this, however, there seems to have been widespread agreement that although self-help existed, and there was a tradition of self-help within black communities, overall self-help organisations tended to be predominantly white and middle class (although this could of course be related to biases in the formal recognition of self-help groups in contrast with the more informal organisational patterns of minority groups). 'Self-help organisations have an abysmal track record with members of minority groups' Powell concluded, in the late 1980s (Powell, 1987 p. 21). Amongst the largest US groups were weightwatchers, with some two million members, and Alcoholics Anonymous with some half a million US members in the 1980s (with a total of over a million worldwide). There had been a proliferation particularly of health-related groups (such as Mended Hearts for those who had undergone heart surgery, and Stroke clubs) with smaller groups being (like small businesses) less likely to survive than larger groups.

The growth of self-help has been linked to growing challenges to professional dominance. But both Powell, in relation to the US experience, and Richardson, in relation to the British experience, also stressed the potential for positive relationships between self-help organisations and professionals. Powell explained that professional attitudes had undergone some change, and that there were professionals who had consciously welcomed self-help as a means of changing professional practice, improving services and empowering clients/patients. Particular professionals had actually played key roles in establishing certain self-help groups (such as Parents Anonymous and Epilepsy Self-Help). On their side, self-help groups were not necessarily anti-professional so much as wanting more effective, more user-sensitive and more accountable professional services. There were instances where professionals referred clients to self-help groups for support, and vice versa; self-help groups referred clients needing professional counselling, for example. Similarly, in the British context, Richardson argued that self-help groups could benefit from professional support, together with financial and administrative assistance. Whilst the value of collaboration between professionals and self-help groups has been widely identified, some caveats have however been expressed. Wann, for instance, has pointed to the relatively lower success rate of self-help groups established *by* professionals *for* people with particular problems, as defined by the professionals concerned. Professionals have to accept being challenged and questioned by lay people, and professionals have to learn to share power with the people they are trying to help. 'But when a dialogue is established and a more equal relationship develops, there are clear benefits for both sides', she concluded (Wann, 1992, p. 167).

It was clear, then, that self-help groups were not in general attempting to substitute for professional and official forms of provision. Whilst there were examples of such a view being put forward, the majority of self-help groups were not attempting to supplant professional services, but rather to make professional services more responsive and appropriate, whilst offering complementary self-help. Powell put this point particularly forcefully, arguing that self-help groups and professionals each have specific roles and remits. 'What is bankrupt, however', he argued, 'is the policy to substitute self-help services for professional ones. Nothing in self-help implies the elimination or cutting back of professional services' (Powell, 1987, p. 3).

Self-help groups have covered a range of perspectives as well as a range of activities. And whilst many have combined mutual aid and support with pressure-group and campaigning functions, not all have done so (for instance AA has not included campaigning in its functions, concentrating instead on individual and group support and personal change and development). Nor have they necessarily been concerned with empowerment in the sense of collective action, aimed at empowering the most powerless and combatting institutionalised discrimination and disadvantage in society. But typically they have shared a concern to put the client/patient first, and to combat official and professional hierarchies of control.

More generally, however, issues related to community empowerment and equal opportunities *were* emerging on the agendas of the more traditional as well as the newer voluntary and community organisations (alongside issues of professional accountability and user control). By the 1980s, for instance, the National Federation of Community Associations, renamed the National Federation of Community Organisations, had adapted its thinking and structure to take account of changing pressures. In addition to rethinking commitments to participation and democratic pluralism, the organisation also committed itself to an increasingly active concern with tackling problems of social deprivation, and with equal opportunities and antiracism (Clarke, 1990, pp. 168–9).

Similar influences made their impact, too, on other well-established organisations within the voluntary sector. For example, at the end of the 1980s, the National Council for Voluntary Organisations was responding to debates about the contract culture with similar references to the importance of promoting 'community development and local empowerment; to ensure the voices of consumers and users are heard and have a chance to influence policy and practice', as well as the importance of mobilising voluntary effort (NCVO, 1989, p. 2). The paper went on to list (amongst the basic principles which must be preserved in any approach to contracting) user involvement, local involvement (including community groups' involvement, independence and advocacy, (that is, maintaining campaigning as well as service provision) and equal opportunities.

In parallel, towards the end of the 1980s, in arguing for local authorities to develop strategies towards the voluntary sector, the London Voluntary Service Council emphasised, amongst the distinctive features of the voluntary sector, that 'Voluntary organisations are linked integrally with local communities, and have an important empowering and enabling function in providing a means whereby local communities can take action themselves to address problems'. The report goes on to propose that local authorities should set up their voluntary-sector strategies through joint working parties, including truly representative and accountable voluntary-sector membership. 'An essential part of the entire process', the report continues, 'will be to ensure adequate representation for groups who traditionally face discrimination and exclusion, for example, black and ethnic minority people, women, lesbians and gay men, and people with disabilities' (LVSC, 1988, p. 8).

The Policy Prospectus for Community Development and Local Democracy, 'Taking Communities Seriously', which was launched by the Community Development Foundation and the National Coalition for Neighbourhoods in 1991, summarised a number of these trends. The policy prospectus started from the importance of a community development approach in terms of local democracy and active citizenship. 'Community development is an approach to social, economic and environmental renewal that starts by changing the relationship between people and institutions such as central and local government' (CDF, 1991, p. 3). The policy prospectus went on to emphasise the relationship between a community-development-based approach and equal opportunities. 'It also recognised that voluntary organisations are themselves often becoming large service-providers with professional staff. They too are partners in regeneration and should be as accountable as any other agency' (ibid., p. 9).

The policy prospectus had no official status, of course, although it was prepared by organisations with wide-ranging support (and the CDF was itself funded by the government's Voluntary Service Unit, as well as from other sources). The policy prospectus set out an agenda for the future of community development, rather than necessarily commenting on existing practice. But it does summarise the approach taken at the beginning of the 1990s: a perspective on self-help, mutual aid, community participation and development, active citizenship, wider democracy and equal opportunities, an approach which could be applied within the traditional mainstream of the voluntary sector in general, as well as within central and local government.

Meanwhile, long-standing working-class self-help and commu-nity-based organisations were also undergoing processes of change. In particular the tenants' movement has been identified as having revived and widened some of its concerns over this period. Willmott, for instance, referred to the growth of tenants' organisations in the 1970s (Willmott, 1989).

Tenants' organisations have a long history in Britain, both in terms of organising around specific issues such as rents and repairs, and in terms of organising to campaign for wider changes in housing policy (as demonstrated by tenants' organisations in the First World War, and the interwar period, in areas such as Clydeside). Tenants' movements have been particularly active during specific periods and around specific issues. One factor in the growth and revival of tenants' organisations in the 1970s was the Housing Finance Act, 1972, an act which has been described as having the goal of achieving 'a regulated free market rent' throughout all rented accommodation, a goal which entailed some significant rent increases (Cowley, 1979, p. 88). There was local resistance, within the framework of a national campaign, and there were instances where local authorities held out against implementing the act in response to organised tenant pressure.

There were also private tenant campaigns in the late 1960s and early 1970s around issues of urban renewal and change, as the property development boom in particular cities, especially London, led to increasing pressures on private tenants to move out to make way for more profitable uses of the land. In areas such as Barnsbury, Islington and Camden, tenants organised to resist this pressure and to press for alternatives, including local-authority purchase of the properties in question so that they might be kept in the rented sector at affordable rents (Cowley, 1979). Once again, then, there were campaigns around immediate issues (to prevent particular individuals or groups of private tenants from being displaced) and there were campaigns centred on alternative approaches to housing policy.

Urban renewal led to a range of different types of campaigning. In addition to the upsurge of organisation in response to plans for redevelopment, there were also campaigns in response to unsatisfactory aspects of redevelopment and rehousing (dampness, for instance, and the all too frequent lack of community facilities on redeveloped estates). The Association of Community Workers publication, *Successes and Struggles on Council Estates* (Henderson, Wright and Wyncoll, 1982), provided case studies of campaigns on such issues, including, for example, tenant campaigns to improve the quality of housing provision and maintenance in the 'new slums – damp-ridden, insanitary, nine-year old council flats' in the Gorbals, a former Glasgow slum that had been redeveloped (Bryant, 1982, p. 60).

Whilst tenants' campaigning, in these different cases, was based upon traditional working-class forms of organisation, support was also provided in some cases by community activists, including socially and politically aware and committed community activists (for example Cowley, 1979). So there were, at least in some cases, examples of the cross-fertilisation of ideas and approaches between the different strands of community activity. And there have also been examples where tenants' organisations have received crucial organisational support, information and advice from professionals, whether these were professional community workers or professional architects or planners, for example.

Towards the end of the 1980s there were further revivals of tenants' organisations in response to legislation, in particular the 1988 Housing Act, which included provisions for local-authority tenants to opt out of local-authority control, to 'choose' a landlord, or alternatively for the government to transfer council housing, in selected areas, to Housing Action Trusts (HATs). These proposals were followed up in 1989 by legislation affecting housing finance which resulted in a further squeeze on council tenants, through increased pressures on rents. These measures came in the context of a decade of massive reductions in local-authority building, the sale of over a million council houses to their occupants, and provisions for private landlords and housing associations to charge higher rents. In this context of the relative decline of council housing, and the reduction of affordable alternatives (as private and housing-association rents were also under pressure), many of those council tenants who remained in the public sector (having been unwilling or unable to afford to buy their homes) became increasingly anxious. There were pressures for them to leave the public sector, yet they feared that they would be unable to find secure and affordable alternatives.

There was, then, a relative upsurge of tenants' organising and campaigning. Some of this was directed at resisting attempts to transfer council housing to HATs or private landlords ('Better the devil you know', as one local authority described this apparent upsurge of loyalty from their previously far-from-contented tenants). But there were also moves to develop alternative approaches, based on tenants' organisations taking more control of their housing. Chapter 7 looks at some tenants' experiences when working to develop new approaches, albeit in the context of shrinking resources.

More generally, in relation to housing and other aspects of community activity, a number of local authorities were by this time prepared to provide support and resources to enable community organisations to operate effectively. For example the Tenants' Resources and Information Service (TRIS) was launched in 1991, with support from a number of local authorities, to provide information, training, research and advice to tenants' organisations and federations, on their own terms and taking full account of equal-opportunities considerations. As the publicity leaflet explained, 'The Service will be run by tenants for tenants and will adopt a comprehensive equal opportunities policy' (which was carried at the 1991 launch).

Local authority responses to change

This brings the discussion on to the changing role of a number of local authorities in relation to community activism, and to their support for this through community work and community development. Local authorities, as providers of public services, were in the frontline of growing criticism and campaigning (see for example Cockburn, 1977). The local authority housing department was the first port of call for dissatisfied tenants whose repairs were not being carried out, just as local authority planners bore the brunt of criticisms from individuals and community organisations opposing local plans. And it was through local authority departments that institutionalised sexism and racism was experienced, for instance in relation to housing allocation. As has been argued, local authorities faced a barrage of criticism, too, from the end of the 1970s and early 1980s, from the new right. Local authorities had a major rehabilitation job to face if they were to respond to these criticisms and improve their image, demonstrating that local government did not necessarily have to be heavily bureaucratic, ineffective and inefficient, or excessively controlling and paternalistic.

Chapter 3 has already discussed some of the better-known cases where local authorities embarked upon alternative approaches in the early to mid-1980s. The experiences of authorities such as the GLC and Sheffield related to conscious attempts to demonstrate that there *were* alternatives to new-right policies and that these policies could and did work in practice, providing locally relevant jobs and services. These experiences were also strongly influenced by debates around self-help and community activity, and the need for local authorities to work in new partnerships with local people and local organisations. As has already been argued, too, by the mid- to late 1980s, the scope for such approaches had been severely reduced; the GLC had been abolished and local-authority finance was more tightly constrained than ever before, forcing local authorities to consider other survival strategies and other partners (including, increasingly, private-sector partners).

In this increasingly problematic climate, however, a number of local authorities did continue to develop strategies and policies that took account of the upsurge of self-help and community activity, and of the movements for equality, from the 1960s and 1970s. These experiences had a far lower profile than the more confrontational experiences of the early 1980s; but they can be related to committed attempts by a number of authorities to develop community participation, supported by community-development and community-education strategies.

In 1989 the Association of Metropolitan Authorities published a booklet on community development that summarised the work of a coordinating group of members and officers representing different committees and areas of expertise. In addition a wide range of community and self-help organisations contributed to the document, organisations which included the Association of Community Workers, the British Council of Churches, the Community Projects Foundation, the National Association of Arts Centres, the National Council for Voluntary Organisations, the National Coalition for Neighbourhoods, the National Federation of Community Organisations, the National Federation of Self-Help Organisation, the National Out of School Alliance, the National Federation of Community Work Training Groups and the Standing Conference on Community Development. The document started from 'the need for a proactive and coherent expression of support for community development as an approach and a process' (AMA, 1989, p. 5). 'In essence community development is about working with and alongside people rather than for and on behalf of people in order to tackle discrimination and disadvantage and the feelings of powerlessness experienced by many people in Britain today' the document continued (ibid., p. 6). Whilst the document made it clear that community development was not a panacea, it could form an important element in 'any local authority's anti-poverty and equal opportunities strategies' (ibid., p. 10). It could also form a key part of strategies for local authorities to become 'enabling' rather than paternalistic.

Through community development strategies, it was argued, the enabling authority could build upon spontaneous developments of self-help and community activity to enable people to achieve things for themselves. In practice this involved, it was argued, a strategic, corporate approach, crossing traditional departmental boundaries.

Local authorities needed to develop more active forms of consultation and participation if services were to be more responsive and relevant, and local authorities needed to develop strategies to support the voluntary sector, including self-help and community activity, in the community sector, and to provide grant aid, and assistance with training and evaluation (along the lines suggested in the LVSC proposals). The document went on to illustrate community development in practice, in relation to council-wide strategies to improve services (for example around quality of service review and decentralisation) and around specific issues such as tenant participation in housing, local economic development, community social work, play and youth, health issues, leisure, recreation and the arts and community education. These, in turn, were illustrated by case studies from eight local authorities. Only two of these were London authorities, incidentally, and only one authority, outside London, had been associated with some of the better known examples of local authority alternative strategies in the early 1980s. The document was firmly rooted, then, in rather lower key developments, which had taken place subsequently, in the latter part of the 1980s.

In the year following the launch of the AMA's paper on community development a further document was produced, this time in association with the Federation of Community Work Training Groups, on participative training for community work, starting from the same value base and definitions of community development (AMA, 1991). According to this perspective, training for community development would not be about experts imposing solutions, but about building upon peoples' experiences and actively promoting models that challenged existing power relationships in society (e.g. Black/White, male/female). According to this view-point, 'Practised in this way community work is no longer a marginal activity but one which is central to the operation of an enabling authority' (ibid., p. 92).

The reality, however, as the document also pointed out, was more varied and far more problematic: 'Whilst the 1980s have seen the proliferation of jobs with a community tag', indicating perhaps, some increasing awareness and recognition by local authorities of the need to respond positively to new pressures and changes in their local communities, 'the number of actual community worker posts had declined through the period'. The document does not provide detailed evidence of the number of posts, so it is not possible to make a straightforward comparison between the number of community workers employed in the late 1980s with the total of five thousand community workers (working in local authorities and elsewhere) identified in the study by Francis and others in 1984 (Francis *et al.*, 1984). But the document goes on to raise further qualifications about the ways in which community workers had been employed, qualifications which can be related to evidence from other studies. 'Increasing emphasis on cost effectiveness within local authorities, who, themselves, are threatened by central government legislation has, in many places, marginalised community work' (AMA, 1991). In addition community workers suffered from being employed in a range of different departments, 'often managed by people who have no direct community work experience. As a result community workers are often inappropriately managed and expected to conform to practices which are unsupportive of and contradictory to their work, or, they are left relatively unmanaged until a crisis occurs.' Neither approach, the document argued, 'results in good practice' (ibid., p. 84).

A local authority that had provided a case study of good practice for the first AMA document ironically provided, in the face of wider funding crisis in 1991, a case study of precisely this marginalisation of community work and community-development strategy. The London Borough of Haringey had featured both in terms of public involvement in participation and in terms of including training support, as part of the borough's overall support for the community sector (including support for many black, ethnic-minority and women's projects). In 1990, the council handbook for the voluntary sector explained that Haringey was 'proud of the example it has established within London and nationally in developing a constructive and accountable relationship with the community sector.' (Haringey Voluntary Sector Resources Handbook, 1990, p. i). However as a result of the financial crisis Haringey's community development strategy, community-work staff and its grant-aid programme were cut drastically. This was an extreme, but not a unique example of community-development cutbacks by increasingly beleaguered local authorities.

Whilst the issue of diminishing resources has been central to experiences of the 'enabling local authority', in practice there have of course also been examples of local authorities mismanaging the resources they have made available for community development. For example the study of local-authority community work by Davies and Crousaz (1982) found that community workers within social-service departments tended to be isolated and marginalised. Although they did perform useful work, for example in mobilising resources for particular client groups such as children and the elderly, and although they did do some work of a more campaigning nature (for instance with tenants' groups), overall they were marginalised and had not instigated wider changes within the authorities. Barr's study of community work within social services in Strathclyde identified similar problems of marginalisation and insufficient connections between community work and policy development at corporate level. Community workers tended to be of the opinion that their managers had very limited interest in their work, seeing community work as being concerned with mobilising volunteers and self-help rather than also being concerned with community participation and empowerment. Yet this was despite the fact that, in general, Strathclyde Regional Council *had* recognised these latter objectives for community work, and had even recognised and begun to identify ways for community workers to deal with any conflicts of interest that could be expected to arise between community organisations and the council (Barr, 1991).

Conflicting pressures in the early 1990s

To describe the situation in the early 1990s as contradictory would seem to be something of an understatement. Some of the basic principles of community development had achieved relatively widespread sympathy by the beginning of the 1990s. In his foreword to Barr's study of community work in Strathclyde David Donnison wrote that there were both scientific and moral principles at stake. The scientific basis stemmed from 'the recurring observation that we do not fully understand human problems, and cannot therefore formulate fully effective responses to them if we do not give the people who experience them a voice both in the analysis of the problems and in the formulation of the solutions. Other voices must be heard too. But a study of the needs of the unemployed (or of one-parent families or people with AIDS, or whoever. . .) which does not give a voice to those people will – to some degree at least – get it wrong'. In addition there were, he suggested, moral principles at stake in terms of courtesy and humanity, and in terms of honestly addressing the power relationships involved. Donnison observed, too, that these community-based ways of working had exerted wider influences on other professions and services. 'Lord Scarman' he pointed out, 'after the Brixton riots, gave the same advice to the police: crime prevention has to be a community-based, hearts-and-minds operation or it is worthless. The medical profession – another with strongly authoritarian traditions – is increasingly adopting the same principles'. Donnison concluded by raising questions about the implications of this approach for professional education and training; how, for instance, could mental patients contribute to the education of doctors and psychiatric nurses, or council tenants to the training of housing managers? And how could more education and training be provided for the customers of the services concerned? 'How do we teach – and learn from – the people who are (in Barbara Wootton's immortal phrase) "more planned against than planning"?' (Donnison, 1991).

Whilst such an approach might have commanded widespread support, the government was more ambivalent. With the launching of the Citizen's Charter in 1991 the government was actively promoting active citizenship, and user and consumer rights. There was cross-party political support for these notions of user and consumer rights, and for the development of quality services geared to meeting users' requirements rather than bureaucratically or professionally determined requirements. But, as was suggested in the Introduction, these official approaches to citizenship, even active citizenship and consumer rights were based predominantly upon individualised concepts of citizenship.

Some of the limitations of this approach were discussed in a collection of essays on citizenship (Andrews, 1991). For example, the essay by Paul Hirst considered the government's failure to locate the debate within wider positive planning policies to provide citizens across regions, including relatively disadvantaged regions, with economic opportunities. Ann Phillips raised important criticisms about individualised approaches to citizenship in relation to the need for collective and political pressures to widen opportunities for women, both in the workplace and in the home. And Bhikhu Parekh raised key issues about the need for wider changes to promote equal rights and opportunities for ethnic-minority communities (Hirst, Phillips and Parekh; ibid.)

It was not even the case, however, that the government was only emphasising the rights of individual users and consumers to participation and quality services at the expense of more collective, community-based approaches. The reality was more complex. The government *was* in some cases concerned to promote community based-approaches; but around specific issues, where a community-based approach would relate to wider policy objectives. Two of the more frequently quoted examples of government interest in community-based approaches were in relation to community policing and community care. Willmott, for example, singles out law and order and community care as representing major concerns of government (Willmott, 1989).

As a number of studies have demonstrated, law and order became a key issue for the government in the 1980s, acquiring the status of a moral panic, according to some commentators (for example Harding, 1987). Despite incarcerating increasingly large numbers, the penal system appeared to be failing to stem the growth of crime. Whilst there were alternative explanations of just how serious this crime wave really was (or how far it actually represented changes in the reporting and recording of particular crimes), there clearly was widespread concern. And, in the wake of the Brixton riots, the Scarman Report's emphasis on the need for preventative action and community-based policing gained widespread interest. Typically, community-based approaches included efforts by the police to become locally better known, involved and trusted, and efforts by the probation service to become more actively involved in community work and community development. Some of the tensions inherent in working to empower disadvantaged clients and communities whilst maintaining responsibility for other aspects of probation work – including the supervision of punishment within the community – were explored, for instance, in Broad's study of community-based approaches within probation (Broad, 1991).

In addition, there were widespread developments of neighbourhood crime-prevention schemes, typically promoted with the active support of the police. Of course there were cases where communities actively rejected this neighbourhood-watch approach on a number of grounds. For example it was argued that the schemes encouraged prying, with vulnerable groups (such as black youths) being disproportionately at risk of being further harassed as a result of complaints of 'suspicious behaviour ' by over-zealous white neighbours. And there were suggestions that neighbourhood-watch schemes advantaged well-organised, middle-class areas, which would merely succeed in pushing the criminals out of their areas into less-organised working-class areas. But whatever the criticisms, large numbers of neighbourhood-watch and community-policing schemes were launched. There was also evidence to support the contention that people in working-class areas were as concerned as people in middle-class areas, if not more so, by the fear of crime, and that these fears were restricting people's lives (particularly the lives of women and the elderly who were afraid to go out at night in high crime areas) (Hough and Mayhew, 1985). So although the government's support for community policing could be considered as part of the controlling functions of the state, it would be far too simplistic to imply that community policing did not also have considerable community support as a result of genuinely held community fears (whether or not these fears corresponded at all closely with the actual risks for the different groups concerned).

The other prime area of government interest in community-based approaches was community care. The government's support for key recommendations within the Griffiths Report on community care (Griffiths, 1988) fitted into their wider concerns to reduce expenditure on costly institutional forms of care for the elderly, the mentally ill and people with physical or mental disabilities. Previous chapters have already considered some of the implications of this move towards community care policies, together with some of the criticisms raised about plans for their implementation, including the criticism that community care was being promoted in the absence of adequate resources and without realistically identifying what was actually meant by community care, or who was actually going to be able to do the caring (would the burden fall, disproportionately, on women, as daughters, daughters-in-law, wives and mothers, who would feel pressured into stepping into the breach despite the lack of adequate public support?) Sir Roy Griffiths himself raised questions about the adequacy of the resources that would be guaranteed for community care, and the adequacy of the planning and monitoring systems that would be essential to the policy's successful implementation. As he pointed out in the run-up to implementation, 'if the government wishes to see its policies effectively implemented, then clarity of policy, timescales for achievement and reasonable certainty as to the availability of the required money are necessary' (Griffiths, 1992, p. 21).

Despite all these criticisms however, overall it was not the notion of community care that was under attack so much as the probability that community care would be under-resourced and inadequately implemented. As has already been suggested, community care was in any case already a widespread reality, in the sense of the actual extent of informal family and neighbourly care. And as the next chapter will illustrate, a wide range of community organisations, including organisations that took part in campaigning-type activities, included the provision of community care within their remit (even if this was not explicitly recognised as being community care). The development of community-care plans by local authorities has also raised the possibility of increased community involvement. Levick, for instance, has pointed to the progressive potential of actively engaging local people in community-care plans, drawing upon the experiences of local authorities such as Islington and Humberside, which had already been developing decentralised approaches to service delivery and to user participation more generally (Levick, 1992). Oxfordshire's Community Care Plan, for example, also illustrated some of the potential for community organisations to become directly engaged in the planning process. The Oxfordshire Community Care Plan for 1992–3 included a section on what was wanted by clients and carers, a section which drew directly on the contributions of such organisations as the Oxford Pensioners Action Group and others, a form of public recognition that was clearly welcomed by the organisations concerned. The key question of how far these requests were actually met, remained, of course, to be answered in practice.

Meanwhile, in addition to government support for community policing, and community care, there was also some official recognition and support for community based approaches to child care and child protection. For example, the Children Act 1989 included recognition of the preventative role of community-based initiatives, and there was recognition of the need for support for family centres, within the framework of preventative services within localities. But once again resources to support family centres were not clearly identified and earmarked. Nor were there clear policy directions on the functions of family centres. Yet in practice, family centres had developed in different ways within the voluntary sector, (for example the Children's Society) as well as within the statutory sector, and different centres had different approaches. Some set out to provide community resources for families and their children, resources which were available to all who felt the need for them, operating as they did on open-door policies (see for example Phelan, 1983). Linked to this were family centres that fitted into wider community-development approaches within their neighbourhoods to respond to need on a non-stigmatising basis, stimulate self-help, demystify professionalism and promote empowerment in deprived areas where there were disproportionate numbers of parents experiencing difficulty in raising their children (for example the approach described and advocated by Holman, 1983). A study by Jane Gibbons and Sally Thorpe refers to the growth of such centres in the 1980s, with an emphasis on 'mutual help, user participation and local control' (Gibbons and Thorpe, 1989, p. 2).

Alternatively there were family centres that focused on providing counselling and support to particular families who had been referred for treatment because their children were considered to be 'at risk'. This was a different approach, and not necessarily one which was readily compatible with the open-door, community-development-type approach. So once again there were potentially major contradictions.

Similarly there were potentially different approaches to the Children Act's provisions on child minding and collective child care. The Act clarified local authorities' responsibilities for registration and inspection, and extended the age range covered by registration. Whilst the recognition of the importance of quality child care was seen as positive, there were also anxieties that unless adequate resources were to be made available to small-scale community organisations such as parent and toddler groups, which were providing play groups and play schemes on a shoestring, then these projects would be in jeopardy if they were unable to meet the required standards.

It was not just that government policy towards community-based initiatives and community development were ambiguous and contradictory (although they were). Nor even that the government failed to provide adequate resources, expecting community care, for instance, or community-based child-protection work and child care to emerge spontaneously. The government was also pursuing other policies that potentially could undermine community-based approaches. The constraints that government placed on local authority expenditure were of key importance here because local authorities were the major source of funds for the voluntary sector, including community work in the voluntary sector (Francis, Henderson and Thomas established that 85 per cent of community workers in the voluntary sector were dependent on statutory funding in 1984, with local authorities playing a key role, whether directly or indirectly, for example by contributing to urban aid – Francis *et al.*, 1984).

The NCVO produced a report on the impact of one area of local-government finance – the community charge, or poll tax – on the voluntary sector in 1991 (NCVO, 1991). Despite government support for the sector, the report argued in relation to community care and the Children Act, the reality was that in 1991 the talk was of cuts and redundancies in the voluntary sector. 'At best activity is at a standstill, at worst jobs, services and whole community organisations have been lost in the past year or so as millions of pounds are slashed from grant budgets'. London had been hardest hit; it was estimated by LVSC that £15 million had been lost in grant aid. And this process continued. NCVO estimated that from 1990/1 to 1991/2 there were cuts of £30 million in real terms (NCVO News, 1992). Although these cuts originated from financial pressures relating to central-government policies, local authorities also played their part in implementing the decisions, including in some cases the decision to cut the grants of some of the most vulnerable groups.

Faced with these mounting pressures, community organisations and community workers increased their efforts to put forward constructive alternatives. These included pressures for alternatives from local government. For example the increasing recognition of the importance of developing coherent strategies towards the voluntary sector, and towards community development, was related to the LVSC's paper, which had called for such strategies to be developed and proposed ways of achieving this.

During the 1980s there had also been developing interest in promoting a more coherent national approach to community development. In 1982 the Caloustie Gulbenkian Foundation set up a working party to look into the feasibility of a National Centre for Community Development. Such a centre would have been expected to provide a national reference point, to maintain a data base and to provide training, research and support for practitioners. This scheme had parallels with the model of the National Institute for Social Work.

What followed from the report of the working party in 1984 was a process of consultation, a process which fundamentally altered the outcome. In place of the original proposals, it was agreed that there should be a more 'bottom up' type of approach to national coordination, which would be more in keeping with the principles of community development. The Standing Conference for Community Development (SCCD) would be a more decentralised structure, based on principles of accountability to local, regional and special-interest groupings and with a strong emphasis on equal opportunities.

The Voluntary Services Unit, at the Home Office, took three years to be persuaded of the value of this approach, but eventually some funding was provided and the SCCD was officially launched in Nottingham in 1991. Symbolically, a major role in promoting the event was played by Advocacy in Action, an organisation of people with learning difficulties. Community groups were to contribute actively to the development of the organisation, speaking for themselves rather than being defined as the recipients of services run by others.

After the launch, the SCCD began the challenging task of developing and supporting local networks. The organisation also worked with other groups to promote community development at national level. For example, the SCCD, the CDF and the National Coalition for Neighbourhoods jointly appointed a parliamentary officer to assist in their efforts to put community development onto the national agenda.

In 1991, the CDF and the National Coalition for Neighbourhoods launched a policy prospectus for community development, *Taking Communities Seriously* (which was referred to earlier in this chapter). This launch was part of a parallel attempt to put forward the positive case for community development. As the prospectus argued, after some twenty years of piecemeal support for a range of innovative community-led development schemes, it was time for government to recognise that this was not enough. Community development, it was argued, did not necessarily happen spontaneously. A strategic approach by central government was required to complement the efforts of local authorities and voluntary agencies and the efforts of communities themselves (CDF, 1991).

As an initiative with cross-party political support, the prospectus set out the positive case. Understandably enough in this context, the prospectus did not highlight the extraordinary contradictions of government policy towards community development, contradictions with massive negative implications which were being increasingly forced upon local authorities, even upon local authorities that had previously taken more positive and more strategic approaches. Active citizenship, self-help and community care were supposed to be key ingredients in achieving quality services in Britain in the 1990s. Yet active community organisations were winding down, and there were widespread cuts and redundancies in the community sector, as a direct result of other aspects of public policy at both national and local-government levels.

7

Community Participation in Planning and Community Service Provision

The conclusions of the previous chapter pointed to a situation of contradictions. In Britain, as in so many other countries, government-developed community policies at the beginning of the 1990s were marked by formal commitments to community-based approaches, with multi-party support for community-based systems of social care. But there were widespread criticisms too. Governments had been accused of failing to take account of sociological analyses of that ambiguous concept of 'community', or to recognise the policy implications of the reality to which these analyses pointed; including the reality that the concept of 'community' takes on different meanings in different social contexts, depending on such factors as class, location, age, ethnicity and gender (for example Bulmer, on the work of Abrams, 1986). The patterns of social networks and the relative strengths or weaknesses of community involvement and organisation have varied in relation to these, as well as in relation to other factors of local history and geography. Community policies in general, and specifically policies to promote community care, needed to address these underlying issues if they were to be realistic. But at the outset of the 1990s there was insufficient evidence that this was happening at government level. And although the previous chapter provided examples of local-authority strategies for community development at the beginning of the 1990s there was a major gap in the development of effective strategies to complement these efforts, at the national level. This gap has to be set in the context of the wider criticisms of the wider resources, and the wider context of restrictions on local authority powers and expenditure, over the same period (Broady and Hedley, 1989, p. 1).

Still, despite this and despite the many other difficulties experienced by local authorities during the late 1970s, and 1980s, as the previous chapter argued, there were positive examples of developments at this level. This had been the starting point, for example, for a study by Broady and Hedley, which looked at a range of examples to illustrate their view that at the end of the 1980s, 'many local authorities were trying to relate their services to their constituents, and to develop strategies for community development, in their areas'.

More generally, as the previous chapter also argued, some of the pressures from below, pressures to take seriously such issues as equal opportunities and community empowerment to tackle social deprivation, had also had an impact on some of the better-established sections of the voluntary sector. These issues were at least emerging onto the agenda. So national-government policies for the mixed economy of welfare, and for the community sector, were not simply taken up by the voluntary sector without critical discussion of some of their implications (NCVO, 1989).

This chapter looks at some of these issues and dilemmas from a different set of perspectives; the perspectives of community organisations themselves. The shifting boundaries of the mixed economy of welfare have posed a number of dilemmas for self-help and community organisations. What were the major issues for them, and how did they perceive some of the dilemmas and choices that were opening up to them? How far, in fact, did community groups believe that they had enjoyed or were currently enjoying enhanced choices, in this changing scenario? Or did they, at least in some cases, feel that they were enjoying/enduring, if anything, fewer opportunities to make strategic choices about their changing role within the mixed economy of welfare, being increasingly preoccupied with more immediate problems; such as how to keep their own organisation alive, and how to keep up the pressure on service providers to offer some minimally acceptable level of service, despite the surrounding background of cuts?

Before looking at some of the pressures faced by community organisations as a result of the shifting boundaries of the mixed economy of welfare, however, it may be relevant to focus on some of the continuing pressures and dilemmas that community organisations were already facing (drawing upon well-established discussions in sociological and community-work texts), because some of these seemingly novel pressures have actually related to more perennial dilemmas, dilemmas which have been endemic to the experiences of community organisations and to the experiences of the community workers who have provided them with professional support.

Typically, getting started in the first place has been a problematic process. Effective community organisations have arisen spontaneously and/or have been established with the support of external agents such as community workers. But in either case this has generally required some form of catalyst, at least in the sense that potential members have needed to come to recognise that they have shared interests and/or needs which could be furthered by a collective approach. Abrams, for instance, raised the question of whether the most effective catalyst, in the development of longer-term community-care networks, might be the experience of common campaigning around a shared issue (Bulmer, 1986 p. 228). Henderson and Thomas also recognised the significance of external threats (such as the threat of a major road being planned in a high-density housing area, or the threat of a school closure, or inadequate housing repairs or rent rises) in triggering off the development of community organisations. They also recognised that the catalyst could be more positive if it took the form of new resources or the possibility of change, arising from a shift in local party-political control, for instance (Henderson and Thomas, 1980, p. 155). So people have tended to come together not just because they shared an interest or a problem (which may have been the case for some time anyway), but because they have recognised that there could be, or at least that there urgently needed to be, some change.

Forming a community organisation is the first hurdle then. But effective community organisations also have to be built and maintained over time (with or without external support). And typically, organisation building and maintenance has presented its own challenges. For example how to go about building the organisation and the membership and renewing the pool of activists whilst avoiding becoming a self perpetuating clique (Henderson and Thomas, 1980). How to take genuine account of equal opportunities, and actively involve all sections of the community, including black and ethnic-minority groups. How to avoid gender stereotypes (such as women providing the caring services and organising the socials and refreshments, whilst men represent the organisation on formal occasions, such as negotiating with the local authority; or even, more fundamentally still, defining some issues, such as jobs or housing, as key 'political' issues, to be tackled by the male leadership, whilst relegating other issues, such as childcare or play, to some secondary status, as subsidiary 'women's' issues). How to keep the membership actively involved when community organisations shift their focus over time (whether this shift is from campaigning towards taking on direct service provision, for example, or whether the shift is vice versa, from providing a self-help service towards campaigning for improved public-service provision). How to deliver tangible benefits to the membership, through developing effective working relationships with public service providers (for example getting housing repairs done), whilst maintaining the community organisation's own independence and rights to criticise.

Another aspect of this particular dilemma is how to remain effective without being either coopted by the service providers in question or marginalised and labelled as unrepresentative trouble-makers, if the right to criticise is not accepted as legitimate by the service providers in question. Dearlove's study of North Kensington in the 1970s, for example, demonstrated how an unreceptive local authority could systematically coopt those community organisations which councillors and/or officers deemed 'acceptable', whilst marginalising and undermining the legitimacy of those less acceptable and more challenging groups which were labelled 'trouble makers' (a tactic described by Dearlove in terms of the 'control of disturbance' – Dearlove, 1973). Similar points were made, for example, by Bryant when evaluating the lessons of community campaigns against poor housing and dampness in Glasgow, during the 1970s (Bryant, 1982, p. 71). As social polarisation gathered momentum in the 1980s, with poorer families, unemployed people, the homeless and single parents increasingly housed together on particular council estates, the marginalisation and labelling of community organisations and community activists in those areas as 'unacceptable', 'unrespect-able', 'unrepresentative' and so on became even easier for those officials and/or politicians who were attempting to cope, in the face of increasing pressures and diminishing resources, through strategies for 'controlling disturbance'.

This relates in turn to a further set of problems for community organisations. How to relate effectively, not only to officials and to elected representatives, but also to professionals in relevant service-providing organisations. How to use professional knowledge, skills and expertise creatively, without allowing the community organisation to become dominated by professional perspectives. How to draw a boundary between different forms of accountability (professional, bureaucratic and community-based). And how to define where the boundaries should be drawn between paid professional responsibilities and unpaid volunteering. Whilst this particular set of problems came to the fore in the context of debates about the mixed economy of welfare, there have been much longer-term debates about the relationship between professionals and voluntary activists, including debates about the relationship between trade unions representing public-sector workers and community organisations receiving (or campaigning to receive) the services of public-sector workers.

Community organisations have typically also faced dilemmas relating to the nature and timing of any resourcing they have received. As was suggested in the previous chapter, one of the key demands of the Policy Prospectus for Community Development was that realistic time scales should be established for the support of community organisations. Whilst some local authorities have recognised that community organisations need to develop over time, with consistent support through their ebbs and flows, central government's, and indeed much of charitable foundations' support for community organisations has tended to be time limited and project based. In Britain community organisations, especially in poorer areas, have found difficulty in becoming self-financing, and local authorities have themselves been under increasing financial pressures since the 1970s and therefore have been reluctant to take on these time-limited projects. The situation has been different, of course, in contexts where community organisations have achieved financial viability (the model of Alinsky's approach to community organisation in the USA for example).

This in turn raises another set of problems around monitoring, evaluation and accountability more generally. Where community organisations have received public funds they have generally had to account for these in some way. As the subsequent discussion will argue, the changes in accountability and the closer procedures for monitoring and evaluation that are associated with the 'contract culture', may enforce more systematic forms of monitoring and evaluation. There are potentially positive benefits here for community organisations in terms of clarifying their goals and mutual expectations, and in terms of stability, where grant contracts run over several financial years. This point was recognised by the Association of Metropolitan Authorities in their publication *Contracts for Social Care*, which specifically recommended giving voluntary organisations longer contracts (three to five years) rather than annual ones (AMA, 1990). But there may be other problems, particularly if contracts are over restrictive and/or focus on monitoring and evaluating areas of work that do not correspond with the community organisation's own priorities, potential problem areas which the AMA paper also recognised, and sought to resolve, on the basis of developing partnerships, rather than developing increasingly managerial and controlling relationships with the voluntary sector in their areas.

Finally, of course, community organisations have had to face the problems of death and decent burial. Community organisations have, in particular cases, had to recognise situations in which they have become effectively redundant. This may be because they have fulfilled their original purpose, whether because community needs have changed – or because of some other reason (such as internal differences or personality conflicts within the organisation that cannot be resolved). But winding up community organisations can be effected, in positive ways, valuing what has been achieved and moving on, avoiding situations in which unrepresentative rumps preserve the facade of defunct and tokenistic organisations, or situations in which the survivors become engaged in divisive disputes over any remaining assets.

To summarise then, community organisations typically faced a series of obstacles and pressures even before they faced the increasing pressures of the shifting boundaries of the mixed economy of welfare. Skills and determination were required to organise community groups effectively in the first place, to motivate members to become involved at all, and to believe that community efforts could change policies and/or service delivery, even at local level, let alone to believe that they could take on the delivery of local services themselves.

In Barr's study of community workers in Strathclyde, he noted that community workers tended to comment on the limited aspirations of their client community groups. No less than 83.1 per cent of his respondents thought that their client community groups were primarily concerned to resolve the particular, and essentially parochial, concerns that had brought them into being in the first place (Barr, 1991, p. 102). At one level, as Barr recognised, this was self-evident; although he went on to contrast these rather limited aspirations with some of the wider aspirations and policy concerns that the community workers seemed to hold in relation to these groups. Insofar as there was a gap to be explained here, one possible explanation for this could be that so many people have so little confidence that their efforts are likely to produce significant changes; a view which may rest upon the concrete reality of less-than-successful experiences of attempts to achieve such changes in the past. And they may, understandably, be far too preoccupied with their own and their families' daily struggle for survival to spend time on campaigning for changes that they doubt can be achieved on the basis of such local efforts.

The reality, then, may be that there needs to be more recognition of the extent of the extraordinary achievement of those community activists who have succeeded in building broadly based and genuinely representative community organisations that have survived over time (sometimes over periods of ten to twenty years or more, as in the case of some of the following examples) and have made appropriate changes, in response to changing circumstances and needs, remaining effective without surrendering their organisation's independence or becoming fatally marginalised in the process and maintaining positive relationships with officials, councillors and professionals without allowing them to set their agendas for them. To achieve all this might seem almost incredible; but, as some of the examples quoted in this chapter show, there certainly have been community organisations that have achieved significant progress in response to each of these different dilemmas.

Whilst many of the dilemmas which community organisations face are by no means unprecedented then, they can and often do take on new force in the changing context of the shifting boundaries of the mixed economy of welfare. And they can take on added force as a result of separate but related aspects of national government policies, including policies that have led to the restriction of resources either for local service delivery or for preventative work, including community development work.

Debates about the mixed economy of welfare may not be directly related to increasing pressures and problems in setting up effective community organisations. But new groups can also be expected to experience increased difficulties as they have to struggle to cope with the increasingly formal requirements of grant aid under the contract culture.

Perhaps the most important source of increased pressure, however, could be anticipated around developing and maintaining community organisations over time. In particular, the shift from campaigning group to service-providing organisation entails its own set of problems, such as how to deal with these new responsibilities, including, typically, the responsibilities associated with becoming an employer – gaining the new skills and expertise which this requires whilst maintaining the broad support and active involvement of the entire membership, from all sections of the community; and avoiding the situation in which the management committee gains the necessary skills at the price of becoming a small clique, increasingly removed from the grass roots membership. How to deliver services effectively, working cooperatively with officials, councillors and professionals, without renouncing the wider right to campaign or to criticise public policies, and how to make the time and conserve the energy to do both. How to relate in new ways to professionals, including taking on the new role of becoming the employer of professional staff, using their skills and expertise creatively, without allowing professional perspectives to take over. How to redefine the boundaries between paid and unpaid workers without allowing the latter to become a cheap substitute for the former, using the skills and expertise of professionals whilst offering training and opening up new opportunities to community activists to develop theirs. How to ensure that resources are used effectively, and that there is adequate monitoring and evaluation, without allowing community organisa- tions to become dominated by criteria based on viability and profitability in the contract culture, rather than by criteria based on social need and the community's own goals for meeting these. And finally, how to survive, in the midst of all these difficulties, without losing sight of longer-term strategic goals, becoming so preoccupied with the daily maintenance of the community organisation that there is no time to raise wider questions about future developments, new ways of involving the membership and new ways of promoting strategies for developing community empowerment.

As has already been argued, in both the USA and Britain there have been doubts and scepticism about the probable outcomes of these additional pressures on community organisations in the changing context of the mixed economy of welfare. The Association of Metropolitan Authorities identified some of the potential problems, for instance, in a 1989 survey of contracting in care provision. In addition to the risk that other voluntary-sector functions, such as advocacy, would be squeezed out, the AMA report also raised other implications 'for the smaller voluntary organisations if local authorities indulge an already identified preference for entering into contractual arrangements with larger, more experienced and better resourced voluntary organisations'. There was a danger, the report continued, that 'less established organisations, particularly organisations representing Black and Minority Ethnic interests and organisations representing fragmented and changing client groups, such as people with a mental illness, could lose out in the race for contracts' (AMA, 1990, p. 7).

Meanwhile where community organisations do engage in contracts with statutory organisations, whether this is for new services or simply to codify and formalise arrangements for their grants for existing services, these contracts risk being more restrictive, tying community groups to service provision at the expense of their wider campaigning roles and/or undercutting service provision in the public sector. As the NCVO paper on *Contracting In or Out* argued, voluntary organisations 'must not allow the voluntary sector to be hijacked for other ends; nor must they allow their own missions to become distorted through the imposition of inappropriate mechanisms' (NVCO, 1989, p. iv). One of the basic principles set out in the NCVO paper was that there should be a balance between service provision and campaigning and advocacy. The AMA paper made similar recommendations on this issue of balance. The evidence so far in Britain, however, does not corroborate these fears. One 1990 study, for example, concluded that although it was still too early to comment definitively, by and large projects were not unhappy with the contracts that had been drawn up. Only one of the contracts examined in this study had been agreed as the result of a bid under the compulsory competitive tendering process, and there was no evidence that that contract had undercut previous public-sector arrangements (Davies and Edwards, 1990). Sceptics might of course have argued that this was still early days; and that anyway there was plenty of evidence of the public sector undercutting itself, reducing wages and conditions and cutting back on services, in their efforts to win contracts and avoid community-charge capping (Whitfield, 1992), just as there was plenty of evidence about wider pressures on voluntary organisations as a result of the same problems of capping and consequent cuts in grants.

There were related anxieties that shifts in the mix of the mixed economy of welfare could lead to greater unevenness in service provision. As Chapter 1 pointed out, there have been longstanding doubts about the voluntary sector's spread of services, with provision typically best developed in areas with the most established traditions of volunteering, whether or not these related in any way to the patterns of social need; indeed they may have been inversely related (Brenton, 1985). Any shift towards greater provision in the voluntary sector in general, or via community organisations in particular, risked exacerbating these patterns of inequality. This also raised, once again, the issue of community organisations' representativeness; how far were they really representing and meeting the needs of all sections of their constituencies, taking full account of equal opportunities considerations?

One of the other major areas of anxiety concerning the probable effects of shifts in the mixed economy focused around changes in the relationship between professionals and volunteers. There had been a history of concern that these changes would not necessarily lead to greater collaboration between partners who were equal although different; rather, this could effectively lead to the colonisation of the latter by the former. Abrams, for instance, expressed reservations about such possibilities (although Bulmer also referred to Abram's growing interest in the potential as well as the difficulties of developing creative relationships between formal bureaucracies and informal community initiatives (Bulmer, 1986). One particular aspect of these potential tensions (also raised by Abrams amongst others) was the issue of paid versus unpaid work, including the material pressures on working-class people and their need for paid work, which could cut across the volunteering ethos and/or lead to token payments, which would bring the additional problem of potentially undercutting rates and conditions and undermining paid jobs in the public sector. Some of these dilemmas clearly *had* taken on additional force in the community organisations described in subsequent sections of this chapter.

Perhaps one of the most frustrating problems of all, for community organisations, related to the wider context and policy framework. Participation and campaigning work, and service delivery work have had inherent problems enough for community organisations, even where there has been strong commitment from the relevant local authorities. As has already been pointed out, there was increasing recognition of the importance of local authorities developing effective ways of consulting with consumers, community representatives and service-user groups, and especially so in the more challenging and competitive climate of competitive tendering. This was emphasised for instance by the Audit Commission (Audit Commission, 1988), and by the Local Government Training Board (Local Government Training Board, 1987). As the Local Government Information Unit's publication *Consumer Liaison and Compulsory Tendering* described, a number of local authorities did take steps to develop such mechanisms, both to develop more effective feed-back mechanisms for individual customers and to develop user groups and forums for continuing consultation and participation, learning from past inadequacies and criticisms. In the mid-1980s Beresford and Croft's study, for example, demonstrated that progress in this direction had been slow and uncertain so far, especially in relation to participation around issues of social-service provision, even where other potentially relevant changes, such as decentralisation, had been carried out. They had concluded that democratisation and participation in social services could not be said to have failed because it had not yet been properly tried (Beresford and Croft, 1986). The importance of taking such criticisms seriously, and developing more effective approaches, was increasingly recognised by the end of the 1980s, even if progress towards implementation remained more obstinately problematic. Beresford and Croft were amongst those who continued to work on the issue of user empowerment in the social services in the 1990s (Clode, 1992; Beresford and Croft, 1993).

The problem of maintaining effective links with their membership and their service users can be particularly acute when community organisations are taking up issues and/or delivering services to those who are most vulnerable in the community, such as the very elderly or those who have been suffering from mental illness. The difficulty of being effective *and* in close touch with their constituencies could be expected to be exacerbated where the relevant authorities lacked either the will or the means to deliver their side of the bargain of the mixed economy of welfare. Where local authorities fail to meet their obligations or to respond to community organisations' pressure for improved service delivery, whether this is because they lack the political will or the resources or the powers to do so, community organisations risk becoming caught between the loss of effectiveness and the loss of credibility on all sides. The shifting boundaries of the mixed economy of welfare could result in community organisations becoming the first target of frustrated clients rather than the statutory authorities, let alone the government or the wider economic context, which may ultimately be more responsible for the causes of their frustrations. Beresford and Croft raised this issue when they pointed to some of the difficulties of getting people involved in participation processes, where that effectively entailed local people's participation in the rationing of seriously inadequate service provision. 'It is questionable', they argue 'to call for people's involvement at a time of grossly reduced resources if all that involvement entails is being drawn into a divisive process of rationing, or being left with the responsibility to maintain services without the means to do so' (Beresford and Croft, 1986, p. 231).

So, as previous chapters have also suggested, community organisations have had much to make them anxious. In the following sections of this chapter, a number of examples are set out to illustrate some of the ways in which community organisations were experiencing these problems, at the beginning of the 1990s, together with some of the ways in which they were developing creative responses to these challenges without losing their wider concerns with participation and campaigning. These community organisations have been selected on the basis of the author's personal contacts with them, primarily (but not exclusively). through training programmes for community organisations based at Ruskin College (For an account of the approach upon which these training programmes were based, see the William Temple Foundation and Ruskin College Oxford, 1989). In principle, it would have been desirable to have selected examples on the basis of wider survey data, to ensure their representativeness and to allow for comparison and contrast. But in the absence of sufficiently systematic and contemporary data on community organisations in Britain, these examples have been selected for two broad reasons. Firstly, their experiences do relate to the dilemmas that have been explored in the literature so far, and the issues they raised in training sessions pointed the trainers towards particular areas (and gaps) in the relevant literature. And secondly, whilst these community organisations had been active in areas with high incidences of economic and social problems, in terms of social indicators such as unemployment, low income and poor housing, they had all had access to considerable levels of support, including support in terms of training and community work and/or other forms of professional resources, such as relevant local research. So their experiences may throw some light on the possible benefits, the potential problems and remaining gaps in the support that community organisations may require if they are to continue to develop creative responses to new challenges.

Ferguslie League of Action Groups (FLAG) and Ferguslie Park Partnership, Paisley, Scotland

The Ferguslie Park council housing estate on the outskirts of Paisley was developed from the interwar period to the 1960s. The Strategy for Regeneration, which was developed by the relevant statutory authorities in consultation with local people in 1989, described poverty as endemic in Ferguslie Park. Unemployment stood at almost 40 per cent, well over twice the regional average and some four times the district average. Overall the estate suffered from negative stereotyping as a 'problem estate', a negative image that had been reinforced by earlier housing-allocation strategies; Paisley Council had in the past set aside a special area of some forty-five houses for 'problem families', who were given daily supervision, training and instruction, so that 'in due course, when they have proved they can manage their own affairs, domestic, financial and otherwise, they can return to a better house in a more desirable neighbourhood' (Report by a Sub-Committee of the Scottish Housing Advisory Committee, 1967). Unsurprisingly this reinforced Ferguslie's stigmatised reputation, a reputation which added further disadvantages for the residents.

But despite all these negative features Ferguslie Park had a strong and positive tradition of community activity dating back to the interwar period. There was a long history of community involvement, with the local umbrella organisation, the Ferguslie

League of Action Groups (FLAG) being the established voice for the community. FLAG's history dated in turn from the days of the government's Community Development Project (CDP) there was a local CDP project covering the Ferguslie Park area from 1972–7. By the mid-1980s, FLAG activists saw themselves as having won a positive reputation with local-authority departments, who had come to recognise them as the representative community organisation in Ferguslie. In addition to its campaigning and participatory role, FLAG was also involved in the provision of a range of practical services and support to local people. The CDP had supported the development of such practical initiatives as local employment and community-enterprise projects. After the demise of CDP in 1978, FLAG established an information and advice centre with Urban Programme funding, and from 1978–84 it employed both community-work and welfare-rights staff to support a range of social, recreational and employment activities.

The value of this was recognised in 1984, when the local (Renfrew District Council) and regional (Strathclyde Regional Council) authorities agreed to develop a Joint Area Initiative, to work with each other and with the local community to provide relevant services and to work for community regeneration. This was a contributory factor in the Scottish Office's choice in 1988 of Ferguslie Park as one of its four, nationally selected 'partnership' estates, to promote regeneration through partnerships between the different statutory authorities at all levels, community organisations and the private sector.

As mentioned, the partnership programme was one of four such partnerships aimed at regenerating 'new life for urban Scotland' (the other partnerships were set up in Castlemilk in Glasgow, Wester Hailes in Edinburgh and Whitfield in Dundee). The programme was to run for ten years, which was recognition of the criticism that so many community initiatives were shortlived, and that significant regeneration in partnership with local communities was a long-term project. Initially some £60 million was to be made available for the programme, which would be developed by an implementation team working with the 'partners', who in Ferguslie were to be represented by the Scottish Office, the local authorities (regional and district), other statutory agencies (including the Scottish Development Agency, the Training Agency and the local health board) and the local community. Overall there was official commitment to the principle 'of residents taking greater control over and responsibility for their communities' together with the 'full involvement of the private sector and of partnership between the communities and the public and private sectors' (Secretary of State for Scotland, p. 2).

In Ferguslie Park the partnership developed its strategy, working directly on the basis of inputs from the local community, through FLAG, which was accepted as the umbrella organisation representing the different community interests. FLAG was based in the central part of the estate, in a centre that was leased at no cost from the district council. The regional council provided a grant, and Urban Aid covered the community transport project and the community health project, both of which had been developed by FLAG itself. In addition the regional council's social-work department located community work staff at the FLAG centre, together with welfare-rights support.

In summary then, FLAG could reasonably claim to be broadly representative of the different community interests in Ferguslie Park, as well as being in touch with a wide range of local people who came in and out of the centre to use the different community services and projects housed there. On average some fifty to one hundred people would bring their individual problems to the centre each week, problems such as welfare benefits or housing problems. The prospects for active partnership must have seemed positive.

Two years later the secretary of state for Scotland produced a progress report, *Urban Scotland into the 90s: new life two years on*, which summarised the achievements of the partnerships so far. This report concluded that 'A sound foundation has been built and achievements are beginning to flow' (Secretary of State for Scotland, 1990, p. 7). In Ferguslie, the report pointed to the 200 job placements that had been achieved for the local unemployed, together with the 160 people placed on recognised training schemes. The local district council had spent some £4 million on housing improvements in the area and Scottish Homes had contributed £1.5 million, mostly spent on the first phase of a cooperative housing scheme. A new road link was planned, which 'should open up other major housing opportunities' (ibid., p. 15). Educational opportunities were to be improved through closer links between homes, schools and employers. The image of the estate had been improved; the Prince of Wales had visited the estate and a business support group had been established. The Top End Youth Action Group had won an award in a UK-wide competition organised by the journal *Social Work Today*. And Ferguslie was to be made safer through increased community policing and building a police station on the estate. A new day centre had been built for the elderly, and the first phase of a new sports centre had been completed. 'Ferguslie Park', the report concluded, 'is being changed for the better. Local people are responding enthusiastically to the opportunities which have been created' (ibid., p. 15).

So how did FLAG evaluate the partnership? Clearly some of the developments were welcomed unreservedly. Others were welcomed more cautiously. Some of the developments would, it was suggested, have taken place in any case, whether or not the partnership had been in existence (for example the local-authority-housing improvements). Other developments were welcomed in principle, but it was suggested by some activists that local people had benefited less than had been anticipated. In relation to employment, which was widely agreed to be one of, if not the greatest, key problems on the estate, the achievements on job placement were recognised. But these were set against the relative lack of local jobs and training opportunities involved in the regeneration process itself (for example local building jobs), or in the surrounding local economy (some thirteen people were currently chasing every vacancy in the area), the relative lack of perceived commitment from private-sector 'partners' so far, and the low pay and poor training prospects of the few jobs that were on offer in the local job centre (based in the partnership offices building).

Other proposed developments were seen as potentially problematic, and there was concern that the consultation process had been so rapid that some local activists felt that they had not had sufficient time to absorb the implications of some of the changes being put in train. Anxiety was expressed about the role of the private sector here, in relation to housing, land and property development. The partnership's approach was based on the recognition that, in the current climate, local authorities did not have the resources to make major investments in housing, nor were they likely to have such resources under existing government policy. So the private sector was looked to as the source of housing investment, both for owner occupation and for social housing, typically housing-association rented homes (via Scottish Homes). But some community activists expressed anxiety about the long-term implications of such a strategy: if new/renovated housing proved unaffordable for local people, the result could be that outsiders who *could* afford it would move in, leaving the original tenants increasingly marginalised in the remaining and less desirable sections of the estate. Parallels were drawn with the experiences of other redevelopment schemes which had been criticised for being property led rather than people led (for example in London's Docklands).

In principle such an outcome could not happen, it had been suggested, because local people represented Ferguslie's community organisations in the partnership. But community activists also expressed concern about the partnership process itself.

The partnership process exerted powerful pressures on community organisations and community activists. The sheer intensity and the pace of meetings – one estimate was that some eighty to ninety meetings were taking place per month – put massive pressure on those involved, especially those with plenty of pressure in their own lives already, such as working women with young families. Not surprisingly most interviewees felt that this was a major reason for relatively few members being prepared to come forward to actively seek leadership roles within the FLAG organisation' (ibid., para. 5.8). It was also widely felt that although FLAG appeared to be relatively well resourced, in fact the resources were not at all adequate to the tasks in hand in relation to the partnership.

More generally, there were also suggestions that the partnership was contributing to reducing the role and status of local-government structures, whether by intention or whether because the partnership simply accepted the reality of central government's position towards local government, as exemplified for instance by the lack of resources for local-authority housing in the area. And there were anxieties that the focus of attention on Ferguslie Park as a result of the partnership could actually result in the reinforcement of the negative stereotypes held by residents in surrounding areas, coupled with fears and resentment that Ferguslie might be receiving a disproportionate share of scarce public resources.

But focusing on the worst-case scenario only highlights the negatives. In reality there did also seem to be important positives in the Ferguslie Park experience. There had been massive inputs of time and energy from local people over a period of some twenty years. Local services were provided, and skills, experience and self confidence were acquired by local community organisations and individuals.

Pinehurst People's Centre, Swindon

The Pinehurst People's Centre is a multi-purpose community centre in Swindon. It was set up as a 'centre which would pool the talents of the volunteer and the professional and would integrate economic and social activities' (Pinehurst People's Centre). Housed in a former secondary school that was officially reopened as a community centre in, May 1990 following a major local campaign, the People's Centre provides accommodation for a range of community organisations. By 1991 (when the centre was becoming fully operational) some 1650 people were using the facilities in a busy week. In 1989 Pinehurst People's Centre won *The Times*/RIBA Community Enterprise Scheme Award, which was presented to them by the Prince of Wales.

This tremendous achievement was the result of lengthy campaigning work by community organisations and activists, who had been concerned about service provision and community facilities on the estate and in surrounding parts of Swindon.

Pinehurst had been developed as a housing estate in the interwar period following demonstrations for more housing at the end of the First World War. Local activists recalled that in the interwar period the estate, which was physically relatively isolated from the rest of Swindon, developed a strong sense of local community and had well-developed groups, such as a tenants' association and a youth club. In the absence of a community centre, these groups used premises in the local secondary school. During this period Swindon, overall, was generally described as a town with a strong labour movement and a powerful sense of occupational community, based around the dominant industry – the railways.

After the Second World War Pinehurst gained further dwellings when Swindon expanded, as an overspill town, in the 1950s. The local authority was anxious to promote expansion as part of its strategy to diversify the local economy away from the railway industry, which had begun to decline even before the Second World War. The local authority was actively concerned to plan for the social aspects of expansion too, recognising the need to provide community halls on housing estates, with social development officers employed to combat social isolation amongst newcomers. This local-authority perspective provided a positive tradition of support for community development, a tradition which had considerable subsequent relevance for community organisations in Pinehurst. Broady and Hedley's study of local authorities' initiatives in community development in the late 1980s, included a case study of Thamesdown, Swindon. The study described this background of local authority support for community development, and analysed the successes and the limitations of these attempts to develop partnerships between statutory and voluntary sectors in Swindon (Broady and Hedley, 1989, pp. 95–111).

Despite Swindon's location within the relatively affluent M4 corridor, by the end of the 1980s, the local economy was suffering from the loss of traditional employment in the railways, and Pinehurst was characterised by high levels of deprivation, a situation which was exacerbated by the social polarisation which resulted from the increasingly marginal and residual position of public housing over this period, as rehousing was confined to those in more and more desperate housing need. So, at the end of the 1980s, Pinehurst's deprivation could be measured in terms of statistics, such as the fact that 80 per cent of children were entitled to free school meals because of the low incomes of their families.

In summary then, the People's Centre, which was set up as the result of sustained community campaigning, aimed to continue to press for and participate in the planning and delivery of the most effective and appropriate services for the local community, whilst tapping community self-help and stimulating the active involvement of community volunteers, both in running the centre and in providing services and activities within it.

Four years later, when more fully established, the Pinehurst People's Centre had succeeded in maintaining its original vision and ethos. It had preserved its commitment to participating in efforts to improve services, working in new ways with officials, councillors and professionals, and campaigning, where necessary, to achieve better service provision. And the People's Centre had maintained its commitment to working in non-hierarchical ways to involve all sections of the community in running the centre itself and in providing services.

There was ample evidence to demonstrate the relevance and value of particular services and projects. And there was ample evidence to demonstrate that the People's Centre's policy commitment to equal opportunities was being taken seriously, in relation to disabilities issues as well as in relation to race and gender. For example, the

Pinehurst Training Initiative offered computer training in small groups to break down the mystique surrounding new technology. There were courses specifically designed to meet the needs of women, including women returners, and there were programmes such as home-tuition programmes for people with disabilities. Partly as a result of the training, qualifications and personal support offered by the project and partly as a result of the subsequent support with job placements, some two thirds of trainees who were looking for work found paid employment after completing their courses (Pinehurst Training Initiative, 1988).

There was evidence, too, that projects within the People's Centre were succeeding in carrying out preventative work and rehabilitative work, using the skills and experiences of both professionals and volunteers.

Whilst there were excellent examples of collaboration with statutory agencies, however, there were also pressures. Typically this was not because there was seen to be competition between the two spheres. Nor were there instances where the People's Centre had become involved in direct competition with statutory services through the contracting-out process. This did not happen; and the People's Centre made it clear that it was not in the business of attempting to undermine or undercut public-sector services. On the contrary, there were common problems and pressures which were affecting both statutory and community-based services. Resources were a key issue here, with cuts in the public sector having knock-on effects in the voluntary sector.

Relationships between community activists and volunteers and the People's Centre's own paid staff had to be worked through too. Becoming an employer poses major challenges to community organisations, both in terms of the practical and technical skills involved (such as becoming responsible for employees' tax and insurance) and in terms of the relationships involved. Initially, community representatives on committees that have taken on the employment of staff, and especially professional staff, may tend to assume that professionals know best; that professionals simply need to be allowed to get on with their jobs. Over time however, the management committee at the People's Centre, developed skills and confidence as an employer. For example, the committee was able to cast off some of the professionals' initial assumptions about the roles of volunteers by ensuring that volunteers were to be offered challenging tasks, and given the training to tackle these effectively, rather than being relegated to routine tasks only.

Management itself produced other challenges, too. There were technical skills to be developed in managing a centre of this size, and in ensuring the long term viability of the centre and its component parts. Over the four years in question, the management committee developed considerable skills and experience. By 1991, for example, there was far greater clarity about the nature and location of financial problems, so there was a clear understanding of where shortfalls might be anticipated. But the problem of how to manage such a shortfall was not simply related to the acquisition of technical skills and competencies. There was also the problem of applying these market-related skills to achieve community goals and values. The management committee was concerned that the People's Centre should continue to be value-led rather than market-led, so that particular projects and activities might still be supported even if they could not fully pay their way, according to market criteria, because of their importance to the centre's aims and objectives; but the decision to subsidise any aspect of the centre's work would be taken consciously and in a business-like way, according to agreed criteria.

Unsurprisingly the process of acquiring these managerial skills, and applying them to the management of the People's Centre without jettisoning its values, aims and objectives, was a continuing one. As one set of problems were worked through, new ones emerged. And new community representatives had to catch up on the learning process, just as new volunteers had to receive training and induction. Unless special efforts were made to achieve this, there was a risk that these skills and experiences would be increasingly confined to the group that had already learnt so much, making it harder and harder for new members to become involved. In 1991 the People's Centre's 'Away Day' for training and evaluation included an examination of some of these issues, as well as some of issues around relationships between staff and volunteers. In addition there was some consideration of ways of involving more Pinehurst residents, including new members, in the management of the centre (these proposals included some well-tried and tested community-work practices such as producing newsletters and posters, and conducting personal discussions, on an individual basis, to encourage people to come forward and take on new responsibilities).

But there was a view that, over time, it was becoming more difficult to recruit volunteers to the take on the challenge of the general management of the People's Centre. A number of reasons were suggested to explain this. Firstly, the loss of industrial jobs had also entailed the decline of traditional experiences of trade-union organisation. In addition, this loss of organisational skills was believed to have been compounded by the closure of two local churches which had also developed local organisational skills. Meanwhile local housing had been increasingly occupied by families who were already experiencing a number of problems and stresses of their own, and so had less time for community involvement. Volunteering itself had also become more pressurised, it was believed, so that those who were already involved in specific projects at the centre had become increasingly caught up in fund-raising activities in order that their own projects could survive at all. In view of all these factors, it was therefore believed that it was becoming harder and harder to involve volunteers in the overall management of the People's Centre. Many of these factors were also experienced by volunteers involved in other community initiatives, including the tenant management initiatives that are discussed further on in this chapter.

Meanwhile, in working through these issues, the Pinehurst People's Centre had considerable support, including the community-work support that was available through the local authority, together with access to low-cost, local-authority-run training programmes for community organisations. In addition they had taken up an offer of places on community-education and training weekends, along with community organisations from other areas, at Ruskin College, Oxford. But this level of support needed to be maintained in order to meet the changing needs of the People's Centre whilst providing training and induction for new community representatives and volunteers.

Overall the experiences of the People's Centre demonstrated the strength of the centre's collective development, as well as the strength of its collective commitment. These experiences also provided examples of individual development and growing self confidence. Through their involvement at the People's Centre, as volunteers and community activists and through their responsibilities on the management committee, individuals gained skills and self-esteem; a process which led a number to go on to apply successfully for education and training courses and/or gain paid employment. This was particularly marked amongst women (women being, predictably, disproportionately represented amongst the centre's volunteers), including single parents who first came to the centre needing support and advice themselves. Two women successfully applied for paid jobs as community workers, for example, and one gained a place on a professional social-work course. These outcomes were by-products of their developing self-confidence, through their involvement in the People's Centre, outcomes which were way outside their original aspirations for themselves. Whilst their departure represented a loss for the centre, there was also positive recognition of the gains for the individuals concerned. This by-product of community activism for the individuals involved, their developing skills, increasing self-confidence and widening aspirations for further training and paid employment, emerged in other cases too, as the concluding section of this chapter considers.

Tenant Management Cooperatives in Camden, London

Like the development of the Pinehurst People's Centre, tenant management cooperatives in Camden developed in response to new threats posing new challenges to community organisations and leading eventually, in each case, to the development of schemes for the communities concerned to manage resources and services themselves. Like both the Pinehurst People's Centre and Ferguslie League of Action Groups, these tenant initiatives were built upon a longer history of community involvement and community action and campaigning in the localities.

The history of tenants' organisations around housing issues has already been discussed in Chapter 6. As Chapter 6 has also set out, the Housing Act of 1988 was perceived as a new threat, leading to a resurgence of tenant activity. As the experiences of the tenant management cooperatives demonstrated, there had been a persistent history of dissatisfaction with the council's performance in terms of basic issues such as repairs and maintenance; issues which had absorbed the energies of tenants' associations and their representative structures. But the 1988 Act was perceived as a qualitatively different challenge, requiring new approaches. This was because the

Act was seen as facilitating the shift of public-sector housing out of the public sector and into the private sector. Tenants reported rumours that particular property developers were expressing an interest in their estates. They feared that if this were to happen, they, as tenants, would be priced out of their homes. These fears emerged as a key factor in motivating tenants to come together to explore new solutions.

Tenant management cooperatives were one of the solutions developed by tenants' organisations in Camden, with the support of the Federation of Tenants and Residents, as well as the support of the borough council. Those tenants' associations which opted to become a management cooperative would remain within the public sector, with all the security of tenure this entailed, as an alternative to transferring into the private or cooperative/housing-association sectors. But the tenant management cooperative would take over key aspects of running the estate, which would give the tenants greater control and enable them to tackle the continuing saga of poor repairs and maintenance. Tenant management cooperatives had already been developed in a number of places (for example in Glasgow, and in neighbouring Islington in London), along with related options, such as estate management boards (which offered some, but not all of the aspects of community control offered by tenant management cooperatives). So Camden tenants drew upon these ideas and experiences.

Once they had expressed an interest in forming a tenant management cooperative, tenants' associations were able to receive professional support in exploring this option. Feasibility studies were carried out by consultants (Solon Coop Housing Services Tenant Initiative Unit), who also provided training and advice, in preparation for implementation, for those tenants association which voted decisively in favour of setting up a management cooperative. (This support was funded, at the time, jointly by the Department of the Environment and the local council.)

These feasibility studies started by consulting the tenants, providing them with information, and finding out from them their concerns and aspirations, to see how far these could be met through a tenant management cooperative. From these studies there was clear evidence to bear out the view that tenants were moved by both fear, in view of the perceived threat of the 1988 Housing Act, and frustration at the history of poor and deteriorating service delivery, especially in relation to repairs and maintenance. For example the feasibility study for the Kilburn Vale Estate referred to 'vociferous criticism of a whole range of council services. Although, it was acknowledged that some of the decline in services had arisen from recent cuts as a result of government imposed constraints many strongly felt that the decline had set in several years previously' (Solon CHS Ltd, 1988, p. 5). Another feasibility study (Highgate Newtown) referred to reported waiting times for repairs ranging from two months to over six years. Caretaking and ground maintenance also came in for criticism, together with refuse collection. So tenants' interests in setting up management cooperatives to take matters into their own hands, were based upon long dissatisfaction with the council's performance as a landlord, coupled with fears that any alternative landlord might be even worse (and especially so in terms of security of tenure). The attractions of enhanced community control and empowerment, per se, seem to have appealed to a minority only, at this stage.

Kilburn Vale Estate was the first tenant management to be formally launched, in 1991. The estate consisted of some two hundred units, made up of flats built in the 1950s and some sheltered flats and some houses dating from the 1970s. There had been an active tenants' association in the 1950s which had been revived (with some participation from the original membership) in the 1980s, when there had been major problems over heating over a two-year period. In addition to taking up these types of repairs and maintenance issues, the tenants' association had organised social and welfare activities. This background of community activity, and the shared 'sense of community', was felt to form an important basis for further cooperative work.

The tenant management cooperative (TMC), which was finally launched in 1991, took over management and maintenance responsibilities from the council, which stated its intention to give the members of the cooperative the right to participate in controlling, managing and maintaining the housing in which they lived so that they may achieve the benefits that come from cooperation. On its side the TMC had to have a democratic constitution and equal opportunities policies and practices, which were to be the subject of regular monitoring, together with monitoring of the TMC's financial operations and standards of maintenance. This agreement was for three years, in the first instance, with safeguards to ensure that the cooperative would only continue in the future if the tenants still wanted this.

So was the TMC successful? Over the first year in which it was effectively (although not yet formally) operating, (1990–1), the TMC achieved a surplus of some £15 000 whilst providing a significantly improved service. Small repairs were being completed in one to two weeks, with a twenty-four hour coverage for emergencies (the council's target for making significant improvements over the three years from 1991/2 to 1993/4 aimed to reach 24 per cent of priority, urgent repairs within ten days. Although these are not directly comparable figures, they illustrate the extent of the gap between the TMC's actual achievements and the council's targets, let alone the council's actual performance). As an article in the Federation paper, *Camden Tenant*, described the situation within six weeks of the TMC taking effective control in April 1990, 'The estate looks absolutely spick and span and even people walking through on their way to the shops are commenting on how different it looks. Everyone is delighted with the new caretaker/handyman, Harry, as he is visibly working round the estate in the morning and doing small repair jobs most afternoons' (*Camden Tenant*, June 1990). 'It sounds like a great beginning', the article concluded, 'congratulations, Kilburn Vale tenants'.

The coop administrator, who was employed directly by the coop, believed that it had been important that tenants should see rapid improvements over these first weeks to justify their confidence in the venture. It had been possible to achieve these changes through careful and flexible on-the-spot management. Nor was it the case that savings were being achieved through undercutting trade-union rates and conditions. The TMC's own staff were employed on local-authority scales and conditions and were trade-union members, and the TMC only used contractors who met minimum standards on such issues as health and safety and equal opportunities. So the savings did seem to be the result of greater efficiency and better management. And there were direct contributions from tenants in terms of their voluntary labour to assist with particular jobs, such as cleaning up the estate environment.

In summary, all this represented a major achievement for the TMC; although it could, of course, alternatively be seen as an indictment of previous housing-management systems. As will be suggested subsequently, some of the improvements could also have been achieved by the local authority through changes such as estate-based management, changes which have been demonstrated to have produced significant benefits in housing management more generally (Power, 1987). As it was, the improvements were the result of sustained effort over a period of some four years, backed by significant inputs of support, including training. The tenants paid tribute to the coop employees' efficiency and dedication in making these improvements, although they themselves had clearly contributed enormous amounts of time and energy to the development of the TMC.

The staff expressed strong commitment to their jobs with the TMC. More generally it was important that the TMC staff were also committed to working collaboratively with colleagues in the local authority. This included being committed to working in ways which did not undermine or undercut public-sector provision or trade-union rates and conditions. As a result positive relationships were developed, despite the fact that, initially, the trade unions had been suspicious of the TMC's approach.

It was recognised that the management committee would need to renew itself constantly by training new management-committee members if it was to remain both representative and effective in maintaining its energy and enthusiasm. The management committee used a range of tactics to maintain communication and increase involvement, such as newsletters and social events. Unsurprisingly fewer people came forward to serve on the management committee in the second year, however, as the first year's work had been seen to be so demanding (although a 'fun day' to celebrate the formal launch in 1991 had been very well attended, and some volunteers had been brought in as a result of the follow-up to that event). Active pensioners were keen to involve more younger people, with a view to sustaining the organisation in the future, but there were difficulties in getting families to commit their time, especially where there were young children and both parents were working.

There were also efforts to improve the balance of the management committee in terms of equal opportunities. This evidence of an active commitment to translating the TMC's equal-opportunities policy statement into practice applied to their own organisation as well as to the employment of staff and the provision of services. Each of these areas had also been the subject of training, in preparation for the establishment of the TMC, a practice which had been built into the council's approach towards the development of TMCs. This is not of course to imply that all equal-opportunities issues were resolved; only to make the far more modest claim that equal-opportunities issues had been firmly lodged on the agenda, with training programmes and council monitoring processes to try to ensure progress. There was recognition that without such conscious efforts TMCs would not necessarily move in that direction; on the contrary, debates about increasing tenant control more generally had included the expression of concern that this could result in further social polarisation in general, and further racism in particular (Willmott and Murie, 1988, p. 89).

Overall then, the tenants of Kilburn Vale, and especially those who were active on the management committee, had made a very considerable effort, and put in enormous amounts of time to make their TMC successful, both in terms of delivering a quality service and in terms of achieving this in genuinely democratic and anti-discriminatory ways. As a result there was increased self-confidence, both collectively and for the individuals concerned. This had a knock-on effect for individuals in terms of their confidence, for instance, in applying for further training or education. One example of this was provided by one of the TMC committee members, who had gained the confidence to apply for a training course in word processing to improve her skills in producing the newsletter (sadly she was turned down because of her age, rising seventy-five years old). These positive benefits were valued, and there was considerable pride in the TMC's achievements altogether.

On the other hand, there was also an example of a tenants' association, Highgate Newtown, deciding to pursue the TMC option, on the basis of an 80 per cent majority in 1988, only to back off when the time came to make this final decision (in 1991, after the feasibility study and consultation process had been carried out). The original motivations for exploring the TMC option were the same as those in Kilburn Vale (fears generated by the 1988 Housing Act, coupled with frustrations about repairs and maintenance), and like Kilburn Vale, Highgate Newtown was also building upon a history of an active tenants' association committed to finding solutions within the public sector. The same consultants carried out the feasibility and consultation process, too, and in similar ways. So the drop in active support between 1988 and 1991 came as something of a surprise (in the event there was majority support for a TMC, but the poll was low so it was decided that there was insufficient active support for a TMC to be viable). Possible explanations included the fact that this was a relatively large estate (600 units) and that support had not jelled sufficiently across the different sections of the estate. It was also suggested that there was some anxiety about the time and commitments a TMC would entail, especially amongst younger people in work and/or with family commitments. And there had been fears and anxieties raised by an anonymous leaflet urging people to vote against the formation of the TMC. This leaflet, which had been circulated throughout the estate, suggested that, because a former councillor was involved, the TMC would actually be a vehicle for council 'spies' to keep a watch on tenants and keep files on individual tenants for 'big brother Camden'. 'Come May day' the leaflet pronounced, 'there will be a gay parade' (playing upon stereotypes of municipal socialism in the early 1980s). The leaflet concluded by suggesting that the elderly would be 'winkled out and decanted elsewhere'. Unsurprisingly considerable anxiety was aroused amongst the elderly on the estate.

Ultimately the reasons for the loss of enthusiasm for the TMC option in Highgate Newtown can only be conjectured. But the fact that this happened at all, does emphasise that tenants' associations may have serious reservations about taking on the TMC option. Clearly the launch of TMCs did require enormous inputs of time, organisational abilities and skills, and sheer energy. All of these may be in increasingly scarce supply, and especially so with an increasingly elderly population (as older people are less likely to volunteer, in general, and as more women are returning to the workforce to provide for their families, aspects of the 'crisis of supply' in volunteering which were identified in the NCVO collection of essays on volunteering – Hedley and Davis Smith, 1992, pp. 1–3). If the council had been providing an adequate service, then some tenants may have chosen not to pursue the TMC option in the first place; and if the council were to improve its services significantly, then some of those who had chosen the TMC option could, conceivably, opt to return to full council management. One view was that the very existence of successful TMCs, far from undermining the council's own service, actually constituted pressure to improve that service. Far from constituting a threat to the mainstream of public-sector housing in the borough, according to this perspective, TMCs were actually reinforcing tenants' pressures for improved services.

Meanwhile, however, the borough-wide context was changing too. Improvements to housing repairs and maintenance were threatened by further cuts, which were implemented in 1991 as part of renewed financial pressures on the council as a whole. This raised the longer-term question of what would happen to funding for the TMCs. In the short term of their three-year agreements, they might be protected from such cuts, although if that were to happen it could create tensions between the TMCs and the rest of the tenants' associations, which would bear the full brunt of the cuts in the borough. Alternatively, if such cuts were to be passed on, TMCs could find themselves eventually unable to deliver a satisfactory service to their members, dashing the expectations which had been raised with the establishment of the TMCs. Ultimately the TMCs would not be insulated from the problems and pressures affecting the rest of the tenants' movement, both in the borough and beyond.

The Afro-Caribbean Organisation, King's Cross, London

The Afro Caribbean Organisation (ACO), based near King's Cross in London, provided a further example of a community-based organisation deeply affected by wider pressures and resource problems in the London borough of Camden and beyond. Like the TMCs, ACO's services developed out of a history of campaigning to combat inadequate and discriminatory public services, rather than from any initial commitment to take over the running of these services within the Afro-Caribbean community. Whilst ACO shared some of the reservations other organisations expressed about becoming a service-providing agency (including the reservation that this might leave them with little time or energy to continue campaigning for more appropriate and less inadequate public-service provision), ACO members did believe that the experience of running services themselves had entailed positive features for the group, as well as for individual volunteers who had developed confidence and skills in the process.

ACO was established at the end of the 1960s, by a group of activists who had worked together in North London to campaign against increasing immigration controls, and to combat racism more generally. From the beginning ACO built links with Afro-Caribbean groups elsewhere in Britain (and with a group in Holland), as well as maintaining connections with other black groups in the area. There were also strong connections with the trade-union movement, as a number of founder members were active trade unionists committed to campaigning for racial equality within the workplace.

It was through campaigning on social issues that ACO first became involved in direct service provision. Housing was a major problem, and ACO was actively involved in campaigns against poor housing conditions and homelessness, working alongside other community organisations in the early 1970s (the period when the Camden Federation of Tenants and Residents was established). ACO was also concerned to combat discrimination, including discrimination in the allocation of public housing to black tenants, as well as becoming increasingly concerned with the particular problems of young, black, homeless people. In desperation, when the council failed to respond to continuing pressure to tackle this problem, ACO located an old property that was suitable for housing young homeless people and squatted in it. Following this direct action, the council agreed its use as a hostel. The Community Relations Council (subsequently the Commission for Racial Equality) provided £100 for materials, ACO provided volunteer labour to renovate the building, and 'Paul Robeson' house began to provide accommodation for young black people. Over the five years of its life, from 1975 to 1980, 267 young black people passed through this hostel.

Meanwhile ACO was developing activities in other service areas. In 1978 the organisation gained Urban Aid funding to set up a base in the King's Cross area to take forward the work that ACO had been developing around the provision of information, guidance, advice, counselling and advocacy. This base became a haven where Afro-Caribbeans had the confidence to go for advice and support, including young Afro-Caribbeans who were dubious about encounters with more formal agencies (and particularly so in the case of young people who were in conflict with the law). Whilst the centre was mainly targeted towards meeting the needs of the Afro-Caribbean community, however, young white people also used its facilities, including the provision of advice and guidance on employment issues, which was a major concern for young people arriving in London in search of work in the capital city (ACO's centre was within a five-minute walk of Euston, King's Cross and St Pancras stations). The drop-in centre was also used by young women at risk in the area (which had the reputation of being a red-light area, used by prostitutes, including young girls recently arrived in the capital city, and their clients). Subsequently, with legal changes in the 1980s, immigration issues became another key area of the centre's concern.

The drop-in centre initially had one paid worker (later two). In addition each ACO committee member worked as a volunteer for one evening or more a week. Other professionals provided services on a voluntary basis, including several lawyers who provided legal advice and otherwise supported the centre's 'aid for bail' scheme, working with ACO volunteers to try to keep young people out of custody, wherever possible (for example by finding accommodation and/or standing bail for them).

From the original group of about twenty people who formed ACO at the end of the 1960s, the organisation grew to a total membership of some five hundred, of whom some two hundred were actively involved in the centre in some way. ACO was chaired by a woman, reflecting the strength of women's involvement in the organisation. The organisation's self-confidence grew apace as they developed their experience of running the centre. Although ACO began as a campaigning rather than a service-providing organisation, the members did feel that they had gained status and self-esteem from the centre's success in this latter respect. And individuals clearly gained wider opportunities, including wider employment opportunities on the basis of their expanding skills and self-confidence as volunteers.

More generally, ACO was strongly in favour of the council's equal-opportunities policies. ACO also believed that it was vital that equal opportunities should be firmly built into community-based services. Whether consciously or not, white community organisations could operate in discriminatory ways unless there were countervailing tendencies. ACO recognised the potential risks inherent in community control; but they also recognised the potential advantages of community initiatives such as tenant management cooperatives. The solution, it was felt, was not to avoid these initiatives but to ensure that the council developed, supported and monitored equal-opportunities policies and practices in the community sector, as well as in the mainstream of direct council service provision.

This fitted in with ACO's wider conclusions about the potential for developing partnerships between community organisations and the public sector. There was no way, ACO believed, in which community organisations could or should substitute for mainstream public service provision. But organisations such as ACO could play a key role by ensuring that public services met particular communities' needs and exploring new ways of developing alternative forms of service provision. If they were to achieve these goals, however, community organisations needed continuing access to core funding, as well as to training and other forms of back-up support, without political strings.

Sadly this was precisely what ACO lacked. After a decade of financial support, ACO lost its council funding in 1991 (as part of a wider series of cutbacks due to financial difficulties in the borough). The organisation found itself with bills for the premises in King's Cross which could not be met on a long-term basis, together with bills for the salaries of the two workers, who were then made redundant because their salaries could not be met either. Inevitably this was an extremely painful process for the organisation, a process which raised fundamental questions about its future.

Some wider implications

By themselves, case studies do not constitute proof of theories about the changing role of the community sector, in the mixed community of welfare, of course, even in their own specific regional and national contexts. And the experiences of community organisations have varied even more across international frontiers. As has been suggested in previous chapters, the history of community organisations has differed, for example, in North American cities, where there has been a tradition of community organisations playing a greater role in direct service provision, together with a history of community organisations finding their own resources and support mechanisms. These histories can offer valuable lessons.

Meanwhile, in a far more limited way, the British examples could be used to assist in illustrating and perhaps helping to clarify some of the questions posed at the beginning of this chapter, questions about some of the issues which need to be addressed when community organisations take on new roles, or expand their previously established roles and responsibilities, in the changing climate of the mixed economy of welfare.

Each example illustrated some of the positive aspects of community participation and community self-management of resources and service provision. There were examples where statutory provision had been improved and/or made more relevant, with new relationships being developed between professionals and the communities they were employed to serve. And there were examples of community organisations successfully taking on the management of resources and services. As a result of working through the problems and dilemmas associated with these new tasks and responsibilities, community organisations have provided examples of increased self-confidence and a growing sense of empowerment, collectively. And individuals, especially women, developed personal confidence and skills through these experiences, going on to pursue wider training and employment opportunities as a result.

But where these positive outcomes were achieved, this had been the result of major inputs of local people's time and energy, typically building upon long histories of community activity and organisation in their area. This was clearly the pattern in every case. Community participation and community management did not just arise spontaneously. And in each case local efforts received considerable support in terms of funding for staff and premises, together with other forms of professional input, and access to training, including training for equal opportunities. It was noticeable, too, that professionals provided both technical skills and community-work support. And professionals from a range of disciplines, including, for example, housing cooperative administrators with backgrounds in housing management, worked with community groups in ways that were sensitive to community work-aims and objectives, supporting the development of the cooperative as a group, as well as providing a technical housing-management service. This was precisely the type of outcome that Donnison identified as positive when he argued that 'If they are sound, the principles of community work apply to every profession that works with people' (Donnison, 1991, p. viii). But even here, in situations where community organisations received such effective and appropriate support, the demand for resourcing, including training, still outstripped the supply. This raises questions about why this was so, especially given that the community organisations concerned were relatively well-established and self-sufficient, with their own histories of success over considerable periods of time. If they needed so much support, how much more support might less-established community organisations require if they were to take on such tasks of community management effectively?

This relates back to the increased demands of the mixed economy of welfare. In each case there were examples of ways in which community organisations were faced with increased pressures. There were pressures to acquire new skills and technical expertise, often at a very rapid rate, and then to apply these skills and expertise to attaining the particular goals of their community organisations without jettisoning their values on the way. These pressures generated further pressures, as community activists on management committees and formal representative structures gained new skills and expertise, which the rest of their memberships had still to acquire. Community organisations have traditionally faced the recurring challenge of how to keep their memberships in touch, and how to keep renewing their leaderships democratically. But this was exacerbated by the pressures that were generated, for example, when community organisations took on community management responsibilities.

In addition there were illustrations of the problems of maintaining, let alone expanding, the pool of volunteers and activists in the face of socio-economic and demographic change. Active pensioners, who were the mainstay of a number of the community organisations in question, were particularly concerned that their organisations were finding it increasingly difficult to find younger active members who would be able to replace them in the future. These anxieties were partly related to practical pressures on families, especially on families where both parents were in paid employment and on single-parent families. And they were partly related to fears about the loss of other, transferable organisational experiences and skills, especially the loss of organisational skills and experiences gained through the trade union movement as trade-union membership fell during the 1980s and early 1990s. This is not of course to imply that trade-union forms of organisation were necessarily the most appropriate model unless these were adopted for the varying needs of community-based organisations, let alone that such organisational forms would necessarily remain appropriate and effective, in changing circumstances, in the future; but being active in the trade union movement provided experience that could be built upon, and skills that could be transferred to other situations. It may be that community organisations could be expected to need even more resourcing and support to offset these losses, and to find new and more appropriate ways to build and develop their organisations in the future.

As it was, the examples illustrated that these community organisations did not take on major managerial responsibilities because they sought community control and empowerment, let alone because they sought to undermine or undercut the mainstream of public-sector provision. On the contrary, they usually became involved because of unsuccessful attempts to obtain or maintain satisfactory public provision. In these instances community management clearly led to significant improvements, as well as to personal growth and increased self-confidence and it was achieved in ways that did not undermine or undercut public-sector provision. All this was achieved as a result of conscious and determined effort, for example, through careful negotiations to reach common positions rather than confronting or undermining those trade unions which were affected by the establishment of tenant management cooperatives.

Similarly, there were examples of conscious strategies to promote equal opportunities, rather than expecting progress on this front to occur spontaneously. This applied to equal opportunity in employment and service delivery, and to strategies to promote the democratic participation of all sections of local communities. But, as has already been suggested, the examples illustrate commitments and strategies to make significant *progress* torwards equal opportunities, backed up with training and monitoring from grant-giving agencies; they certainly did not claim to represent the full *achievement* of equal opportunity, which will entail far longer-term and wider changes at national and international as well as at local level.

This raises the more general issue of the connection between community participation structures, community-managed services and resources, and the wider policy context. Each case illustrated different ways in which community organisations were affected by the contextual framework, whether, for example, this was because cuts were undermining or threatening to undermine voluntary and community services as well as statutory services, or whether wider policies were failing to reinforce or were even working against local-community regeneration policies. Ultimately this raised the question of the point at which community organisations might decide to pull out of participatory structures or wind up their organisations, if these were in effect being used to substitute for or cover up inadequate public services or inappropriate public policies for their communities.

Finally, if communities are to be offered genuine participation and real choice, then this must include the choice *not* to manage community services as well as the choice to do so. This means that public service provision must be satisfactory and appropriate if it is to represent a real choice. In the case of tenant management cooperatives for instance, many of the significant improvements in housing management achieved by the TMCs were improvements that had already been clearly recommended to the public sector via local estate-based management, which resulted in significant improvements in priority estates in the 1980s (Power, 1987). If such improvements had been effected and adequately resourced, then some (although not all) of the pressure to set up the TMCs in the first place would have been removed, and some tenants might have preferred *not* to have had to expend so much time and energy via the TMC in order to achieve acceptable standards of housing for themselves and their families. In any case, as the example of the Highgate Newtown tenants' decision not to set up a TMC illustrated, unless the commitment to giving this time and energy is unequivocal then a TMC is not in any case going to be viable. In practice, if community organisations are not enthusiastically as well as realistically committed to running services and managing resources, then community management will not stand much chance of providing a successful option. But where community organisations do opt to run particular services themselves they require resourcing, including education and training, for an extended period to enable them to gain the necessary technical skills and expertise without losing sight of the community organisations' values, goals and objectives.

Some of these issues are developed in the concluding chapter, together with some of the wider policy issues around the shifting boundaries between the public, private and non-statutory voluntary and community sectors.

8

Conclusion

The Introduction posed a series of questions about the changing boundaries of the mixed economy of welfare. Can the role of community/non-profit organisations be developed in partnership with a more democratically accountable public sector? Can community participation and community development be supported in ways that improve the quality and appropriateness of services and planning? Can such improvements be achieved whilst safeguarding broad principles of equity, including equity in terms of class, race and gender? And can such changes be promoted without further undermining the mainstream of public-sector provision, or the pay and conditions of public-service workers, including already low-paid frontline service workers, typically women from the communities (including black and ethnic minority communities) in question? Even if these conditions can be met, can an enhanced role for the 'community sector' be achieved without placing an even greater burden on those who are already most vulnerable in the community, including the imposition of a third burden on women who are already struggling with their double burden of coping with the demands of family responsibilities and paid employment?

The evidence over the past decade or more has been contradictory to say the least, both in Britain and beyond. As previous chapters have argued, there has been official support for community participation and community development from international agencies through to government and local-government organisations. But there have been reductions in mainstream programmes, and reductions in grant aid to precisely the types of community organisations that have been mobilising self-help efforts, as well as reductions in grant aid to more directly campaigning community organisations. Cuts in local-authority grants to the voluntary sector, in real terms, have continued in Britain, despite government support for an enhanced role for voluntary effort in the mixed economy of welfare. As Gutch has argued, 'at the very time when local authorities should be increasing investment in the infrastructure for local voluntary action in order to implement the D of H's community care policies, it appears a policy of disinvestment is taking place – as a direct result of the Department of the Environment's policies towards local government' (Gutch, 1992, p. 9). Meanwhile funding from individual and corporate voluntary donations has been squeezed as the recession has deepened. As *Charity Trends* (1991) commented, 'it would be surprising if the charitable world had been exempted from the recession altogether' (p. 6). Yet social needs have been increasing, whilst both public and voluntary sector resources for meeting them have been decreasing.

In spite of this situation, previous chapters have pointed to examples of community organisations that have succeeded in surviving and maintaining their missions, whether these missions have been to provide services directly or to campaign for improved public-service provision, or both. And these examples have included cases where community organisations have been working in partnership, rather than in competition with the public-sector, working alongside professionals and reinforcing rather than undercutting the contributions of frontline public-sector workers and their trade-union organisations. New relationships between the public sector and the non-profit sector and community organisa-tions *could* be developed, to extend and enhance rather than undermine public provision and public planning, even in this difficult period. But in the meantime the financial pressure on community organisations have been increasing. In line with this trend, two of the community organisations discussed in Chapter 7, have had to make members of their own staff redundant.

The preceding chapters have already discussed the importance of overall resourcing. As has been argued throughout, there is no way in which the voluntary sector, self-help or community initiatives can realistically substitute for the mainstream of public provision and resourcing. The voluntary sector itself has been absolutely clear about this. Any further attempts to achieve this can be expected to result in yet more polarisation, between those who can afford to pay for services on the one hand, and those who are dependent upon diminishing and increasingly fragmented public and voluntary provision on the other.

Public resourcing includes both direct financial provision and access to education and training. The importance of adequate and continuing education and training, both for individuals and for community organisations, emerged in both First and Third-World situations (and in the case studies in Chapter 7). Individuals and community organisations needed training in a variety of specific skills, ranging from the management skills required to bid for, manage, monitor and evaluate contracts for community service provision in Britain, to the particular construction skills needed for building self-help housing projects in Nicaragua and Zambia. More generally, both individuals and community organisations needed access to broader educational opportunities, too, if they were to develop and sustain their distinctive missions most effectively, critically analysing and taking appropriate account of the different socio-economic and political contexts in which they were operating.

Active participation in community organisations has itself been shown to have provided education and training in the widest sense of these terms. This was clearly the case for those volunteers and community activists who gained the confidence and skills to move on to further education, training and career development. Chapter 7 provided a number of examples of this. The 1991 National Survey of Volunteering in the UK, for example, provided wider evidence of the way in which a proportion of volunteers, especially women volunteers, believe that their involvement offers them broader experiences and opportunities to develop their confidence as well as their skills. Skilled, semi-skilled and unskilled working-class people were (unsurprisingly) rather more likely than managerial or professional people to value these perceived opportunities to learn new skills, to get 'out of myself', and even to move on to acquire recognised qualifications.

Clearly the numbers involved should in no way be exaggerated, however important these routes of opportunity to new careers may have been to the individuals concerned. Nor should the fact that a minuscule proportion of individual men and women from working-class and black and ethnic-minority communities became profess-ionals in local caring services be in any way taken to imply that this, of itself, will result in fundamental changes in the way in which those services are organised and delivered. The nature of the power of professionals working in the caring professions is, of course, more complex, relating as it ultimately does to the controlling as well as the caring functions of the welfare state. Clients, in any case, it has been argued, tend to perceive professionals as 'middle class' regardless of their actual class origins, separated from their clients through the exercise of their professional power, as well as through their education and use of professional language (Hugman, 1991). On both sides of the Atlantic there have been examples of the tensions and difficulties, as well as examples of some of the potential benefits and achievements, of professionals attempting to work in new ways with working-class and black and ethnic-minority clients and community organisations (for example Clavel and Wiewel, 1991). Increasing the number of professionals, even senior professionals who come from working-class backgrounds will not, by itself, alter these tensions, just as increasing the number of women and black and ethnic-minority professionals will not, by itself, be sufficient to challenge inherent biases in terms of gender and race. But Hugman, for instance, has also argued that such changes in the composition of the caring professions could *contribute* to wider and more fundamental strategies for change.

Meanwhile tensions remain in the relationship between volunteering and community involvement on the one hand and paid employment on the other. These tensions have also emerged in Third-World contexts too. Lund, for instance, has commented on such tensions in South Africa. 'A current project which Nozizwe Madlala and I are working on is concerned with developing training materials and strengthening support structures for community-based lay carers (family members or neighbours) of black elderly people living in their own homes, in rural and urban areas. Both in this project and in the community health workers study, the situation has arisen where project leaders have frowned on the fact that women carers see this voluntary participation as possibly opening doors for jobs, through receiving skills training, making connections, becoming visible outside the home. It is as if this motivation is seen by the (well-paid) leaders as betraying the notion of altruistic service to the community – wanting a job is seen as somehow greedy or selfish' (Lund, 1991). Lund concludes that these economic and employment issues need to be studied seriously in their own right, and be related to women's needs and interests in relation to informal caring.

Similar issues and debates have emerged in Britain and other First-World countries. For example, the research of Abrams and others in Britain identified working-class women's interest in providing social care as waged work (which coexisted alongside working-class notions of social care in terms of reciprocity), in contrast with middle-class women's concepts of volunteerism and philanthropy (Abrams *et al.*, 1989). In addition to the discussion about the development of individual pathways to paid employment and career progression, Chapter 3 also considered the potential for community-based employment through the provision of caring services. US examples included cases in cities such as Chicago, where well-organised community groups negotiated contracts with progressive administrations (for example Wintermute and Hicklin, 1991, p. 160). Individuals gained opportunities, but within the framework of collective approaches to meeting community needs.

This brings the discussion to the more collective aspects of education and training, and to some of the connections between adult and community education and community participation and development, connections which have, of course been central to the history of community development (linked to mass education in the British colonies). Adult and community education, in fact, provide further examples of the two-way processes of learning between First and Third Worlds, north and south, which were identified in Chapter 5, in place of the more traditional approach to comparative social policy, an approach which emphasised the transmission of learning as a one-way process only – from north to south.

Active participation has itself been seen as a form of education in the broadest sense. One study, based upon comparisons and contrasts between some eight hundred voluntary organisations in three areas in Britain estimated that a third of all adult learning is undertaken through voluntary organisations, if informal as well as formal learning activities were to be included (Perry, 1988). Groups as well as individuals learn from such experiences, gaining both general and specific skills and competencies. Similar findings have emerged from studies elsewhere; for example a survey of participants in community activities in a rural setting in the USA identified significant learning that was associated with community participation, and the greater the level of participants' involvement, the greater the learning (Lackey and Dershem, 1992).

Community education has been associated with the acquisition of knowledge and skills to enable individuals and communities to cope more effectively with particular problems and situations (unemployment for example). The liberal tradition has also included support for individuals to become more actively involved in social and political life; active citizenship in fact. And conversely these approaches have been contrasted with the radical tradition within community education, linked with community action (Lovett, Clarke and Kilmurray, 1983). Collective experiences of the radical tradition of adult education can be central to the growth and development of community organisations in relation to their abilities to analyse critically and then to challenge the structures that reinforce their disempowerment. Adult education of this type can be linked to, and reinforce, wider movements for social and political change. Cowburn identified the powerful influence of such challenging adult learning experiences, through short courses at the Northern College, by working back from the impact that these courses had made on community organisations in Sheffield (in the locality). 'In our fieldwork', he said, 'we were led to Northern College by the impact it had upon the people associated with our projects' (Cowburn, 1986, p. 197). Community education, then, has been characterised in terms of its dual and contradictory potential, accommodating or challenging, traditional or radical, just as community development and community participation have also been characterised in terms of competing definitions and contrasting approaches.

Similarly conflicting conclusions have been drawn about the impact of that most influential adult educator, Paulo Freire. Freire's work has already been quoted as a key influence on community education and community development programmes across a range of contexts in Third-World countries (for example in Brazil and in South Africa, as Chapter 5 illustrated). Freire's ideas have also been applied in First-World countries, including Britain. For example Kirkwood and Kirkwood have provided an account of a project to implement Freire's ideas in a project in Scotland from 1979 (Kirkwood and Kirkwood, 1989). In fact Freire's work has travelled to and fro, across First and Third-World countries, north and south. Starting from Freire's work, for instance, Hope and

Timmel developed their own version of community-development education, training for transformation, which they used in different contexts in Southern Africa, writing up manuals which were then also used creatively in First-World training contexts, including community-development courses in Northern Ireland (Hope and Timmel, 1984). (There have of course been a number of reasons why parallels and lessons have been drawn between Northern Ireland and Southern Africa, particularly South Africa itself, including the lessons to be drawn from different communities' efforts to survive in a context of violence, both state violence and intercommunal violence).

These ideas of Freire have been traced to Christian influences, to humanist Marxist influences and to existentialist thinking (Grabowski, 1972). And given this diversity, it is perhaps unsurprising (as Youngman, for instance, has pointed out) that Freire has been interpreted in widely differing ways, and for widely differing purposes and political projects (Youngman, 1986). Marxists have been critical of Freire's ideas for a number of reasons. It has been argued for instance, that his approach has lacked coherence (ibid.). And it has been suggested that he overemphasised the role of ideas in social change and the importance of the development of individual consciousness, whilst underemphasising the importance of developing strategies for structural change. But Marxist critics such as Youngman have also recognised the importance of the debt owed by adult educators to Freire, and the importance of his work, emphasising the political nature of adult education and the potential contribution it can make to the development of consciousness to combat cultural domination.

From the context of the 1990s, Freire's contribution to adult and community education may seem to have potentially more relevance than ever, notwithstanding some of its limitations. Freire has been concerned to develop a pedagogy based upon dialogue and problem posing, to enable oppressed people to develop their own under-standing and definitions of themselves and their situations in order to achieve change, gain confidence and understanding, and become 'subjects' rather than 'objects'. Students become critical coinvesti-gators in dialogue with the teacher, rather than docile listeners, as in the 'banking' approach to education, the traditional approach to filling essentially passive students with knowledge.

In *Pedagogy of the Oppressed*, Freire contrasted the 'banking' approaches of right-wing and leftist sectarians: the right 'imagines a 'well-behaved' present', seeing adult education in terms of domestication, fitting docile people into existing slots within the status quo; the leftist version sees the future as preordained. Quoting the journalist Alves he argues that both 'suffer from an absence of doubt' (Freire, 1972, p. 18). 'The revolutionary society which practises banking education is either misguided or mistrustful of men [sic]. In either event, it is threatened by the spectre of reaction', he argued (ibid., p. 52). Such a comment could perhaps usefully be related to more recent debates about the different causes of the collapses of socialist governments, twenty years on.

Meanwhile the right sectarian approach could be related to increasing pressures, during the late 1970s and 1980s, for adult education to be increasingly narrowly defined in terms of vocational training (Evans, 1987). Griffin, for instance, has argued that 'The progressive liberal-welfare model of adult education as social policy has been transformed out of recognition in recent years, and is now both fragmented and displaced as adult education has been increasingly discussed in terms of the needs of the economy and manpower planning' (Griffin, 1987 p. 94). Yet, paradoxically, this narrowing of focus has been criticised for being ultimately self-defeating, even in its own terms. Adult learning does not actually fit into such neat categories, and what may be educational and recreational for one person may be vocational for another. In the parliamentary debates on the Further and Higher Education Bill these arguments were developed from different perspectives. From the Labour perspective, Baroness Blackstone criticised the bill's 'unworkable distinction' between so called 'leisure' education courses, which were to be provided by the local education authorities, and the vocational courses and access courses, which were to be provided by the new further-education funding council (Hansard, 1991, col. 1032). And Baroness Seear developed comparable arguments from the Liberal Democrat perspective. She also argued that the distinction between vocational and non-vocational studies was a false one. 'Even flower arranging at adult colleges', she argued, 'can be vocational' even if people jeer at it. 'One can set up a florist's shop and do it very well' (ibid., col. 1038). In any case, participation in adult education was potentially valuable for a number of reasons, including the confidence that people gained in themselves, confidence which could then help people to 'go out and get a job'. Similar points were argued back in 1982, for instance in a report by ACACE: 'We do not think that it is useful to draw artificial boundaries between education and training, between vocational and general education, or between formal or informal systems of provision', the report concluded. Adult learning was taking place in many contexts. Provision needed to recognise this, by being flexible as well as comprehensive (ACACE, 1982).

Ironically too, there have been examples of employers recognising the importance of developing unified approaches towards education and training in both Britain and the USA. Whilst, in general, employers have tended to focus only on the provision of training that is specific to their own needs, there have been recent cases of employers coming to the view that their needs would also be served by the provision of access to more general education that would allow their employees to gain enhanced flexibility and adaptability (for example basic English and maths may be required before employees are able to benefit from more job-specific training, including new-technology training) (Mayo, Meyer and Rosenblum, 1992). Which brings the discussion back to some of the wider connections between community education and training, local economic development strategies, community participation and community development more generally.

Community participation and community development; towards an integrated approach?

So far this chapter has concentrated on issues of resourcing for community participation, community-based service provision and community development. Resources for community participation and community development, including resources for education and training, have been highlighted in terms of their central importance. But even if there were to be a coherent framework for community participation and community development, backed up by continuing resources guaranteed by the public sector, and even if this framework were to include relevant education and training opportunities for community activists and workers as well as for the range of other professionals who work with communities, this would still leave other central questions to be addressed.

In this final section the argument returns to some of the wider questions about the climate for community participation and community development. From the outset the positive contributions of communities, whether in Britain, the USA, Europe or Third-World countries, were set against the effective limits on these contributions, in the context of economic recession, restructuring, structural adjustment and polarisation between rich and poor, both within and between populations in different states. Chapter 3 picked up on some of these themes in relation to goals and strategies for community-based economic development. From the early British colonial programmes for mass education and community development through to contemporary initiatives, in both First and Third Worlds, in urban as well as rural contexts, economic development has been placed upon the community development agenda. Across these very different situations, both official organisations and community-based initiatives have recognised that issues such as community health, housing, education and training cannot be effectively tackled without confronting related issues around poverty and the lack of economic opportunities. These issues have been raised within working-class communities and within women's groups and black and ethnic-minority organisations. And organisations of people with disabilities have similarly raised demands for economic opportunities, and for an end to discrimination in employment and training, as part of an integrated attack on the social creation of dependency (see for example, Oliver, 1990).

Of course the extent to which issues of poverty and lack of economic opportunities can be tackled through community economic development is extremely limited. 'In introducing community economic development it is all too easy to fall into the trap of claiming too much', as a guide to community economic development in the 1990s has pointed out (Henderson, 1991, p. 25). As Chapter 3 emphasised, there has been no suggestion that community economic development could in any way substitute for the economic and political strategies that would be required to make a significant impact on the wider context on a long-term basis. That was not the issue.

But there have been arguments for attempting to make connections, to develop an integrated approach, arguments which have been developed both in Third-World contexts and, more recently, in the European Community. In relation to the development of an integrated approach to development from a community-work perspective at EC level, Frazer, for example, has set out the following features of a model. This model is area based, in geographical terms. It is holistic, recognising the interdependency of social, cultural, recreational, environmental, economic and other factors. There is emphasis on coherent planning and coordination. There is concern for environmental factors. And this approach is based upon participative development, with local people's active involvement in the planning, management and implementation of development (Frazer, 1991).

Frazer accounts for the increasing interest in this type of approach in terms of the need to respond to the failure of economic growth to trickle down, the impact of economic recession, increasing social polarisation and the growth of poverty, concentrated in particular areas in the EC. In addition Frazer argues that there is evidence from specific programmes to demonstrate that an integrated approach can be more effective. But, on the basis of experiences in Ireland for instance, he argues that this will not just happen 'just by someone deciding it should. It needs committed workers and resources' (Frazer, 1991, p. 73).

Nor can integrated local approaches, by themselves, provide solutions to wider problems of poverty and inequality. Frazer is clear that society as a whole has to face up to these issues. Otherwise, if integrated development is offered to poor and disadvantaged communities as a substitute for wider strategies for change, rather than as an integral and complementary aspect of such wider economic, social and political strategies, then the 'frustration, anger and alienation of those who are marginalised will merely be contained and policed in certain areas. . . . 'And Community workers will be in danger of being used as part of this containment process' (ibid., p. 74). The point, then, is absolutely not that community economic development, integrated development, or any other type of community based development could or should be substituted for regional, national or international strategies for development. But local communities' demands for jobs as well as for services do raise these questions about the need for alternative agendas.

The new-right agenda, which relies on market forces to resolve the problems of international recession, has not resulted in sustained economic revival. And far from the benefits of economic growth trickling down, new-right policies have led to increasing polarisation and marginalisation for those who have already been disadvantaged and excluded. Galbraith has described the trickle-down approach as 'the less than elegant metaphor that if one feeds the horse enough oats, some will pass through to the road for the sparrows' (Galbraith, 1992, p. 108). The trouble is that during the eighties the sparrows received proportionately less, despite (or indeed because of). the increased share of the horses. But what alternatives have been on offer?

One of the themes of this book has been that alternative agendas *have* been worked at, at least in terms of developing debates about alternative ways of planning and delivering welfare-state services. Despite all the difficulties there have been attempts to develop more accountable services, with more effective community and user participation, and greater scope for community-based provision of services on a non-profit basis, complementing rather than undermining the jobs of public-sector employees, within the overall framework of a more democratic and more pluralist public sector. There are a range of questions here, questions which could be taken further.

But there seems to have been less discussion of how to link these debates with debates on alternative agendas for economic and social change at national and international level. The new right has been committed to shifting the focus of the policy agenda away from economic and social planning altogether. But this reliance on market mechanisms has proved to be contradictory, even in terms of the new right's own agenda. Galbraith, for instance, has argued that government intervention and planning is 'inescapable as regards the deeply inherent and self-destructive tendencies of the economic system. The dismal consequences, not least for those involved, of the great speculative (and frequently larcenous) activity of the 1980s are wonderfully evident. These could have been averted by timely and responsible regulatory action' (ibid., 1992, p. 179). And Galbraith went on to argue that public action was urgently required to tackle the problems of the underclass, problems which he identified as the 'greatest threat to long-run peace and civility. . . . . Life in the great cities in general could be improved', he argued, 'and only will be improved, by public action – by better schools with better-paid teachers, by strong, well-financed welfare services, by counselling on drug addiction, by employment training, by public investment in the housing that in no industrial country is provided for the poor by private enterprise, by adequately supported health care, recreational facilities, libraries and police. The question once again, much accommodating rhetoric to the contrary, is not what can be done but what will be paid' (ibid., pp. 180–1). But Galbraith was not optimistic about the early prospect of such policies being implemented.

Galbraith has not been alone in arguing that relying too heavily on market mechanisms has proved to be counterproductive, even in its own terms, let alone where issues of social justice have been concerned. Hambleton for instance has argued, on the basis of experiences in both Britain and the USA, that 'as the limitations of relying too heavily upon market mechanisms are becoming apparent, it is possible to foresee a renewed commitment to planning on the part of governments in the 1990s. Even property developers', he went on to argue, 'now recognise the desirability of having clear planning frameworks which give stability to their investments' (Hambleton, 1991, p. 18). This more strategic planned approach to the social, economic and physical environment needs to be balanced, he argued, by greater citizen involvement in public affairs, with transformed relationships between those providing public services and those wishing or needing to use them. 'Somehow a renewed public spirit has to be recreated, Hambleton concluded, 'Without it fire engines will continue to be stoned by the alienated and the angry' (ibid., p. 19). So the case for economic and social planning was to be put back on the agenda, in terms of the enlightened self-interest of those with some stake in the market economy, as well as in terms of the interests of the disadvantaged, the alienated and the angry.

Meanwhile socialist approaches to planning were subjected to so much criticism, both from the new right and from former supporters, that during the 1980s sections of the former left lost confidence in planning altogether, a trend which was exacerbated by the collapse of the former Soviet Union at the end of the decade. But the problems that economic and social planning had been attempting to address remained obstinately unresolved. And for the left that still leaves a series of urgent questions about alternative approaches to planning and the development of socialism that are both effective and take account of the need for greater participation and democracy. This book has emphasised that community-based initiatives cannot and should not be used to substitute for wider strategies for economic, social and political change. But wider strategies to develop alternative and more democratic approaches to economic and social planning could also be related to community-based approaches, developed at local level, drawing upon critical evaluations of actual experiences of community participation and community development.

References

Introduction

Abrahamson, P. (1989) *Future Welfare: Solidarity Towards Year 2000, Summary of Postmodern Welfares: Market, State and Civil Society.* (Roskilde: Institute of Economics and Planning, Roskilde University Centre).

Batley, R. and G. Stoker (1991) *Local Government in Europe* (London: Macmillan).

Berry, L. (1988) 'The Rhetoric of Consumerism and the Exclusion of Community', *Community Development Journal*, vol. 23, no. 4 (October) pp. 266–72.

Blackburn, R. (ed.) (1991) *After the Fall* (London: Verso).

Boddy, M. and C. Fudge (eds) (1984) *Local Socialism* (London: Macmillan), p. 7.

Bowles, S., D. M. Gordon and T. E. Weisskopf (1984) *Beyond the Wasteland* (London: Verso).

Brandt, W. (1980) *North–South: A Programme for Survival* (London: Pan).

Brittain, V. (1992) 'Third World cries out for a 21st century Keynes', the *Guardian*, 24 April, p. 13.

Corrigan, P. (1979) 'Popular Consciousness and Social Democracy', *Marxism Today*, December.

Deakin, N. and A. Wright (eds) (1990) *Consuming Public Services* (London; Routledge).

Duncan, G. (1989) 'A Defence of the Welfare State', in G. Duncan (ed.), (1989) *Democracy and the Capitalist State* (Cambridge University Press).

Friedman, M. (1962) *Capitalism and Freedom* (University of Chicago Press).

Galbraith, J. K. (1990) 'Back to the future', *Observer*, 30 December.

Gaster, L. (1991) *Quality at the Front Line* (Bristol: SAUS).

George, V. and I. Howards (1991) *Poverty Amidst Affluence* (Aldershot: Edward Elgar).

Glennerster, H. and J. Midgely (eds) (1991) *The Radical Right and the Welfare State* (London: Harvester Wheatsheaf).

Harrison, B. and B. Bluestone (1988) *The Great U-Turn* (New York: Basic Books).

Hoggett, P. (1987) 'Political Parties, Community Action and the Reform of Municipal Government in Europe', in P. Hoggett and R. Hambleton.

Hoggett, P. (1990) *Modernisation, Political Strategy and the Welfare State: An Organisational Perspective* (Bristol: SAUS).

Hoggett, P. and R. Hambleton (eds) (1987) *Decentralisation and Democracy* (Bristol: SAUS).

Johnson, N. (1990) *Reconstructing the Welfare State, a Decade of Change* (London: Harvester Wheatsheaf).

Jowell, R., S. Witherspoon and L. Brook (eds) (1989) *British Social Attitudes; Special International Report* (Aldershot: Gower).

Karger, J. H. (1991) 'The radical right and welfare reform in the United States, in H. Glennerster and J. Midgley, 1991.

Le Grand, J. (1990) *Quasi-Markets and Social Policy* (Bristol: School of Advanced Urban Studies).

Le Grand, J. and R. Robinson (eds) (1984) *Privatisation and the Welfare State* (London: Allen and Unwin).

Lipsky, M. and S. Smith (1989–90) 'Nonprofit Organisations, Government and the Welfare State', *Political Science Quarterly*, vol. 104, no. 4.

Loney, M. (1986) *The Politics of Greed* (London: Pluto).

Miliband, R. (1991) 'Reflections on the Crisis of Communist Regimes', in R. Blackburn.

Millar, J. (1991) 'Bearing the Cost', in S. Becker (ed.), *Windows of Opportunity* (London: CPAG).

Mishra, R. (1990) *The Welfare State in Capitalist Society* (London: Harvester Wheatsheaf).

Moser, C. (1989) 'Community Participation in Urban Projects in the Third World', in D. Diamond, J. McLoughlin and B. Massam, *Progress in Planning*, vol. 32, part 2 (Oxford: Pergamon).

Papadakis, E. and P. Taylor Gooby (1987) *The Private Provision of Public Welfare: State, Market and Community* (Brighton: Wheatsheaf).

Phillips, K. (1990) *The Politics of Rich and Poor: Wealth and the American Electorate in the Reagan Aftermath* (New York: Random House).

Rentoul, J. (1989) *Me and Mine* (London: Unwin Hyman).

Social Trends (1992) (HMSO).

Speaker of the House of Commons (1990) *Encouraging Citizenship*, report of the Commission on Citizenship (London: HMSO).

Stewart, J. and K. Walsh (1990) *The Search for Quality* (Birmingham: INLOGOV).

Thatcher, M. (1992) 'Don't undo what I have done', the *Guardian*, 22 April.

Tobin, J. (1981) 'Supply Side Economics; What Is It? Will It Work?', *Economic Outlook*, Summer 1981.

US House of Representatives (1992) 'Overview of Entitlement Programs, 1992 Green Book', Washington, DC, US Government Printing Office, 15 May 1992, pp. 1. 356, quoted in P. Townsend, 'The power of one', in *New Statesman & Society*, 18 September pp. 18–20.

Van Rees, W. (1991) 'Neighbourhoods, the State and Collective Action' in van Rees W. *et al.*, *A Survey of Contemporary Community Development in Europe* (The Hague; Dr Gradus Hedriles-Stichting).

Whitfield, D. (1992) *The Welfare State* (London: Pluto).

Wilson, E. (1991) *The Sphinx and the City* (London: Verso).

1 The Mixed Economy of Welfare

Adams, R. (1990) *Self-Help, Social Work and Empowerment* (London: MacMillan).

Albrow, M. (1970) *Bureaucracy* (London: Pall Mall Press).

Barclay, P. (1982) *Social Workers, Their Roles and Tasks* (London: Bedford Square Press).

Brenton, M. (1985) *The Voluntary Sector in British Social Services* (London: Longman).

Calnan, M. (1991) 'Early to bed with a nice cup of tea', the *Guardian*, 29 March.

Charities Aid Foundation (1991) *Charity Trends 1991* (Charities Aid Foundation).

Crossman, R. H. S. (1976) 'The role of the volunteer in the modern social services; Sidney Ball Memorial lecture 1973', in A. H. Halsey (ed.), *Traditions in Social Policy* (Oxford: Blackwell).

Dale, J. and P. Foster (1986) *Feminists and State Welfare* (London: Routledge and Kegan Paul).

Ferris, J. and E. Graddy (1992) 'Production costs, Transaction costs and Local Government Contractor Choice' unpublished paper, University of Southern California, quoted in R. Gutch.

George, V. and P. Wilding (1976) *Ideology and Social Welfare* (London: Routledge and Kegan Paul).

Gibbons, J. (1990) *Family Support and Prevention: Studies in Local Areas* (London: NISW/HMSO).

Ginsburg, N. (1979) *Class, Capital and Social Policy* (London: MacMillan).

Gough, I. (1979) *The Political Economy of the Welfare State* (London: MacMillan).

Gutch, R. (1992) *Contracting, Lessons from the US* (London: National Council for Voluntary Service Publications).

Hadley, R. and S. Hatch (1981) *Social Welfare and the Failure of the State* (London: Allen and Unwin).

Hayek, F. (1973) *Law, Legislation and liberty: vol. 1 Rules and Order* (London: RKP).

HMSO (1992) *Social Trends* (London HMSO).

Illich, I. (1973) *Deschooling Society* (Handsworth: Penguin).

Johnson, N. (1981) *Voluntary Social Services* (Oxford: Blackwell).

Kramer, R. (1981) *Voluntary Agencies in the Welfare State* (Berkeley: University of California Press).

Kramer, R. and P. Terrell (1984) *Social Services Contracting in the Bay Area* (Berkeley, California: Institute of Governmental Studies, University of California).

Le Grand, J. (1985) 'Making Redistribution Work: The Social Services', in H. Glennerster (ed.), *The Future of the Welfare State*, 2nd edn, (Aldershot: Gower).

Lipsky, M. and S. R. Smith (1989–90) 'Nonprofit Organisations, Government and the Welfare State', *Political Science Quarterly*, vol. 104, no. 4 (Winter) pp. 625–49.

Miliband, R. (1969) *The State in Capitalist Society* (London: Weidenfeld and Nicolson).

Mishra, R. (1990) *Welfare State in Capitalist Society* (London: Harvester Wheatsheaf).

Murray, C. (1990) *The Emerging British Underclass* (London: The IEA Health and Welfare).

Navarro, V. (1986) 'The 1980 and 1984 elections and the New Deal', in R. Miliband, J. Saville, M. Liebman and L. Panitch (eds) *Socialist Register 1985/86* (London: Merlin Press).

NCVO News (1992) no. 31 (Jan./Feb.) (London: National Council for Voluntary Service).

Nyden, P. and W. Wiewel (eds) (1991) *Challenging Uneven Development* (New Brunswick: Rutgers University Press).

Offe, C. (1984) J. Keane (ed.), *Contradictions of the Welfare State* (London: Hutchinson).

Ruzek, S. B. (1978) *The Women's Health Movement* (New York: Praeger).

Sugden R. (1984) 'Voluntary Organisations and the Welfare State', in J. Le Grand and R. Robinson (eds) *Privatisation and the Welfare State* (London: Allen and Unwin).

Titmuss, R. (1963) 'The Social Division of Welfare', in R. Titmuss, *Essays on the Welfare State* (London: Allen and Unwin).

Titmuss, R. (1968) 'Welfare State and Welfare Society', in R. Titmuss, *Commitment to Welfare* (London: Allen and Unwin).

Titmuss, R. (1970) *The Gift Relationship* (London: Allen and Unwin).

Titmuss, R. (1974) *Social Policy* (London: Allen and Unwin).

Voluntary Action Research (1991) 'The (1991) National Survey of Voluntary Activity in the UK' (Berkhamsted: The Volunteer Centre, UK).

Walker, A. (1984) 'The Political Economy of Privatisation' in J. Le Grand and R. Robinson (eds) *Privatisation and the Welfare State* (London: Allen and Unwin).

Ward, C. (1976) *Housing, an Anarchist Approach* (London: Freedom Press).

Webb, A. and G. Wistow (1987) *Social Work, Social Care and Social Planning* (London: Longman).

Whitfield, D. (1992) *The Welfare State* (London: Pluto).

Wilensky, H. and C. Lebeaux (1965) *Industrial Society and Social Welfare: the impact of industrialization on the supply and organization of social welfare services in the United States* (London: Collier Macmillan) reprint.

Williams, F. (1989) *Social Policy* (Cambridge: Polity Press).

Wilson, E. (1977) *Women and the Welfare State* (London: Tavistock).

2   The Shifting Concept of Community

Association of Metropolitan Authorities (AMA) (1989) *Community Development: The Local Authority Role* (London: AMA).

Alinsky, S. (1971) *Rules for Radicals* (New York: Vintage).

Baldwin, S. and J. Twigg (1991) 'Women and Community Care', in Maclean, M. and D. Groves (eds) *Women's Issues in Social Policy* (London: Routledge).

Bamberger, M. (1988) *The Role of Community Participation in Development Planning and Project Management* (Washington: World Bank).

Barrett, M. and M. McIntosh (1985) 'Ethnocentrism and Socialist Feminist Theory', *Feminist Review*, no. 20.

Bell, D. (1956) 'The Theory of Mass Society', *Commentary*, July, 1956.

Bryant, R. (1972) 'Community Action', *British Journal of Social Work*, vol. 2, no. 2, pp. 206, 208.

Bulmer, M. (1987) *The Social Basis of Community Care* (London: Allen and Unwin).

Byrne, D. (1989) *Beyond the Inner City* (Milton Keynes: Open University Press).

Caloustie Gulbenkian Foundation (1968) *Community Work and Social Change: A Report on Training* (Harlow: Longman).

Carby, H. (1982) 'White Women Listen, Black Feminism and the Boundaries of Sisterhood', in Centre for Contemporary Cultural Studies, *The Empire Strikes Back* (London: Hutchinson, with Centre for Contemporary Cultural Studies).

Cary, L. (ed.) (1970) *Community Development as a Process* (Columbia: University of Minnesota Press).

Castells, M. (1977) *The Urban Question* (London: Edward Arnold).

Castells, M. (1978) *City, Class and Power* (London: Macmillan).

Castells, M. (1983) *The City and the Grassroots* (London: Edward Arnold).

Colonial Office (1943) *Mass Education in African Society* (London: Colonial Office).

Cooper, J. (1989) 'From Casework to Community Care', *British Journal of Social Work*, vol. 19, p. 183.

Craig, G. and D. Corkey (1978) 'CDP: Community work or class politics', in P. Curno (ed.), *Political Issues and Community Work* (London: Routledge and Kegan Paul).

Du Sautoy, P. (1958) *Community Development in Ghana* (Oxford University Press).

Fainstein, S. and N. Fainstein (1991) 'The Changing Character of Community Politics in New York City', in J. Mollenkopf and M. Castells (eds) *Dual City* (New York. Russel Sage Foundation).

Finch, J. and D. Groves (eds) (1983) *A Labour of Love: Women, Work and Caring* (London: Routledge and Kegan Paul).

Gans, H. (1962) *The Urban Villagers* (New York: Free Press).

Griffiths, Sir R. (1988) *Community Care: Agenda For Action* (London: HMSO).

Habermas, J. (1980) *Legitimation Crisis* (London: Heinemann) reprint.

Harvey, D. (1989) *The Urban Experience* (Oxford: Basil Blackwell).

hooks, b. (1982) *Ain't I a Woman?: Black Women and Feminism* (London: Pluto).

Keane, J. (ed.) (1984) *C. Offe: Contributions of the Welfare State* (London: Hutchinson).

Kramer, R. (1969) *Participation of the Poor* (New Jersey: Prentice-Hall).

Loney, M. (1983) *Community Against Government* (London: Heinemann).

Lowe, S. (1986) *Urban Social Movements* (London: Macmillan).

McAdam, D. (1988) *Freedom Summer* (Oxford University Press).

Manghezi, A. (1976) *Class, Elite and Community* (Uppsala: The Scandinavian Institute of African Studies).

Meikins Wood, E. (1988) 'The Uses and Abuses of "Civil Society"', in A. Melucci, *Nomads of the Present*, J. Keane and P. Mier (eds), (London: Hutchinson).

Melucci, A. (1988) *Nomads of the Present*, J. Keane and P. Meir (eds) (London: Hutchinson).

Miliband, R. and L. Panitch (eds) (1990) *Socialist Register 1990* (London: Merlin).

Milson, F. (1974) *An Introduction to Community Work* (London: Routledge and Kegan Paul).

Moser, C. (1989) 'Gender Planning in the Third World: Meeting Practical and Strategic Needs', *World Development*, vol. 17, no. 11.

Moser, C. (1989) 'Community Participation in Urban Projects in the Third World', *Progress in Planning*, D. Diamond, J. McLoughlin and B. Massam (eds), vol 32, part 2 (1989) (Oxford: Pergamon).

Murray, R. (1988) 'Life after Henry (Ford)', *Marxism Today* (October) pp. 8–13.

Nehru, J. (1957) *Community Development* (New Delhi: Ministry of Community Development).

Report of the Commission on Citizenship (1990) *Encouraging Citizenship* (London: HMSO).

Samuel, R. *et al.* (eds) (1985) *The Enemy Within: Pit Villages and the Miners' Strike of 1984–85* (London: Routledge and Kegan Paul).

Scott, A. (1990) *Ideology and the New Social Movements* (London: Allen and Unwin).

Segal, L. (1987) *Is the Future Female?* (London: Virago).

Stacey, M. (1969) 'The Myth of Community Studies', *British Journal of Sociology,* vol. 20, p. 134.

Toennies, F. (1957) *Community and Society* (Lansing, Michigan: Michigan State University Press).

Touraine, A. (1974) *The Post Industrial Society* (London: Wildwood House).

Ungerson, C. (1987) *Policy is Personal: sex, gender and informal care* (London: Tavistock).

Waddington, D., M. Wykes and C. Critcher (1991) *Split at the Seams? Community, continuity and change after the 1984–5 coal dispute* (Buckingham: Open University Press).

Wellman, B. (1979) 'The Community Question: the Intimate Networks of East Yorker', *American Journal of Sociology*, vol 84, no. 5, pp. 1201–31.

Williams, F. (1989) *Social Policy* (Cambridge: Polity Press).

Williams, R. (1976) *Keywords* (London: Croom Helm).

Willmoth, P. (1984) *Community in Social Policy* (London: Policy Studies Institute).

Yeo, E. and S. Yeo (1988) 'On the Uses of Community', in S. Yeo (ed.), *New Views of Co-operation* (London: Routledge).

Young, M. and P. Willmott (1957) *Family and Kinship in East London* (London: Routledge and Kegan Paul).

3 Policies for Jobs and Training

Abel-Smith, B. and P. Townsend (1965) *The Poor and the Poorest* (London: Bell).

Audit Commission (1989) *Urban Regeneration and Economic Development: The Local Authority Dimension* (London: HMSO).

Batten, T. (1957) *Communities and their Development* (Oxford University Press).

Blunkett, D. and K. Jackson (1987) *Democracy in Crisis* (London: Hogarth).

Boddy, M. and C. Fudge (eds) (1984) *Local Socialism?* (London: MacMillan).

Brehm, R. (1991) 'The City and the Neighbourhoods: Was It Really a Two-Way Street?', in P. Clavel and W. Wiewel (eds) *Harold Washington and the Neighbourhoods* (New Brunswick: Rutgers University Press).

Brownhill, S. (1990) 'The People's Plan for the Royal docks: Some contradictions in popular planning', in J. Montgomery and A. Thornley (eds) *Radical Planning Initiatives: new directions in the 1990s* (Aldershot: Gower).

Butcher, H. *et al.* (1990) *Local Government and Thatcherism* (London: Routledge and Kegan Paul).

Byrne, D. (1989) *Beyond the Inner City* (Milton Keynes: Open University Press).

Centre for Local Economic Strategies (1987) *Against the Odds* (Manchester: Centre for Local Economic Strategies).

CIPFA (1985) *Employment and Industrial Development – Local Authority Initiatives* (CIPFA).

Clavel, P. (1986) *The Progressive City* (New Brunswick: Rutgers University Press).

Clavel, P. and Wiewel, W. (1991) *Harold Washington and the Neighbourhoods* (New Brunswick: Rutgers University Press).

Community Development Project (1977) *The Costs of Industrial Change* (CDP, IIU).

Colenutt, B. (1988) 'Local Democracy and Inner City Regeneration', *Local Economy*, vol. 3, no. 2 (August), pp. 119–25, 124–5.

Costello, N., J, Michie and S. Milne (1989) *Beyond the Casino Economy* (London: Verso).

Craig, G. (1989) 'Community Work and the State', *Community Development Journal*, vol. 24, no. 1, (January) pp. 3–18.

Duncan, S. and M. Goodwin (1988) *The Local State and Uneven Development* (Oxford: Blackwell).

Fitzgerald Ely, J. and K. Cox (1990) 'Urban Economic Development Strategies in the USA', *Local Economy*, vol. 4, no. 4, (February) pp. 278–89.

Gaster, L. (1991) *Quality at the Front Line* (Bristol: SAUS).

Gills, D. (1991) 'Chicago Politics and Community Development: A Social movement Perspective', in Clavel, P. and W. Wiewel, *Harold Washington and the Neighbourhoods* (New Brunswick: Rutgers University Press).

George, V. and N. Manning (1980) *Socialism, Social Welfare and the Soviet Union* (London: Routledge and Kegan Paul).

Giloth, R. (1990) 'Beyond Common Sense: The Baltimore Renaissance', *Local Economy*, vol. 4, no. 4, (February), pp. 290–7.

Gough, J. (1986) 'Industrial policy and socialist strategy: Restructuring and the unity of the working class', *Capital and Class*, vol. 29.

Gyford, J. (1985) *The Politics of Local Socialism* (London: Allen and Unwin).

Hambleton, R. (1989) 'Boomtown Houston?', *Local Economy*, vol. 3, no. 4, pp. 273–8.

Henderson, P. (ed.) (1991) *Signposts to Community Economic Development* (London: Community Development Foundation Publications).

Loney, M. (1983) *Community Against Government* (London: Heinemann).

Mackintosh, M. and H. Wainwright (eds) (1987) *A Taste of Power: the Politics of Local Economics* (London: Verso).

Marris, P. and M. Rein (1972) *Dilemmas of Social Reform*, 2nd edn (London: Routledge and Kegan Paul).

Massey, D. (1982) 'Enterprise Zones: a Political Issue', *International Journal of Urban and Regional Research*, vol. 6, no. 4, pp. 429–34.

Mayo, M. (1989) 'Editorial Introduction: Community Development and Jobs: Local Economic Struggles in a Multinational Context', *Community Development Journal*, vol. 24, no. 2, (April) pp. 92–4.

Meyer, P. and R. Kraushaar, (1989) 'The Grass is always Greener', *Community Development Journal*, vol. 24, no. 2, (April) pp. 95–100.

Mishra, R. (1990) *The Welfare State in Capitalist Society* (London: Harvester Wheatsheaf).

Moynihan, D. (1969) *Maximum Feasible Misunderstanding* (New York: Free Press).

Murray, U. (1989) 'Public Sector Jobs and Services for Community Needs', *Community Development Journal*, vol. 24, no. 2 (April) pp. 101–10.

Newman, I. (1989) 'Locally Relevant Job Creation in the U.K.', *Community Development Journal*, vol. 24, no. 2, (April) pp. 120–6.

Newman, I. (1991) 'Surviving in a Cold Climate: Local Authority Economic Strategy Today', *Local Economy*, vol. 5, no. 4 (February) pp. 293–304.

Robinson, F. and K. Shaw (1991) 'Urban Regeneration and Community Involvement', *Local Economy*, vol. 6, no. 1, (May) pp. 61–73.

Shutt, J. (1984) 'Tory enterprise zones and the labour movement', *Capital and Class*, no. 23, (Summer) pp. 19–44.

Smith, T. (1990) 'Community work, the Inner City and Jobs', *British Journal of Social Work*, vol. 20, p. 254.

Tyne and Wear Development Corporation (1988) *Forward to 1991* (Newcastle, Tyne and Wear Development Corporation).

Wiewel, W. (1990) 'Economic Development in Chicago; The Growth Machine Meets the Neighbourhood Movement', *Local Economy*, vol. 4, no. 4, (February) pp. 307–16.

Wiewel, W. and N. Rieser (1989) 'The Limits of Progressive Municipal Economic Development,', *Community Development Journal*, vol. 24, no. 2 (April) pp. 111–19.

Whitfield, D. (1992) *The Welfare State* (London: Pluto).

4 Some International Comparisons from the North

Association of Metropolitan Authorities (AMA) (1990) *Contracts for Social Care* (London: AMA).

Baine, S., J. Benington and J. Russell (1992) *Changing Europe: Challenges facing the Voluntary and Community Sectors in the 1990s* (London: NCVO Publications and Community Development Foundation).

Benington, J. (1991) 'Social Impact of the Single European Market: the Challenges Facing Voluntary and Community Organisations', *Community Development Journal*, vol. 26, no. 2, (April) p. 87.

Brauns, H. and D. Kramer (1989) 'West Germany – the break up of consensus and the demographic threat', in B. Munday (ed.), *The Crisis of Welfare* (London: Harvester Wheatsheaf).

Brenton, M. (1985) *The Voluntary Sector in British Social Services* (London: Longman).

Castles, F. (1978) *The Social Democratic Image of Society* (London: Routledge and Kegan Paul).

Clavel, P. (1986) *The Progressive City* (New Brunswick: Rutgers University Press).

Chamberlayne, P. (1990) 'Neighbourhood and tenant Participation in the GDR', in B. Deacon and J. Szalai.

Conroy, P. (1990) 'The Case of Western Europe: integration and change in the EEC – the Fortress and the Excluded', *Community Development Journal*, vol. 25, no. 4, (October) p. 297.

Deacon, B. and J. Szalai (1990) *Social Policy in the New Eastern Europe* (Avebury: Gower).

Dennett, J., E. James, G. Room and P. Watson (1982) *Europe Against Poverty* (London: Bedford Square Press).

Esping-Andersen, G. (1990) *The Three Worlds of Welfare* (Cambridge: Polity Press).

Evers, A., H. Nowotny and H. Wintersberger (eds) (1987) *The Changing Face of Welfare* (Aldershot: Gower)..

Ferge, Z. (1990) 'The fourth road: the future for Hungarian social policy', in B. Deacon and J. Szalai, 1990.

Fox Piven, F. and R. Cloward (1982) *The New Class War* (New York: Pantheon.

George, V. and N. Manning (1980) *Socialism, Social Welfare and the Soviet Union* (London: Routledge and Kegan Paul).

Gould, A. (1988) *Conflict and Control in Welfare policy: the Swedish Experience* (London: Routledge and Kegan Paul).

Grahl, J. and P. Teague (1990) *The Future of the European Community* (London: Lawrence and Wishart).

Grunow, D. (1986) 'Debureaucratisation and the Self Help Movement', in E. Oyen (ed.), *Comparing Welfare States and their Futures* (Aldershot: Gower).

Gutch, R. (1992) *Contracting: Lessons from the US* (London: NCVO).

Harrison, B. and B. Bluestone (1988) *The Great U-Turn* (New York: Basic Books).

Hegelson, A. (1989) 'USSR: the Implications of Glasnost and Perestroika', in B. Munday (ed.), *The Crisis of Welfare* (London: Harvester Wheatsheaf).

Jacobs, B. (1992) *Fractured Cities: capitalism, community and empowerment in Britain and America* (London: Routledge).

Kohn, R. (1977) *Coordination of Health and Welfare Services in 4 Countries* (Geneva: World Health Organisation).

Lanning, H. (1981) *Government and Voluntary Sector in USA* (London: NCVO).

Lees, R. and M. Mayo (1984) *Community Action for Change* (London: Routledge and Kegan Paul).

Littlejohn, G. (1984) *A Sociology of the Soviet Union* (London: Macmillan).

Lodge, J. (1989) *Social Europe: Fostering a People's Europe* (London: Pinter).

McConnell, C. (1990) 'Foreword', in C. McConnell (ed.), *A Citizen's Europe* (London: Community Development Foundation).

McConnell, C. (1991) 'Community Development in Five European Countries', *Community Development Journal*, vol. 26, no. 2 (April) p. 107.

Matzat, J. (1989) 'Some Remarks on West Germany's Health and Welfare system', in S. Humble and J. Unell (eds) *Self-Help in Health and Welfare in England and West Germany* (London: Routledge).

Meyer, P. and R. Kraushaar (1989) 'The Grass is always Greener', *Community Development Journal*, vol. 24, no. 2, (April) pp. 95–10.

Mishra, R. (1990) *The Welfare State in Capitalist Society* (London: Harvester Wheatsheaf).

Neuberger, H. (1989) *The Economics of 1992* (London: British Labour Group of MPs).

Nunes, H. (1990) 'A View from Portugal' (Community Development Foundation, 60 Highbury Grove, London N5 2AG).

Nygren, J. (1989) 'Sweden', in Council of Europe Standing Conference of Local and Regional Authorities of Europe, conference on 'Free Local Government: Deregulation, Efficiency, Democracy', held in Sweden, 28–30 June 1988 (Strasbourg: Council of Europe Standing Conference of Local and Regional Authorities of Europe).

Parkin, F. (1972) *Class, Inequality and Political Order* (St Albans: Paladin).

Rajan, A. (1990) *A Zero Sum Game* (London: The Industrial Society Press).

Room, G. (1990) *New Poverty in the European Community* (London: Macmillan).

Rossell, T. and C. Rimbau (1989) 'Spain: Social Services in the Post/ Franco Democracy', in B. Munday (ed.), *The Crisis of Welfare* (London: Harvester Wheatsheaf).

Rubiol, G. (1990) 'A View from Spain', in Community Development Foundation.

Sivanandan, A. (1988) 'The New Racism', *New Statesman and Society*, 4 November.

Tausz, K. (1990) 'The Case of Eastern Europe: Why Community development still has to find a role in Hungary', *Community Development Journal*, vol. 25, no. 4 (October) pp. 30–6.

Thomas, D. (1990) 'A View of 1992 from Britain', in Community Development Foundation 1990.

Tricert, J.- P. (1989) 'Community Action to Combat Poverty', *Social Europe* (January) (Luxemburg: EEC) p. 112.

Van Rees, W. (1990) 'A View of 1992 from the Netherlands', in Commission of the European Communities, *A Citizen's Europe* (London: Community Development Foundation, 60 Highbury Grove, London, N5 2AG).

Varga, T. and I. Vercseg (1992) 'An Experiment in Community Development in the Bakony, Hungary', *Community Development Journal*, vol. 27, no. 1, pp. 50–9.

Wilson, D. (1979) *The Welfare State in Sweden* (London: Heineman).

Zapf, W. (1986) 'Development Structure and Prospects for the German Social State', in R. Rose and R. Shiratori (eds) *The Welfare State East and West* (Oxford University Press).

5 Some International Comparisons from the South

Afshar, H. (1991) *Women, Development and Survival in the Third World* (London: Longman).

Botha, T. and S. Kaplinsky (1989) 'Some Preliminary Thoughts on Alternative Housing Strategies for a Free and Democratic South Africa' paper presented at the Seminar on Local Government, under the Auspices of the South African Study Programme, Held in Harare, from 1–4 November (1989.

Boyer, D. (1990) *The role of northern NGOs in the promotion of sustainable development in Africa* (Edinburgh: Centre of African Studies, University of Edinburgh), occasional paper no. 28.

Bryant, J. (1969) *Health and the Developing World* (Cornell University Press).

Burgess, R. (1982) 'Self-help housing advocacy: a curious form of radicalism. A critique of the work of John F. C. Turner', in P. Ward (ed.), *Self-Help Housing: A Critique* (London: Mansell).

Burnell, P. (1992) 'Debate: NGOs and Poverty; Third World Charities in a Changing World', *Community Development Journal*, vol. 27, no. 3 (July) pp. 290–302.

Centre for Development Studies (1990) *Report on the ANC National Consultative Conference on Local Government, Johannesburg, October 1990* (Bellville: Centre for Development Studies, University of Western Cape).

Constantino-David, K. (1990) 'The Limits and Possibilities of Philippine NGOs in Development', paper for University of the Philippines Round Table Discussion on Non-Government Organisations and People's Participation, 9 March (1990).

Darke, R., with D. Alexander, J. Darke and A. Manogue (n.d.) 'Housing in Nicaragua' unpublished paper, University of Sheffield.

Development Dialogue (1982) *Another Development with Women* (Uppsala: Development Dialogue).

Dore, R. and Z. Mar (eds) (1981) *Community Development: Comparative Case Studies in India, the Republic of Korea, Mexico and Tanzania* (London: Croom Helm).

Dwyer, D. (1975) *People and Housing in Third World Cities* (New York: Longman).

Frank, A. G. (1969) *Latin America: Underdevelopment or Revolution* (New York: Monthly Review Press).

Holloway, R. (1989) *Doing Development* (London: Earthscan Publications).

ifda Dossier 79 (1990) 'African Charter for Popular Participation in Development and Transformation', ifda, Nyon, Oct/Dec, pp. 3–16.

Illich, I. (1975) *Medical Nemesis: The Expropriation of Health* (London: Calder and Boyars).

Jain, L., B. Krishnamurty and P. Tripathi (1985) *Grass without Roots* (London and New Delhi: Sage).

Lund, F. (1990) 'Some Issues in the Financing of Welfare in South Africa', paper presented at the Conference on Health and Welfare in South Africa, held in Maputo, April.

Lund, F. (1991) 'Women, Welfare and the Community', paper presented at the Conference on Women and Gender in Southern Africa, Durban, 1991, Centre for Social and Development Studies, University of Natal, Durban.

MacPherson, S. (1982) *Social Policy in the Third World* (Brighton: Wheatsheaf).

MacPherson, S. (1987) 'Social Policy and Development', *Social Policy and Administration*, vol. 21, no. 3, pp. 215–17.

Marsden, D. and P. Oakley (1982) 'Radical community development in the Third World', in G. Craig, N. Derricourt and M. Loney (eds) *Community work and the State* (London: Routledge and Kegan Paul).

Marshall, G., D. Rose, H. Newby and C. Vogler (1988) *Social Class in Modern Britain* (London: Unwin Hyman).

Massey, D. (1987) *Nicaragua* (Milton Keynes: Open University Press).

Matiwana, M. and S. Walters (1986) *The Struggle for Democracy* (Bellville: Centre for Adult and Continuing Education, University of the Western Cape).

Mayo, M. (1975) 'Community Development: A Radical Alternative?', in Bailey, R. and M. Brake (eds) *Radical Social Work* (London: Edward Arnold).

Midgely, J. with A. Hall, M. Hardiman and D. Navine (1986) *Community Development, Social Development and the State* (London: Methuen).

Mitter, S. (1986) *Common Fate, Common Bond* (London: Pluto).

Moser, C. (1989) 'Community Participation in Urban Projects in the Third World', in D. Diamond, J. McLoughlin and B. Massam (eds) *Progress in Planning*, vol. 32, part 2.

Moser, C. and L. Peake (eds) (1987) *Women, Human Settlements and Housing* (London: Tavistock).

Muller, J. (1987) 'People's Education and the National Education Crisis Committee', *South African Review*, no. 4, G. Moss and I. Obery (eds) (Johannesburg: Ravan Press).

Mutiso, R. (1986) 'Kenya and the Future of the Welfare State', in E. Oyen (ed.), *Comparing Welfare States and their Futures* (Aldershot: Gower).

Nash, J. and M. Fernandez Kelly (1983) *Women, Men and the International Division of Labour* (New York: State University of New York Press).

Rahman, A. (1990) 'The Case of Third World Development: People's Self-Development', *Community Development Journal*, vol. 25, no. 4 (October) pp. 307–14.

Rupesinghe, K. (1986) 'The Welfare State in Sri Lanka,' in E. Oyen (ed.), *Comparing Welfare States and their Futures* (Aldershot: Gower).

Schlyter, A. (1984) *Upgrading Reconsidered – The George Studies in Retrospect* (Gavle, Sweden: The National Swedish Institute for Building Research).

Schlyter, A. (1988) *Women Householders and Housing Strategies: the case of George, Zambia* (Gavle, Sweden: The National Swedish Institute for Building Research).

Skinner, R. and M. Rodell (1983) *People, Poverty and Shelter* (London: Methuen).

South African Institute of Race Relations (1990) *Social and Economic Update 5*, 1988 and *Update 9*, July 1989–December 1989 (Braamfontein: South African Institute of Race Relations).

Thomas, B. (1985) *Politics, Participation and Poverty: development through self-help in Kenya* (Boulder: Westview Press).

Turner, J. and R. Fichter (1972) *Freedom to Build: Dweller Control of the Housing Process* (New York: Macmillan).

Vance, I. (1987) 'More than bricks and mortar: women's participation in self-help housing in Managua, Nicaragua', in C. Moser and L. Peake.

Walters, S. (1993) 'Non-Governmental Organizations and the South African State', *Community Development Journal*, vol. 28 (January), pp. 1–10.

Ward, P. (ed.) (1982) *Self-help Housing: a Critique* (London: Mansell).

Ward, P. (1989) *Corruption, Development and Inequality* (London: Routledge and Kegan Paul).

UN Centre for Human Settlements (Habitat) (1989) *Cooperative Housing: Experiences of Mutual Self Help* (Nairobi).

6   The Changing Role and Potential of the Non-Statutory Community Sector in Britain

Andrews, G. (ed.) (1991) *Citizenship* (London: Lawrence & Wishart).

Association of Metropolitan Authorities (AMA) (1989) *Community Development: The Local Authority Role* (London: AMA).

Association of Metropolitan Authorities with Federation of Community Work Training Groups (AMA) (1991) *Learning for Action: Community Work and Participative Training* (London: AMA).

Barclay Report (1982) *Social Workers, their Role and Tasks* (London: National Institute for Social Workers).

Barr, A. (1991) *Practising Community Development* (London: Community Development Foundation).

Brenton, M. (1985) *The Voluntary Sector in British Social Services* (London: Longman).

Broad, B. (1991) *Punishment under Pressure* (London: Jessica Kingsley).

Bryant, R. (1982) 'The New Slums – Community Action Response', in P. Henderson, A. Wright and K. Wyncoll (eds) *Successes and Struggles on Council Estates: Tenant Action and Community Work* (London: Association of Community Workers).

Caloustie Gulbenkian Foundation (1973) *The Community Work Study Group: Current Issues in Community Work* (London: Routledge and Kegan Paul).

Camden Council (1990) *Camden Housing Strategy* (London: Camden Council).

Camden Tenant, July 1991 p. 3.

Chanan, G. (1991) *Taken for Granted* (London: Community Development Foundation).

Charities: A Framework for the Future (1989) Cmnd 694 (London: HMSO).

Clarke, R. (ed.) (1990) *Enterprising Neighbours: The Development of the Community Association Movement in Britain* (London: National Federation of Community Organisations, with the Community Projects Foundation).

Cockburn, C. (1977) *The Local State* (London: Pluto).

Community Development Foundation and the National Coalition for Neighbourhoods (1991) *Taking Communities Seriously: A Policy Prospectus for Community Development and Local Democracy* (London: CDF: Northampton: National Coalition for Neighbourhoods).

Cowley, J. (1979) *Housing for People or Profit?* (London: Stage One).

CPF (1988) *Action for Health* (London: Community Projects Foundation, Health Education Authority, The Scottish Health Education Group).

Davies, C. and D. Crousaz (1982) *Local Authority Community Work: Realities of Practice* (London: HMSO).

Donnison, D. (1991) 'Foreword', in A. Barr, 1991.

Francis, D., P. Henderson and D. Thomas (1984) *A Survey of Community Workers in the United Kingdom* (London: National Institute for Social Work).

Gibbons, J. and S. Thorpe (1989) *Family Support and Prevention: Report to the Joseph Rowntree Memorial Trust* (London: National Institute for Social Work).

Griffiths, Sir R. (1988) *Community Care: Agenda for Action* (London: HMSO).

Griffiths, Sir R. (1992) 'With the Past Behind Us', *Community Care*, 16 (January) p. 21.

Harding, J. (ed.) (1987) *Probation and the Community* (London: Tavistock).

Haringey Council (1990) *Haringey Voluntary Sector Resources Booklet* (London: Haringey Council).

Hatchett, W. (1992) 'Do's and don'ts of campaigning', *Community Care*, 12 March, Issue 906, p. 12.

Henderson, P., A. Wright and K. Wyncoll (eds) (1982) *Successes and Struggles on Council Estates* (Association of Community Workers).

Hirst, P. (1991) 'Labour and the Constitutional Crisis', in G. Andrews (ed.), *Citizenship* (London: Lawrence and Wishart).

Holman, R. (1983) *Resourceful Friends* (London: The Children's Society).

Hough, M. and P. Mayhew (1985) *Taking Account of Crime: key findings from the second British Crime Survey* (London: HMSO).

Knight, B. and R. Hayes (1981) *Self-Help in the Inner City* (London: London Voluntary Service Council).

Johnson, N. (1981) *Voluntary Social Services* (Oxford: Blackwell).

Labour Community Action *Labour and the Voluntary Sector* (London: Labour Community Action) (n.d.).

Levick, P. (1992) 'The janus face of community care legislation: an opportunity for radical possibilities?', *Critical Social Policy*, Issue 34, (Summer) pp. 75–92.

London Voluntary Service Council (1988) *Developing a Voluntary Sector Strategy* (London: LVSC).

Metro Rochdale (1989) *Learning in Action: the Report of Metro Rochdale's Community Education Review* (Metro Rochdale, Community Education Service, Education Department, October).

Metro Rochdale (1991) 'Local Democracy in Rochdale: Further Proposals', Joint Report of Chief Executive and Acting Director of Neighbourhood Services, Neighbourhood Services Committee, 26 May 1991, Policy and Resources Committee 17 June 1991 (Metro Rochdale).

Murray, G. (1969) *Voluntary Organisations and Social Welfare* (Glasgow: Oliver and Boyd).

National Council for Voluntary Service (NCVS) (1989) *Contracting In or Out?* (London: NCVO).

National Council for Voluntary Service (NCVS) (1990) *Cause and Effect: a survey of campaigning in the voluntary sector* (London: NCVO).

National Council for Voluntary Service (NCVS) (1991) *A Contracting Sector* (London: NCVO).

NCVO News (1992) no. 31 (January–February).

Oxfordshire Social Services (1992) 'The Community Care Plan 1992–1993' (Oxfordshire: Oxfordshire Social Services).

Parekh, B. (1991) 'British Citizenship and Cultural Difference', in G. Andrews, 1991.

Phelan, J. (1983) *Family Centres* (London: Children's Society).

Phillips, A. (1991) 'Citizenship and Feminist Politics', in G. Andrews, 1991.

Powell, T. (1987) *Self-Help Organisations and Professional Practice* (Silver Spring, Maryland: National Association of Social Workers).

Powell, T. (ed.) (1990) *Working with Self-Help* (Silver Spring, Maryland: NASW Press).

Richardson, A. (1984) *Working with Self-Help Groups: a guide for local professionals* (London: NCVO).

Ungerson, C. (1987) *Policy is Personal: sex, gender and informal care* (London: Tavistock).

Wann, M. (1992) 'Self-Help Groups: Is There Room for Volunteers?', in R. Hedley and J. Davis Smith (eds) *Volunteering and Society* (London: NCVO).

Willmott, P. (1989) *Community Initiatives* (London: Policy Studies Institute).

7 Community Participation in Planning and Community Service Provision

Association of Metropolitan Authorities (AMA) (1990) *Contracts for Social Care: the local authority view* (London: AMA).

Audit Commission for Local Authorities in England and Wales (1988) *The Competitive Council* (London: Audit Commission).

Barr, A. (1991) *Practising Community Development* (London: Community Development Foundation).

Beresford, P. and S. Croft (1986) *Whose Welfare? Private Care or Public Services?* (Brighton: Lewis Cohen Urban Studies at Brighton Polytechnic).

Beresford, P. and S. Croft (1993) *Citizen Involvement* (London: Macmillan).

Brenton, M. (1985) *The Voluntary Sector in British Social Services* (London: Longman).

Broady, M. and R. Hedley (1989) *Working Partnerships* (London: Bedford Square Press).

Bryant, R. (1982) 'The New Slums – Community Action Response', in P. Henderson, A. Wright and K. Wyncoll (eds) *Successes and Struggles on Council Estates* (London: Association of Community Workers).

Bulmer, M. (1986) *Neighbours: The Work of Philip Abrams* (Cambridge University Press).

Camden Tenant, June 1990.

Clode, D. (1992) 'Users angered by poor services', in *Community Care*, 16 April, p. 5.

Community Care: A Reader (1993) edited by Joanna Bornat, Charmaine Pereira, David Pilgrim, Fiona Williams (Macmillan in association with The Open University).

Davies, A. and K. Edwards (1990) *Twelve Charity Contracts* (London: Directory of Social Change).

Dearlove, J. (1973) *The Politics of Policy in Local Government* (Cambridge University Press).

Donnison, D. (1991) 'Foreword', in A. Barr, *Practising Community Development* (London: Community Development Foundation).

Ferguslie Park Partnership (1989) *Strategy for the Regeneration of Ferguslie Park* (printed in Scotland for HMSO).

Ferguslie Park Area Board (1990) *Evaluation of Ferguslie League of Action Groups: Report by the Joint Evaluation Panel* (Ferguslie Park, Paisley: Ferguslie Park Area Board).

Fielding, N., G. Reeve and M. Simey (1991) *Active Citizens: new voices and values* (London: Bedford Square Press).

Harloe, M. (1975) *Swindon: A Town in Transition* (London: Heinemann).

Hedley, R. and J. Davis Smith (1992) *Volunteering and Society: Principles and Practice* (London: Bedford Square Press).

Henderson, P. and D. Thomas (1980) *Skills in Neighbourhood Work* (London: Allen and Unwin).

Kilburn Vale News (1991) The Newsletter of Kilburn Housing Co-operative, (August).

LGIU (1988) *Consumer Liaison and Compulsory Tendering* (London: Local Government Information Unit).

LGIU (1991) *Going for Quality: results of a survey of quality in local services* (London: Local Government Information Unit).

Local Government Training Board (1987) *Getting Closer to the Public* (Luton: Local Government Training Board).

Loney, M. (1983) *Community against Government: The British Community Development Project 1968–78* (London: Heinemann).

National Council for Voluntary Service (1989) *Contracting In or Out?* (London: NCVO).

Oelschlagel, D. (1991) 'Between Possibility and Restriction: Community Work as a professional strategy in the social field', in W. van Rees *et al.*, *A Survey of Contemporary Community Development in Europe* (The Hague, distributed in Britain by Community Development Foundation, London).

Pinehurst People's Centre (1989) *Half-Year Report – June* (Swindon: Pinehurst People's Centre).

Pinehurst People's Centre (1989) *Annual Report 1988–89* (Swindon: Pinehurst People's Centre).

Pinehurst People's Centre (1991) *Annual Report 1990–91* (Swindon: Pinehurst People's Centre).

Pinehurst People's Centre (no date) *What's behind the Pinehurst People's Centre* (Swindon: Pinehurst People's Centre).

Pinehurst Training Initiative (1988) *Review, June 1987–October 1988* (Swindon: Pinehurst People's Centre).

Pinehurst People's Centre (1991) *'Away Day' for Pinehurst People's Centre Held on 19th May 1991* (unpublished report for Pinehurst People's Centre).

Power, A. (1987) *Property before People: The Management of Twentieth Century Housing* (London: Allen and Unwin).

Report by a Sub-Committee of the Scottish Housing Advisory Committee (1967) *Housing Management in Scotland* (London: HMSO) (quoted in CDP, *Whatever Happened to Council Housing*, CDP, 1976, p. 82).

Secretary of State for Scotland (1990) *Urban Scotland into the 90s: new life two years on* (printed in Scotland for HMSO).

Solon CHS Ltd (1988) *The Kilburn Vale Study: a feasibility study to assess the viability of a tenant management co-operative on the Kilburn Vale Estate, West Hampstead for Kilburn Vale Tenants Association* (London: Solon CHS Ltd).

Solon/Catch (1991) *Highgate New Town, Draft Feasibility Study for Highgate and Newtown Tenants and Residents Association* (London: Solon/Catch).

Specht, H. (1976) *The Community Development Project: National and Local Strategies for Improving the Delivery of Services* (London: National Institute for Social Work Papers, no. 2).

Waddington, P. (1979) 'Looking ahead-community work into the 1980s', *Community Development Journal*, vol. 14, no. 3.

Whitfield, D. (1992) *The Welfare State* (London: Pluto).

William Temple Foundation and Ruskin College (1989) *Learning from Experience: Project work with community groups* (Manchester: William Temple Foundation and Ruskin College, Oxford), occasional paper no. 17.

Willmott, P. and A. Murie (1988) *Polarisation and Social Housing* (London: Policy Studies Institute).

8   Conclusion

Abrams, P., S. Abrams, R. Humphrey and R. Snaith (1989) *Neighbourhood Care and Social Policy* (London: HMSO).

Advisory Council for Adult and Continuing Education (ACACE) (1982) *Report: Continuing Education: From Policies to Practice* (Leicester: ACACE).

Charity Trends (1991), p. 6.

Clavel, P. and W. Wiewel (1991) *Harold Washington and the Neighbourhoods: Progressive City Government in Chicago 1983–87* (New Brunswick: Rutgers University Press).

Cowburn, W. (1986) *Class, Ideology and Community Education* (London: Croom Helm).

Evans, B. (1987) *Radical Adult Education: A Political Critique* (London: Croom Helm).

Frazer, H. (1991) 'Integrated approaches to development', in W. van Rees (ed.), *A Survey of Contemporary Community Development in Europe* (The Hague, distributed in Britain by Community Development Foundation, London).

Freire, P. (1984) *Pedagogy of the Oppressed* (Harmondsworth: Penguin Books).

Galbraith, J. (1992) *The Culture of Contentment* (London: Sinclair-Stevenson).
Grabowski, S. (ed.) (1972) *Paulo Freire: A Revolutionary Dilemma for the Adult Educator* (Syracuse. NY: Syracuse University Publications).
Griffin, C. (1987) *Adult Education as Social Policy* (London: Croom Helm).
Gutch, R. (1992) 'Building site or battlefield', *NCVO News* (January–February).
Gutch, R. (1992) *Contracting: Lessons from the US* (London: NCVO).
Hambleton, R. (1991) *Another Chance for Cities? Issues for Urban Policy in the 1990s* (Cardiff: Department of City and Regional Planning, University of Wales College of Cardiff).
Hansard (1991) House of Lords, 21 November, cols 1032, 1038.
Henderson, P. (ed.) (1991) *Signposts to Community Economic Development* (London: Community Development Foundation/Manchester: Centre for Local Economic Strategies).
Hope, A. and S. Timmel (1984) *Community Workers' Handbook* (Gweru: Zimbabwe Mambo Press).
Hugman, R. (1991) *Power in the Caring Professions* (London: Macmillan).
Kirkwood, G. and C. Kirkwood (1989) *Living Adult Education: Freire in Scotland* (Milton Keynes: Open University Press, in association with Scottish Institute of Adult and Continuing Education).
Lackey, A. and L. Dershem (1992) 'The Process is Pegagogy: What Does Community Participation Teach?', *Community Development Journal*, vol. 27, no. 3 (July), pp. 220–34.
Lovett, T., C. Clarke and A. Kilmurray (1983) *Adult Education and Community Action* (London: Croom Helm).
Lund, F. (1991) 'Women, Welfare and the Community', paper presented at the Conference on Women and Gender in Southern Africa, Durban, Centre for Social and Development Studies, University of Natal, Durban, 1991.
Mayo, M., P. Meyer and S. Rosenblum (1992) 'Workplace-based Education and Economic Development', *Economic Development Quarterly*, vol. 6, no. 4 (November) pp. 444–53.
Oliver, M. (1990) *The Politics of Disablement* (London: Macmillan).
Perry, K. (1988) *Learning in Voluntary Organisations* (Leicester: published by NIACE for UDACE).
Volunteer Centre (1991) *The National Survey of Voluntary Activity in the UK* (Berkhamsted, Hertfordshire: Volunteer Centre UK).
Wintermute, W. and C. Hicklin (1991) 'The Employment Potential of Chicago's Service Industries', in P. Nyden and W. Wiewel (eds), *Challenging Uneven Development: An Urban Agenda for the 1990s* (New Brunswick: Rutgers University Press).
Youngman, F. (1986) *Adult Education and Socialist Pedagogy* (London: Croom Helm).

Index